New Casebooks

J. K. ROWLING
HARRY POTTER

Edited by

CYNTHIA J. HALLETT & PEGGY J. HUEY

palgrave
macmillan

First published 2012 by
PALGRAVE MACMILLAN

Palgrave Macmillan in the UK is an imprint of Macmillan Publishers Limited, registered in England, company number 785998, of Houndmills, Basingstoke, Hampshire RG21 6XS.

Palgrave Macmillan in the US is a division of St Martin's Press LLC, 175 Fifth Avenue, New York, NY 10010.

Palgrave Macmillan is the global academic imprint of the above companies and has companies and representatives throughout the world.

Palgrave® and Macmillan® are registered trademarks in the United States, the United Kingdom, Europe and other countries.

ISBN 978–0–230–00849–6   hardback
ISBN 978–0–230–00850–2   paperback

This book is printed on paper suitable for recycling and made from fully managed and sustained forest sources. Logging, pulping and manufacturing processes are expected to conform to the environmental regulations of the country of origin.

A catalogue record for this book is available from the British Library.

A catalog record for this book is available from the Library of Congress.

10   9   8   7   6   5   4   3   2   1
21   20   19   18   17   16   15   14   13   12

Printed and bound in China

J. K. Rowling's popular series of books about the boy wizard Harry Potter has captivated readers of all ages around the world. Selling more than 400 million copies, and adapted into highly successful feature films, the stories have attracted both critical acclaim and controversy.

In this collection of brand new essays, an international team of contributors examines the complete *Harry Potter* series from a variety of critical angles and approaches. There are discussions on topics ranging from fairytale, race and gender, through to food, medicine, queer theory, and the occult. The volume also includes coverage of the films and the afterlife of the series with the opening of Rowling's 'Pottermore' website.

Essential reading for anyone with an interest in the Harry Potter phenomenon, this exciting resource provides thoughtful new ways of exploring the issues and concepts found within Rowling's world.

Introduction by Cynthia J. Hallett. Essays by: Jim Daems, Charlotte M. Fouque, Lykke Guanio-Uluru, Siân Harris, Pamela Ingleton, Anne Klaus, Em McAvan, Clyde Partin, Fran Pheasant-Kelly, Marcus Schulzke, Tess Stockslager, Robert T. Tally Jr, Roslyn Weaver & Kimberley McMahon-Coleman.

Cynthia J. Hallett is an independent scholar. Her previous publications include *Scholarly Studies in Harry Potter* (2005).

Peggy J. Huey is currently an Assistant Professor at Colorado Technical University Online, USA. She has published a number of articles on the *Harry Potter* books.

This latest series of *New Casebooks* consists of brand new critical essays specially commissioned to provide students with fresh thinking about key texts and writers. Like the original series, the volumes embrace a range of approaches designed to illuminate the rich interchange between critical theory and critical practice.

New Casebooks
Collections of all new critical essays

CHILDREN'S LITERATURE

ROBERT CORMIER
Edited by Adrienne E. Gavin

ROALD DAHL
Edited by Ann Alston & Catherine Butler

C. S. LEWIS: *THE CHRONICLES OF NARNIA*
Edited by Michelle Ann Abate & Lance Weldy

J. K. ROWLING: *HARRY POTTER*
Edited by Cynthia J. Hallett & Peggy J. Huey

FURTHER TITLES ARE CURRENTLY IN PREPARATION

For a full list of published titles in the past format of the New Casebooks series, visit the series page at www.palgrave.com

New Casebooks Series

Series Standing Order
ISBN 978–0–333–71702–8 hardcover
ISBN 978–0–333–69345–2 paperback
(Outside North America only)

You can receive future titles in this series as they are published by placing a standing order. Please contact your bookseller or, in case of difficulty, write to us at the address below with your name and address, the title of the series and the ISBN quoted above.

Customer Services Department, Macmillan Distribution Ltd, Houndmills, Basingstoke, Hampshire RG21 6XS, England

Contents

Series Editor's Preface

Welcome to the latest series of New Casebooks.

Each volume now presents brand new essays specially written for university and other students. Like the original series, the new-look New Casebooks embrace a range of recent critical approaches to the debates and issues that characterize the current discussion of literature.

Each editor has been asked to commission a sequence of original essays which will introduce the reader to the innovative critical approaches to the text or texts being discussed in the collection. The intention is to illuminate the rich interchange between critical theory and critical practice that today underpins so much writing about literature.

Editors have also been asked to supply an introduction to each volume that sets the scene for the essays that follow, together with a list of further reading which will enable readers to follow up issues raised by the essays in the collection.

The purpose of this new-look series, then, is to provide students with fresh thinking about key texts and writers while encouraging them to extend their own ideas and responses to the texts they are studying.

Martin Coyle

Notes on Contributors

Jim Daems teaches in the English Department of the University of the Fraser Valley, British Columbia, Canada. His research focuses on the early modern period and gender studies. He is the co-editor (with Holly Nelson) of *Eikon Basilike* (Broadview, 2005) and the author of *Seventeenth Century Literature and Culture* (Continuum, 2006), as well as articles in *Milton Quarterly, Men and Masculinities, A Reader's Guide to Lesbian and Gay Studies, Topia: Canadian Journal of Cultural Studies*, and *Literature and Ethics*.

Charlotte M. Fouque holds a BA in Creative Writing from North Carolina State University and completed a Master's in English Literature there in 2011. Combining her personal interests and her research, she wrote her thesis on *Harry Potter*, titled "Houses, Blood, and Prophecy: A Deterministic Reading of J. K. Rowling's *Harry Potter* Series." She hopes to be able to expand it to book-length in the future, and certainly intends to keep reading young adult fiction as literature.

Lykke Guanio-Uluru is at the University of Oslo, Norway, where she is working on her inter-disciplinary PhD thesis "Best-selling Ethics: A Literary Analysis of Ethical Dimensions of J. R. R. Tolkien's *The Lord of the Rings* and J. K. Rowling's *Harry Potter* Series." She has an MA in English Literature with an emphasis on fantasy and science fiction. Additional subjects include archaeology, film and video production, and the philosophical history of aesthetics. She is affiliated with the Nordic Network of Narrative Studies and is sponsored by the Ethics Programme at the University of Oslo.

Cynthia J. Hallett is an independent scholar and was formerly Associate Professor of English and Foreign Languages at Bennett College for Women, North Carolina. Her previous publications include *Scholarly Studies in Harry Potter* (Edwin Mellen Press, 2005).

Siân Harris completed her PhD in 2009. Her doctoral research on the Canadian female *Künstlerroman* was catalyzed by her concerns about gender, genre, and creative identity, which intersect with an interest in popular culture. Forthcoming publications include an analysis of the male poet in the contemporary literary biopic, and a consideration of feminist histories in the fiction of A. S. Byatt and

Marina Warner. Siân currently teaches Literary Studies at Newcastle University, United Kingdom.

Peggy J. Huey is an Assistant Professor in General Studies for Colorado Technical University Online and an Instructor for DeVry University Online. She has published articles on a variety of topics including Breton *lais*, Chaucer, Arthurian romances, Renaissance sonnets, Jane Austin, bell hooks, and Harry Potter.

Pamela Ingleton is a PhD candidate in the Department of English and Cultural Studies at McMaster University in Hamilton, Ontario, writing a dissertation on online authorship and the discourses of social media. Recently her work was published in *Flow*, an online publication with the University of Texas at Austin. She was also an invited speaker at the Texas Institute for Literary and Textual Studies (TILTS) symposia at UT Austin, on the topic of "The Digital and the Human(ities)."

Anne Klaus studied English and German at the University of Osnabrück, Germany. Since receiving her certificate of "Erstes Staatsexamen" in 2008, she is employed as research assistant at the University of Osnabrück. She is working on a doctoral thesis on archetypes and savior figures in fantasy fiction for children and young adults. Her research interests lie in the fields of children's literature, the Victorian era, Shakespeare, and Arthurian romance.

Em McAvan is an independent scholar of religion and literature, whose work has appeared in the *Journal of Postcolonial Writing, Literature & Theology* and *Critique: Studies in Contemporary Fiction*. Her first full-length monograph titled *The Postmodern Sacred* is forthcoming with MacFarland.

Kimberly McMahon-Coleman teaches in Learning Development at the University of Wollongong, Australia. Her doctoral thesis examines shamanism and indigenous diaspora in the work of Alootook Ipellie and Sam Watson. Her work has been published in *Australasian-Canadian Studies* and *Kunapipi*, and in R. K. Dhawan and Stewart Gill's book, *Canadian Studies Today: Responses from the Asia Pacific*. She is currently writing a book with Dr. Roslyn Weaver from the University of Western Sydney, focusing on the figure of the shapeshifter in literature and popular culture.

Clyde Partin, MD, FACP, is an Associate Professor of Medicine at Emory University, Georgia, actively involved in teaching residents and medical students. Prior to his academic career, he spent six years as a flight surgeon for the United States Air Force. His interests and publications have dealt with the history of medicine, Sir William Osler, medicine and literature, obscure medical phenomena, Hank Aaron's Hate Mail, and raising chickens. He is a member of the American Osler Society and the American Academy of Poets.

Fran Pheasant-Kelly is MA Award Leader and Senior Lecturer in Film Studies at the University of Wolverhampton, United Kingdom. Her research interests include abjection and space, which form the basis for a forthcoming book *Abject Spaces in American Cinema: Institutional Settings, Identity, and Psychoanalysis in Film* (I. B. Tauris, forthcoming). Imminent publications include "The Ecstasy of Chaos: Mediations of Trauma and Terrorism in *The Dark Knight*" (*Journal of War and Culture Studies*); "Cinematic Cyborgs, Abject Bodies: Post-Human Hybridity in *Terminator 2* and *Robocop*" (*Film International*); and "Authenticating the Reel: Realism, Simulation and Trauma in *United 93*" in C. Dony *et al.* (eds.), *Portraying 9/11: Essays on Representations in Comic Books, Literature, Film, and Theater* (McFarland Press).

Marcus Schulzke is an ABD PhD candidate in political science at the State University of New York at Albany. His primary research interests are political theory, comparative politics, political violence, applied ethics, and digital media. He is currently working on a disser-tation about how soldiers make moral decisions in combat.

Tess Stockslager is Director of the Graduate Writing Center and lecturer in English at Liberty University in Lynchburg, Virginia. She is a PhD candidate in literature and criticism at Indiana University of Pennsylvania. As a Victorianist, her primary research interests are eating and bodies in George Eliot's novels, and the intersection between weight loss and masculinity during the nineteenth century. At the 2011 Southeast Conference on Christianity and Literature, she presented the paper "Lily, Luna, and the Power of Love: How Friendship and Kindness Saved the Wizarding World." She writes short stories and has published a novella.

Robert T. Tally Jr. teaches American and world literature at Texas State University. He is the author of *Melville, Mapping and Globalization: Literary Cartography in the American Baroque Writer*, *Kurt Vonnegut and the American Novel: A Postmodern Iconography*, and the forthcoming *Spatiality (The New Critical Idiom)*. Tally is also the translator of Bertrand Westphal's *Geocriticism: Real and Fictional Spaces* and the editor of *Geocritical Explorations: Space, Place, and Mapping in Literary and Cultural Studies*.

Roslyn Weaver has a PhD in English Literature and is a Postdoctoral Research Fellow in the Family and Community Health Research Group, University of Western Sydney, Australia. Roslyn is the author of *Apocalypse in Australian Fiction and Film: A Critical Study*. Her research interests include medical humanities, children's literature, and popular culture.

List of Abbreviations

CS[A]   J. K. Rowling, *Harry Potter and the Chamber of Secrets* (New York: Scholastic, 1999).

CS[B]   J. K. Rowling, *Harry Potter and the Chamber of Secrets* (London: Bloomsbury, 1998).

DH[A]   J. K. Rowling, *Harry Potter and the Deathly Hallows* (New York: Scholastic, 2007).

DH[B]   J. K. Rowling, *Harry Potter and the Deathly Hallows* (London: Bloomsbury, 2007).

GF[A]   J. K. Rowling, *Harry Potter and the Goblet of Fire* (New York: Scholastic, 2000).

GF[B]   J. K. Rowling, *Harry Potter and the Goblet of Fire* (London: Bloomsbury, 2000).

HP[A]   J. K. Rowling, *Harry Potter and the Half-Blood Prince* (New York: Scholastic, 2005).

HP[B]   J. K. Rowling, *Harry Potter and the Half-Blood Prince* (London: Bloomsbury, 2005).

OP[A]   J. K. Rowling, *Harry Potter and the Order of the Phoenix* (New York: Scholastic, 2003).

OP[B]   J. K. Rowling, *Harry Potter and the Order of the Phoenix* (London: Bloomsbury, 2003).

PA[A]   J. K. Rowling, *Harry Potter and the Prizoner of Azkaban* (New York: Scholastic, 1999).

PA[B]   J. K. Rowling, *Harry Potter and the Prisoner of Azkaban* (London: Bloomsbury, 1999).

PS[B]   J. K. Rowling, *Harry Potter and the Philosopher's Stone* (London: Bloomsbury, 1997).

SS[A]   J. K. Rowling, *Harry Potter and the Sorcerer's Stone* (New York: Scholastic, 1998).

Introduction

Cynthia J. Hallett

As the last pages of *The Deathly Hallows* rustled shut and the final notes of music played while the closing cinematic credits for the final film rolled, some rather relieved critics were throwing a wake for Harry Potter, referring to the millions of Potter fans as mourners attending a funeral, for "finally" the Harry Potter phenomenon was dead. What?! Did they not read the book or see the movie? Have they not caught the wave to Pottermore.com or been whisked away to the Wizarding World of Harry Potter theme park at Universal Studios in Orlando, Florida? "Can you read Bulgarian?" Then off to Potter-Mania.com, or if visiting Bulgaria, get a Potter fix by visiting the exhibition of wax works at the Earth and Man National Museum, Sofia, where there is a Harry Potter corner.

The Internet site Pottermore.com, launched by Rowling herself, is touted as a place to be shaped by fans of the series and is defined as "an exciting new website from J. K. Rowling that can be enjoyed alongside the Harry Potter books. You can explore the stories like never before and discover exclusive new writing from the author. It is FREE to join and use, and is designed to be safe for people of all ages" (Pottermore.com). In addition, the site is intended to function as an outlet for *Harry Potter* ebooks and audiobooks, which have not yet been available to the public in either of those formats. However, Amazon.com has announced that on June 19, 2012, the entire *Potter* series will also be available as ebooks through the Kindle Owners' Lending Library in English, French, Italian, German, and Spanish. Further, the Pottermore site is to include interactive storylines. Even fan art is exhibited on the site. All of these opportunities are intended to give Potter fans both a creative outlet and continuing access to the world of Harry Potter, a world that has been steadily expanding since the phenomenon spread quickly around the globe, hitting Bulgaria in 2000, for example, when the translation was released there.

J. K. Rowling's *Harry Potter* series first sparked the imagination of children and adults alike with the release of *Harry Potter and the Philosopher's Stone* in 1997. The magical tale seemed to provide an antidote to the late twentieth-century complaint that "kids don't read anymore" with the novel drawing in the young readers, combating the poisonous influences of television and computer games on young minds and pulling children into the enchanted world contained in its pages. It is difficult to believe that there ever was a time when no one had heard of Harry Potter, Hermione, or Ron; or of Hogwarts, house-elves, or Horcruxes. With all these fictional wonders, the greatest strength of the *Potter* series is that it can be read on a number of levels and from a variety of perspectives. Although neither a Bible nor a Joycean *Ulysses*, as with both, the Harry Potter phenomenon may well one day spawn its own Compendium, but not this day. Confined and confounded by space and time, the contributors to this collection are able to address but a few of the countless, significant elements of fiction and literary techniques employed by Rowling in the pages of her *Potter* series.

Alive and well, J. K. Rowling's body of work is now ironically splayed forever on the literary analyst's table. Contributors to this New Casebook are among the enthusiastic, celebratory examiners of Rowling's complex and concerted methods as creator of the world that spawned and nourished the character and world of Harry Potter. Finally, those "serious" scholars whom Lana A. Whited titled "The Ivory Tower" have adopted the *Harry Potter* series, for they have recognized its ancestral roots in folklore, myth and legend, psychology, sociology, and certainly popular culture. Rowling may be finished with the series, but the academic world has only just begun tackling the concepts found within Rowling's world.

Certainly, no one book can pretend to touch on all the themes, motifs, allusions, or literary connections in the seven-book *Potter* series. The thirteen essays in this New Casebook include not only the more obvious literary themes such as fairy-tale, *bildungsroman*, and gender roles, but also some less apparent subjects as ethics, politics, and medicine. Much will be done over time on the translation of the series into film; we have one essay that enters this discussion early. Because no one can ignore Rowling's after-the-fact declarations that Dumbledore was gay, we have an essay on queer theory. Necessarily, we had to address religion and the occult. Woven in between the explicit and implicit—the expected and unexpected—are essays on food, free will and ethnicity in Harry's world. Not purposely to reflect the plot of the series, we end with an essay on the afterlife, thinking of what Albus Dumbledore says in a self-conscious comment about Voldemort in particular but literature in general: "'Of house-elves and children's tales, of love, loyalty, and innocence, Voldemort knows and understands nothing. Nothing. That they all have a power beyond his own, a power beyond the reach of any magic, is a truth he has never grasped'."[1]

Reminiscent of the start-of-term banquet in the Great Hall when students first arrive at Hogwarts School of Witchcraft and Wizardry, Siân Harris's essay in Chapter 1, "Glorious Food? The Literary and Culinary Heritage of the *Harry Potter* Series," charts Rowling's treatment of food and eating and draws connections between the *Harry Potter* books and several canonical works of children's literature, including Roald Dahl and Enid Blyton. This examination of the themes of food and feasting in the *Potter* books considers the inter-textual and socio-political dynamics of the series and offers an understanding of Rowling's recipe for literary success.

Is the *Potter* story simply a modern fairy tale gone epic? Surely, most critics agree that Harry's story contains the ingredients of a fairy tale, but Anne Klaus's essay in Chapter 2, "A Fairy-tale Crew? J. K. Rowling's Characters under Scrutiny," looks beyond Harry as a typical fairy-tale hero and questions whether the characters surrounding the young protagonist can also be labeled fairy-tale characters or whether the clear-cut distinction between good and evil becomes blurred as soon as the focus is withdrawn from the hero and his entourage.

One of the more engaging aspects of the Potter story is watching Harry grow up, mature, and do all those things—right and wrong—that form the core of a person's character over time and make each individual what he or she is as an adult, in this case Harry's character (both meanings implied). In Chapter 3, "The Way of the Wizarding World: *Harry Potter* and the Magical *Bildungsroman*," Robert T. Tally Jr. addresses the ways in which Harry's story is Rowling's postmodern *Bildungsroman*, much like Goethe's or Dickens's modern ones; a story about growing up that aids readers in a navigation of their own paths in a perilously complex world and that gives everyone an Everyman hero—both as model and companion with which to explore life.

The cinematic versions of the series allow exactly that, to watch Harry Potter grow. In Chapter 4. "Bewitching, Abject, Uncanny: Other Spaces in the *Harry Potter* Films," Fran Pheasant-Kelly sorts through the eight movies that comprise the collection. She uses Julia Kristeva's theories to explain the concept of "abject" and Sigmund Freud to address the "uncanny" aspects of the films. She was able to include the final movie, as it premiered before the collection went to press.

More than just an epic fairy tale or journey to adulthood, Harry's story evokes the age-old conundrum of life's events as steered by free will or fate. In Chapter 5 Charlotte M. Fouque avers that, while they do make choices, the characters of the *Harry Potter* books are still ruled by the determinism that pervades their world.

An element that readers hear little about with regard to the Potter themes is ethics. The long-standing tension between the discourse fields of literature and moral philosophy may go a long way towards explaining why academic debate on the ethical propositions of J. K. Rowling's vastly popular *Harry Potter* series has been scant so far. To date, few scholars have drawn explicitly on ethical theory in their work on the *Potter* series. This void seems all the more surprising, as a better understanding of the ethical dimension of the series would be a vital supplement and corrective to the religiously inspired controversies that the series has provoked. Lykke Guanio-Uluru addresses this subject in Chapter 6, "Dumbledore's Ethos of Love in *Harry Potter*."

The *Harry Potter* series has faced numerous criticisms from religious leaders—evangelical, Anglican, Catholic, and even Muslim. In Chapter 7, "*Harry Potter* and the Origins of the Occult," Em McAvan analyzes the roots of the evangelical criticisms that have been directed at the series from churches in the United States. McAvan discusses the origins of the reading of fantastic texts as occult and Satanic, from early Puritan theologians Cotton Mather and Jonathan Edwards to twentieth-century evangelical apocalyptic writing, and argues that although the *Harry Potter* novels themselves are fantasy novels, evangelical criticisms sit squarely within a distinctly American tradition of Gothicized theology. By vilifying *Harry Potter*, these criticisms have less to do with the specific properties of the text than with the perennial need to repeat such scapegoating rituals in American Christendom.

Politics may not be the usual topic that comes to mind with the mention of Harry Potter, but the business of politics permeates the series. In Chapter 8, "Wizard's Justice and Elf Liberation: Politics and Political Activism in *Harry Potter*," Marcus Schulzke addresses these and other political themes, demonstrating how they emerge and evolve as the characters age and develop more nuanced views of their world. Political themes shape the course of the seven novels and provide useful analogues for judging contemporary politics. The books offer examples for young and old alike, as they promote a critical, albeit as much as is possible non-ideological, view of politics.

Completely coloring the characters and events in the Potter series is the theme of ethnicity, from half-blood, to house-elf, to full Muggle born. In Chapter 9, "What it Means to Be a Half-Blood: Integrity versus Fragmentation in Biracial Identity," Tess Stockslager sees Rowling as having created a world in which race operates on more than one level. First, though the series is set in present-day, multi-cultural England, characters of non-European descent are few—an issue which, while it may draw criticism from commentators, is not contentious within the world of the books. Rowling more fully explores race in a second sense. The practice of monitoring the percentage of wizard "blood" in one's pedigree allows pure-blood wizarding families to distinguish themselves from those who have Muggle blood—never mind the poor full-blooded Muggles that people the outer world.

What happens to a wizard-in-training when she or he is deformed by a spell gone awry or one falls from the sky during a Quidditch game? That person is taken to Madam Poppy Pomfrey, the Matron and nurse in charge of Hogwart's hospital wing. She is depicted as a stern and professional woman who takes her chosen path quite seriously. However, what do we really know about medicine in the world of Harry Potter? According to Clyde Partin, MD, in Chapter 10 "Magic, Medicine, and *Harry Potter*," the rich tradition of medicine is deeply embedded in the *Potter* novels. The steady undercurrent of medical issues and themes present in the saga has received scant attention from critics and scholars. For example, traditional medical topics such as anatomy, embryology, physiology, and especially pharmacology infuse the books. With the use of gillyweed, the biologic principle that ontogeny recapitulates phylogeny is demonstrated within the biblical framework of re-birth—a remarkably creative and riveting example of storytelling.

Harry Potter would not be "alive" were it not for his mother's love. Roslyn Weaver and Kimberley McMahon-Coleman address the themes of mothers and gender roles in Chapter 11, "*Harry Potter* and the Myriad Mothers: The Maternal Figure as Lioness, Witch, and Wardrobe." While many critical approaches to the *Harry Potter* series have discussed gender, less attention has been drawn to the specifics of certain gender roles, such as motherhood. Weaver and McMahon-Coleman focus on depictions of mothering and motherhood in Harry's world, seeking a greater understanding of the roles and status of the women who perform motherhood duties in the series. Mothering itself is a key theme throughout the seven novels. Harry's early loss of his heroic, biological mother, Lily Potter, leads to a myriad of substitute mothers in both magical and

Muggle worlds, ranging from the cruelly absurd Aunt Petunia, to the loving provider Mrs. Weasley and the authoritative teacher Professor McGonagall. Throughout the series, Harry witnesses other maternal figures who are cruel, neglectful, and eccentric. But his story ends with new hope offered by the mothers of the future in Ginny and Hermione who have received crucial training through their experiences in the books.

Few fans will forget the moment when, during a reading at Carnegie Hall in October 2007, Rowling proclaimed to the world that Professor Dumbledore is gay. Jim Daems addresses this surprising authorial pronouncement in Chapter 12, "'I Knew a Girl Once, whose Hair …': Dumbledore and the Closet." He suggests that, in effect, without textual support for Rowling's claim, positive readings are trapped within negative stereotypes in attempting to see Dumbledore's sexuality as a step towards greater cultural acceptance and cautions readers to be wary of potentially reinforcing these stereotypes.

Finally, Harry died and was reborn. Aspects of a different kind of afterlife are addressed by Pamela Ingleton in Chapter 13, "'Neither Can Live while the Other Survives': *Harry Potter* and the Extratextual (After)life of J. K. Rowling." In comparing Rowling's extratext to the particularly prolific Harry Potter fan community—most notably the production and consumption of Potter fan and slash fiction—Ingleton takes up the question of Rowling's power and influence and examines a component of the *Harry Potter* series almost entirely overlooked in its criticism, but imperative to its understanding: the extratextual (after)life of the books and their author.

Whether Quest-hero or Christ-figure, Harry Potter is *such stuff as dreams are made of*, for literary elements such as these that fill the *Potter* series are all that Dumbledore describes in his response to Harry's question, "'Is this real? Or has this been happening inside my head?' Dumbledore beamed…, 'Of course it is happening inside your head, Harry, but why on earth should that mean that it is not real?'".[2]

The world of *Harry Potter* is an ever-expanding universe. Readers return and new readers join the fold; scholars analyze and teachers include the series in high school and college curricula; Internet sites are mushrooming throughout the Ethernet; and electronic media have become the most recent vehicle of access. Rowling may have stopped writing about Harry Potter, but his reincarnation is something beyond the storyline. The writers of these essays are as diverse in geography, vocations, and interests, as the intended readers are of this collection, which is for novice students and staid academics, as well as general readers and curious Muggles. The *Potter* phenomenon will continue to inspire and to create new thoughts, opinions, debates, and multimedia responses as long as one new reader opens the first book. ... Incoming owl!

Notes

1. DH[B]: 568.
2. DH[B]: 579.

1

Glorious Food? The Literary and Culinary Heritage of the *Harry Potter* Series

Siân Harris

Food is a central theme throughout children's literature, as the focus of celebrations, the currency of bribes and rewards, a solitary pleasure and a social ritual. Whether the characters experience the deprivations of famine or rejoice at bounteous feasts, food occupies a site of narrative and thematic significance that should not be overlooked. Food can be a mundane necessity or a deeply sensuous experience; it is an everyday essential as well as a luxury:

> [T]he subject of food and eating is full of contradictions and a major cause of social anxiety. In our culture food is, paradoxically, compulsively consumed and obsessively consuming [...] Above all, food is never just something to eat: even when it is mundane and everyday it carries meaning.[1]

Food is an effective vehicle by which to explore the literary heritage and social commentary inherent throughout J. K. Rowling's *Harry Potter* series. The starting point of this essay is a consideration of how Rowling uses themes of food and feeding to draw intertextual connections between the *Harry Potter* books and several canonical works of children's literature. The Hogwarts' diet of solid school dinners and illicit dormitory feasts represents a clear continuation of the traditions established in classic boarding-school stories, while the magical sweets available in the wizarding world are instantly evocative of the bizarre confectionary created by Roald Dahl in *Charlie and the Chocolate Factory* (1964).[2] The second section goes on to chart the cultural and political implications of the Hogwarts cuisine, and to question how Rowling uses the theme of food—and, just as importantly, the issue of who does the cooking—to reinforce a socially conservative portrayal of the wizarding world. Notably, the importance of food in emotional terms is a significant factor in the series. Rowling repeatedly uses food as an expression of feelings, a device to strengthen the bonds that exist between family and friends, and as a means of establishing and developing the characters' relationships, the subject of the third section below. These three perspectives on the significance of food, feeding, cooking and eating provide an intriguing insight into the *Harry Potter* universe, at once magical but also familiar and mundane.

Culinary connections: food and intertextual value

From the outset, Rowling has been repeatedly and insistently compared to other successful authors of children's literature—in particular, to Enid Blyton and Roald Dahl. Critics have identified them as "The Famous Three,"[3] while a recent Costa Book Awards poll revealed that "Enid Blyton and Roald Dahl have been named the nation's best-loved writers, beating Harry Potter creator J. K. Rowling into third place and leaving literary giants such as Shakespeare, Jane Austen and Charles Dickens trailing."[4] Through outlining some of the key similarities—and the crucial differences—in how these writers approach the theme of food, this section reveals how Rowling uses intertextual allusions to negotiate with classic works of children's literature and to establish her own place within its canon.

The basis for the comparison between Rowling and Blyton seems primarily rooted in their popularity, their accessibility, and most importantly, in their use of the boarding-school location. Blyton set over thirty books in boarding schools, including the Malory Towers and St. Clare's series, while Rowling's Hogwarts has become one of the most iconic schools in children's literature. In creating Hogwarts, Rowling participates in a tradition of boarding-school stories that dates back to Thomas Hughes's semi-autobiographical *Tom Brown's Schooldays* (1857), and, as Claire Armitstead has noted, the more fantastical elements of the *Harry Potter* universe are firmly established upon the conventions of this tradition:

> Look closer at this comic, gothic world, where pictures speak and every panel may hide a secret tunnel, and readers find a classic boarding school fantasy, complete with dodgy food, sadistic teachers, bullies, and unshakable loyalties [...] fantastical on the one hand, but, on the other, quite conventionally domestic in its depiction of childhood experience.[5]

Food is an essential component of the boarding-school narrative, as Karen Manners Smith has noted: "food might be the most important—almost obsessive—part of boarding school life and stories."[6] This is especially true when it comes to the classic plot device of the midnight feast. In *Upper Fourth at Malory Towers* (1949), the girls smuggle an illicit picnic of "hard boiled eggs, cakes, sandwiches and ginger beer" into their dormitory.[7] Similarly, in *The Prisoner of Azkaban*, when Harry's Gryffindor housemates celebrate their victory at Quidditch, "the party went on all day and well into the night. Fred and George Weasley disappeared for a couple of hours and returned with armfuls of bottles of butterbeer, pumpkin fizz, and several bags full of Honeydukes sweets."[8] Rowling combines these direct echoes with more subtle and humorous revisions of the boarding-school story motifs. At Malory Towers, meals are preceded by a formal blessing or "grace." At Hogwarts, this formality is usually omitted, or on special occasions, replaced by Dumbledore's more whimsical approach: "Before we begin our banquet, I would like to say a few words. And here they are: Nitwit! Blubber! Oddment! Tweak! Thank you."[9] Rowling both upholds and subverts the generic traditions, offering a finely balanced combination of wholesome tribute to and ironic pastiche of predecessors such as Blyton. In other words, when it comes to managing the dynamic between the *Harry Potter* series and the traditional boarding-school story, Rowling manages to incorporate both the old and the new.

Rowling's intertextual relationship with the work of Roald Dahl is slightly more problematic, in that she has repeatedly denied it, insisting in one interview that "[W]hile I think Dahl is a master at what he did, I do think my books are more moral than his."[10] Nevertheless, there are undeniable similarities between them, especially when thinking in terms of food—and in particular, of sweets. Both authors unleash the full extent of their imaginative powers when it comes to confectionary, conjuring up bizarre, delightful, and occasionally downright dangerous concoctions. A direct comparison is illuminating, as can be demonstrated with the following extracts from *The Prisoner of Azkaban* and *Charlie and the Chocolate Factory*:

> There were shelves upon shelves of the most succulent-looking sweets imaginable [...] the strange, splintery Toothflossing Stringmints, tiny black Pepper Imps ("breathe fire for your friends!"), Ice Mice ("hear your teeth chatter and squeak!"), peppermint creams shaped like toads ("hop realistically in the stomach!"), fragile sugar-spun quills, and exploding bonbons.[11]
> EATABLE MARSHMALLOW PILLOWS [...] LICKABLE WALLPAPER FOR NURSERIES [...] HOT ICE CREAMS FOR

COLD DAYS [...] COWS THAT GIVE CHOCOLATE MILK [...]
FIZZY LIFTING SWEETS [...] SQUARE SWEETS THAT LOOK
ROUND.[12]

These creative flourishes constitute a direct, sensory appeal to the
young reader, and present a tantalizing vision of their fictional worlds.
However, the similarities between Dahl and Rowling are not always so
beguiling—despite the sweetness of their imaginative confections, both
authors have the clear potential to turn "nasty."

In Dahl, this is quite blatant. Throughout *Charlie and the Chocolate
Factory*, the 'bad" children are punished in a variety of gruesome
ways, while "good" and meek Charlie survives to inherit the earth
(or at least the factory). Rowling is a little more disingenuous, but
she nevertheless uses food as a means to punish "bad" characters in
the *Harry Potter* series. In *The Chamber of Secrets*, Hermione sedates
Crabbe and Goyle with drugged cakes, knowing that they are greedy
and stupid enough to fall straight into her trap: "Grinning stupidly,
they stuffed the cakes whole into their large mouths. For a moment,
both of them chewed greedily, looks of triumph on their faces.
Then, without the smallest change of expression, they both keeled
over backward onto the floor."[13] Dudley Dursley suffers an even
more unpleasant fate when he helps himself to one of Fred and
George's enchanted toffees in *The Goblet of Fire*: "[H]e was gagging
and spluttering on a foot-long, purple, slimy thing that was protrud-
ing from his mouth. One bewildered second later, Harry realised that
the foot-long thing was Dudley's tongue."[14] These incidents may
not fit well with Rowling's claim to occupy the moral high
ground, but they are undeniably vivid and amusing. The intertextual
importance of food in the *Harry Potter* series, therefore, operates on
several levels. Primarily, it establishes Rowling as a worthy successor
within the realm of children's literature, drawing connections between
her work and that of such canonical figures as Blyton and Dahl.
Rowling's occasionally subversive approach is refreshing, and lends
a new imaginative energy to generic conventions. Perhaps most
unexpectedly, food provides Rowling with an outlet for a darker,
more physical sense of humor, which adds a welcome twist of the
grotesque to the *Harry Potter* universe.

Cultural codes: food and social value

Throughout the *Harry Potter* series, Rowling presents the wizarding
world as a complex and multi-faceted society, with its own particular

codes and traditions. The presentation of food is a crucial component in this process, as a means of reinforcing some of the differences between magical and non-magical communities. However, while some of these differences are immediately evident—the contrast between magical and non-magical confectionary being the most obvious example—the majority of the actual food consumed is perfectly recognizable. As Jann Lacoss notes: "Wizard food, with the exception of children's treats, does not differ considerably from its Muggle counterpart."[15] Rather than create a completely fantastic cuisine, Rowling chooses to signify culinary difference though more subtle and insidious means.

Primarily, the difference is reinforced through superiority. The food available in the wizarding world is consistently tastier and more plentiful than that on offer in the wider world of Muggles. Partly, this reflects Harry's treatment by the Dursleys, and serves to contrast their neglect with the generous way in which Harry is welcomed back into the magical community. In *The Philosopher's Stone*, Uncle Vernon grudgingly allows Harry a "cheap lemon ice lolly,"[16] whereas in *The Prisoner of Azkaban* he receives "free sundaes every half an hour"[17] from Florean Fortescue's ice-cream parlor. With the notable exception of the ghostly banquet in *The Chamber of Secrets*, Harry never attends a bad meal at Hogwarts, and dinners in the great hall are normally characterized by a plentiful supply of his favorite dishes: "He had never seen so many things he liked to eat on one table: roast beef, roast chicken, pork chops and lamb chops, sausages, bacon and steak, boiled potatoes, roast potatoes, chips, Yorkshire pudding, peas, carrots, gravy, ketchup."[18] Rowling describes the Hogwarts meals in such a way as to reinforce both quantity and quality, thereby doubly confirming the superiority of magical over non-magical food. However, what she does not address is the issue of *variety*, and the type of food in question is rather limited to a selection of traditional British classics, leading to endless repetitions on the formula of roast meat and boiled vegetables.

This lack of culinary diversity seems at odds with the apparent commitment to multiculturalism that Rowling exhibits elsewhere in the series. The student population at Hogwarts includes children from a variety of cultural and racial backgrounds, such as Harry's first love interest, Cho Chang, and his Quidditch team-mate Angelina Johnson. However, as Giselle Liza Anatol points out, "the inclusion of people of color does not mean the inclusion of any representation of ethnic difference and cultural practices."[19] Instead, she suggests that Rowling favors a "color-blind" approach to ethnicity, whereby black and Asian students are indistinguishable from their Caucasian counterparts in all but name and fleeting references to physical appearance: "the novels portray not integration and acceptance, but the complete assimilation [...] into the all-white landscape."[20] Similarly, Hogwarts' kitchen does not extend to that much-vaunted symbol of multicultural British cuisine, the chicken tikka massala—described by the then Foreign Secretary Robin Cook as "a true British national dish"[21]—but sticks to its resolutely traditional repertoire. The dining table groans under the weight of pies, puddings, casseroles and stews, without once including a curry, a pizza, or a chow mein.

Instead, it appears that the students' first experience of non-British cuisine does not occur until *The Goblet of Fire*, when the Tri-Wizard tournament prompts the inclusion of some "definitely foreign"[22] dishes on the menu:

> "What's that?" said Ron, pointing to a large dish of some sort of shellfish stew that stood beside a large steak-and-kidney pudding.
>
> "Bouillabaisse," said Hermione
>
> "Bless you," said Ron
>
> "It's *French*," said Hermione. "I had it on holiday, summer before last, it's very nice." "I'll take your word for it," said Ron, helping himself to black pudding.[23]

Ron's palate has been defined by school dinners and the equally traditional British cuisine prepared by his mother at home, so a degree of skepticism towards the unfamiliar is understandable (although it is tempting to speculate how he coped on the Weasley family's Egyptian holiday that precedes *The Prisoner of Azkaban*). However, Carolyn Daniel has noted that Ron does not limit his disdain to the food itself: "He dismisses the bouillabaisse as other along with those who eat it, including Hermione."[24] Tellingly, Hermione has gained her familiarity with French food and culture by going on holiday with her non-magical parents—and therefore Ron's rejection of her insight might also stand as a rejection of Muggle experience. While Daniel finds that there is some humor generated at Ron's expense (after all, he would rather eat congealed blood or offal than try the bouillabaisse), this is implicit rather than overt, and Ron's boorish behavior goes unchallenged. This narrow-minded attitude to international cuisine is not the only cause for concern when considering the social value of food in the series. One must also question the methods of production, for it frequently seems that the role of preparing food is as limited by traditional stereotypes as the type of food on offer.

Initially, the most visible providers of food in the novels are Petunia Dursley and Molly Weasley—and despite their many apparent differences, these women are both traditional housewives, who care for their homes and nurture their children while their husbands go out to work. They are both presented as talented cooks, albeit with drastically opposing motivations for cooking: Petunia exerts herself most to impress her husband's business clients, while Molly is more concerned with feeding up her family and welcoming their friends. Molly is the center of the cozy domestic chaos that flourishes at chez Weasley, bustling about the kitchen with her wand always ready to perform a particularly practical type of magic: "She flicked her wand casually at the dishes in the sink, which began to clean themselves, clinking gently in the background."[25] John Kornfeld and Laurie Prothro draw links between Molly and Samantha from the sitcom *Bewitched*, noting how both women use "cute and funny magical means"[26] to maintain domestic harmony. However innovative Molly's magical methods, her role as a wife and mother remains extremely conventional—hence the parallels to a 1960s television show. In the *Harry Potter* universe, cooking remains a job for witches rather than wizards (Hagrid is a notable exception to this rule, although his food is generally inedible and presented as a source of humor rather than nutrition). This standard does not go entirely unchallenged. When Harry, Ron, and Hermione are on the run in *The Deathly Hallows*, Ron grows increasingly irritable at the lack of food and is quick to complain about Hermione's culinary efforts. He labels the meal she prepares "disgusting" and grows nostalgic for his mother who "can make good food appear out of thin air."[27] Hermione directly confronts his sexist attitude, "Harry caught the fish, and I did my best with it! I notice I'm always the one who ends up sorting out the food; because I'm a *girl* I suppose!"[28]—but her anger is dismissed and her outburst is swiftly forgotten. Less than twenty pages later, Harry wakes up to find that Hermione "was already busy in the kitchen"[29] and her attempt to protest the status quo is presumably curtailed.

It is not the first time that Hermione has questioned the domestic politics of cooking. In *The Goblet of Fire*, she is horrified to discover that the Hogwarts' kitchens are staffed by house-elves, a race of subservient magical creatures who receive no wages for their labors. Essentially, the house-elves are slaves, and their presence at Hogwarts is a disturbing indictment of the wizarding establishment: "[T]he cooking and cleaning at Hogwarts isn't done magically after all, and house-elves are not only possessed by the occasional snobbish family, but are at the heart of wizarding institutions, including the most upright of them."[30] Hermione is appalled and launches into a campaign to promote awareness, but it initially seems that her efforts are undermined by a narrative that repeatedly finds humor at her expense. Her campaign is launched under the unfortunate acronym of S.P.E.W. (Society for the Promotion of Elfish Welfare) and her half-hearted hunger strike is abandoned when the lure of an elf-cooked breakfast proves too much. However, there is also the possibility of reading Hermione's efforts in terms of social commentary rather than slapstick comedy. Karin E. Westman has posited that: "The wizarding world struggles to negotiate a very contemporary problem in Britain: the legacy of a racial and class caste system that, though not entirely stable, is still looked upon by a minority of powerful individuals as the means to continued power and control."[31] This reading highlights the ambiguities and injustices that are as inherent in the wizarding community as in the wider human world: Hermione's efforts with S.P.E.W. can have little impact in a society where the majority hold "the belief that it is simply 'natural' for cultural differences to persist."[32] While subsequent events will prove that the oppression of house-elves can have significant consequences (including the death of Sirius Black), very little actually changes. Indeed, as Harry stumbles to bed following the climactic battle in *The Deathly Hallows*, his thoughts turn to the elf he inherited from Sirius, and he "wonder[s] whether Kreacher might bring him a sandwich."[33] In the post-Voldemort world order, it is evident that some things will stay exactly the same. Behind the magical trappings and fantastic embellishments, a consideration of food and cultural value in the *Harry Potter* series reveals some rather unsavory truths. Just as the apparent multiculturalism of Hogwarts is undermined by its staunchly traditional cuisine, so too the apparent egalitarianism of the wizarding world is undermined by the oppressively traditional roles assigned to women and the continued tolerance of slave labor. The food may well be delicious, but the means by which it appears upon the table becomes increasingly unpalatable, not least because the inequalities portrayed by Rowling help to reinforce the realism of a magical universe.

Comfort eating: food and emotional value

Having considered the intertextual and political possibilities of reading food through the *Harry Potter* series, my focus shifts to a more emotional perspective, and focuses upon the importance of food as a motif for feelings. Throughout the series, food is a primary signifier of emotional state, providing a means by which to chart the characters' development and gather some insight into their inner feelings. It serves as a way of highlighting their moods and state of mind without necessarily having to spell out the details. Food also acts as an indicator of the characters' relationships, and as a means of expressing their feelings towards each other. Reading food from this angle thus provides the chance to re-examine the inner- and inter-personal dynamics of the *Harry Potter* series.

From the beginning, food serves as a metaphor for familial love. We are told that "The Dursleys had never exactly starved Harry, but he'd never been allowed to eat as much as he liked. Dudley had always taken anything that Harry really wanted, even if it made him sick,"[34] which encapsulates the family's prejudice against Harry and their desire to keep him downtrodden, as well as reaffirming their preference for their own son. This bias is taken to a ludicrous extreme in *The Goblet of Fire*, when Harry is deprived of food because Dudley has been placed on a diet: "Aunt Petunia seemed to feel that the best way to keep up Dudley's morale was to make sure that he did, at least, get more to eat than Harry."[35] This attitude is contrasted with the generous way that Harry is welcomed into the Weasley household, thereby juxtaposing the Dursleys' neglect with the love and acceptance that Harry finds among his wizarding allies: "Mrs Weasley fussed over the state of his socks and tried to force him to eat fourth helpings of every meal."[36] As Deborah De Rosa observes, "Leaving the Dursleys ends the Dursley-imposed periods of 'fasting' because Harry encounters adults who nurture him literally and psychologically."[37] The comparison is illuminating, especially when considering the use of food as a tactic by which to punish. The Dursleys discipline Harry by decimating his meager rations, until he thinks that "he'd probably starve to death."[38] However, when Professor McGonagall forbids the disgraced Harry and Ron to attend the school feast, she ensures this does not mean that they go hungry: "a large plate of sandwiches, two silver goblets and a jug of iced pumpkin juice appeared with a pop."[39] Harry's Muggle relatives might deprive him of food and withhold meals in order to punish him, but the generosity of his wizarding allies is unconditional—a true indicator of the parallel between food and familial bonds. Harry's changing diet parallels his changing status, from underfed and unwanted skivvy to healthy and happy hero.

Food also acts as an expression of friendship. In *The Philosopher's Stone*, Harry and Ron first meet each other on the train to Hogwarts. Harry can afford to buy sweets from the snack-trolley, but Ron is on a budget. Harry's first instinct is to share the supplies, which cements the bond between them: "'Go on, have a pasty,' said Harry, who had never had anything to share before or, indeed, anyone to share it with. It was a nice feeling, sitting there with Ron, eating their way through all Harry's pasties and cakes."[40] The episode establishes the friendship between Harry and Ron, while also demonstrating Harry's innate "good" character: this is his first opportunity to spend money on himself, but his instinct is to share the bounty with others. Throughout the term, Harry enjoys both official meals and unofficial feasts with his Gryffindor housemates, fostering a sense of family and community within their ranks. When Harry must return to the Dursleys for the summer vacations, he finds emotional and literal sustenance from the friendships he has formed at school: "The moment he had got wind of the fact that he was expected to survive the summer on carrot sticks, Harry had sent Hedwig to his friends with pleas for help, and they had risen to the occasion magnificently."[41] It is not always easy for Harry and his school friends to keep in touch during the vacation—Ron is baffled by the telephone, and Harry's Uncle Vernon has a nasty habit of padlocking Hedwig in her cage—but the food parcels symbolize their continued connection. However, this close association of food with friendship also has its downside. In *The Order of the Phoenix*, Harry feels that Ron and Hermione are deliberately excluding him from the action, and as a result, he refuses to accept their presents: "In fact, he was so angry with them he had thrown away, unopened, the two boxes of Honeydukes chocolates they'd sent him for his birthday. He'd regretted it later, after the wilted salad Aunt Petunia had provided for dinner that night."[42] Harry's pride, in this instance, is more important to him than his hunger.

Of course, in the *Harry Potter* universe, chocolate has a medical as well as a nutritional value. In *The Prisoner of Azkaban*, when the students are shaken and demoralized by their encounter with the Dementors, Professor Lupin shares out chocolate to restore their spirits: "Harry took a bite and to his great surprise felt warmth spread suddenly to the tips of his fingers and toes."[43] Crucially, while the Dementors have a menacing presence and induce physical symptoms of trauma in their victims, the most disturbing threat they pose is not to the body, but to the mind: "'Dementors are among the foulest creatures that walk this earth. They infest the darkest, filthiest places, they glory in decay and despair, they drain peace, hope, and happiness out of the air around them. [...] Get too near a dementor and every good feeling, every happy memory will be sucked out of you'."[44] The Dementors act as a depressive force, inducing misery and unhappiness in their victims. The use of chocolate as a remedy therefore represents a literal embodiment of the phrase "comfort eating," that reinforces the connection between food and feelings. While the healing properties of chocolate are not dwelt upon at length elsewhere in the series, they are alluded to during a potentially significant scene between Harry and Ginny in *The Order of the Phoenix*. A depressed Harry is brooding over his problems—especially his desire to contact his fugitive godfather Sirius—when Ginny appears to offer sympathy and chocolate: "Harry looked at her. Perhaps it was the effect of the chocolate—Lupin had always advised eating some after encounters with Dementors—or simply because he had finally spoken aloud the wish that had been burning inside him for a week, but he felt a bit more hopeful."[45] Those familiar with the subsequent developments in Harry and Ginny's relationship may read his renewed sense of optimism as having more to do with the company than the confectionary she provides. It certainly suggests that the feelings induced by eating wizarding chocolate are similar if not directly akin to feelings of love, the most powerful and potentially magical emotion in the *Harry Potter* universe.

While the characters primarily bond over "feasts"—whether these be family dinners, formal banquets, or, as with Harry and Ginny, a simple snack—they also experience collective periods of famine (as opposed to Harry's solitary periods of deprivation at the Dursleys). When Harry, Ron and Hermione are on the run in *The Deathly Hallows*, they quickly learn that "a full stomach meant good spirits; an empty one, bickering and gloom."[46] Harry, of course, is accustomed to being hungry, and Hermione is doggedly stoical, but Ron struggles to cope without a regular supply of food: "hunger made him unreasonable and irascible,"[47] and the added pressures of guarding the evil Horcrux aggravate the situation further:

> Whenever lack of food coincided with Ron's turn to wear the Horcrux, he became downright unpleasant.
> "So where next?" was his constant refrain. He did not seem to have any ideas himself, but expected Harry and Hermione to come up with plans while he sat and brooded over the low food supplies.[48]

Initially, this attitude seems to be a simple matter of cause-and-effect, yet the dynamic may be more complex than it first appears. Ron's surly mood-swings are certainly exacerbated by hunger, but he voices nothing that Harry and Hermione are not already aware of: "Harry and Hermione spent fruitless hours trying to decide where they might find the other Horcruxes, and how to destroy the one they had already got, their conversations becoming increasingly repetitive, as they had no new information."[49] They are starved of contact and support as much as they are starved of food. Hunger exposes their fears, but does not cause them. Their hunger reflects their confusion, their lack of direction, and the severity of the situation they are in. If anything, it seems more appropriate to be hungry than to be satisfied; the somber tone of *The Deathly Hallows* renders lavish meals as frivolous indulgences.

This process of reading food through the *Harry Potter* series is illuminating on several levels. It offers a motif by which to understand issues of canonicity, class, race and gender, as well as providing layers of political and psychological meaning. The presentation of food establishes a site of contact between Rowling and her most iconic predecessors in the field of children's literature, and strengthens her intertextual authority. The links between Rowling, Blyton, and Dahl—which are encapsulated in their respective descriptions of food and eating—reinforces the phenomenon of Rowling's rise to popularity, as well as allowing Rowling to demonstrate her understanding and command of certain central conventions in children's literature. Meanwhile, more culturally embedded conventions are left unchallenged, as the production of food reinforces a socially conservative vision of the wizarding world, where the overwhelming majority of meals are prepared by women or servants/slaves. Therefore, while the presentation of food showcases Rowling's descriptive abilities, it also calls attention to certain limitations that may prove to be cause for concern. Perhaps most revealingly, however, food acts as an emotional signifier, and a means by which the characters can express their relationships.

Beyond these possibilities, reading food allows for an expanded appreciation of just how Rowling's literary phenomenon is created and sustained. Daniel has suggested an affinity between literary and culinary creativity, and calls attention to certain similarities between the acts of reading, writing and eating: "[W]hen we actually think carefully about the physical process of eating we can see that it breaks down monolithic structuralisms [...]. The process of writing similarly involves the consumption of material, ideas and words from outside, digesting and re-constructing them."[50] Daniel's striking image of the creative process as consumptive fits perfectly with the *Harry Potter* series. Rowling's writing juxtaposes elements from countless literary traditions—from the *Bildungsroman* and the fairy tale, to the classic boarding-school story or the supernatural thriller—and combines these allusions over seven increasingly intricate novels.

There is a carefully balanced relationship between the old and the new, between the familiarity of Rowling's influences and the originality of her output. This is perfectly demonstrated through her presentation of food in the series, which appeals to the reader's desire for familiar comfort, while invariably adding a certain innovative twist. Reading food therefore provides a consistently complex and intriguing way in which to consider the intertextual and socio-political dynamics of the *Harry Potter* series, as well as a means by which to better appreciate Rowling's recipe for literary success.

Notes

1. C. Daniel, *Voracious Children: Who Eats Whom in Children's Literature* (London: Routledge, 2006): 1.
2. R. Dahl, *Charlie and the Chocolate Factory* [1964] (London: Puffin Books, 1985).
3. J. Briggs, D. Butts, and M. Grenby, *Popular Children's Literature in Britain*, (Aldershot: Ashgate, 2008): 247.
4. A. Berry, "Blyton Is Voted the UK's Best Loved Storyteller," *The Guardian*, August 19, 2008.
5. C. Armitstead, "Review of *Harry Potter and the Prisoner of Azkaban*," *The Guardian*, July 8, 1999.
6. K. Manners Smith, "Harry Potter's Schooldays: J. K. Rowling and the British Boarding School Novel," in G. L. Anatol (ed.), *Reading Harry Potter: Critical Essays* (Westport, CT: Greenwood, 2003): 69–87, at 81.
7. E. Blyton, *Upper Fourth at Malory Towers* (London: Methuen, 1949): 63.
8. PA[B]: 117.
9. PS[B]: 53.
10. As quoted in R. Williams, "The Spotty Schoolboy and Single Mother Taking the Mantle from Roald Dahl," *The Independent*, January 29, 1999.
11. PA[B]: 147.
12. Dahl: 113–15.
13. CS[B]: 102.
14. GF[B]: 47.
15. J. Lacoss, "Of Magicals and Muggles: Reversals and Revulsions at Hogwarts," in L. A. Whited (ed.), *The Ivory Tower and Harry Potter* (Columbia, MO: University of Missouri Press, 2002): 67–88, at 76.
16. PS[B]: 24.
17. PA[B]: 42.
18. PS[B]: 92.
19. G. L. Anatol, "The Fallen Empire: Exploring Ethnic Otherness in the World of Harry Potter," in G. L. Anatol (ed.), *Reading Harry Potter: Critical Essays* (Westport, CT: Greenwood, 2003): 163–78, at 173.

20. *Ibid.*: 174.
21. R. Cook, "Extracts from Speech to the Social Market Foundation," *The Guardian*, April 19, 2001.
22. GF[B]: 221.
23. *Ibid.*: 221, italics in original.
24. Daniel: 18.
25. CS[B]: 34.
26. J. Kornfeld and L. Prothro, "Comedy, Conflict, and Community: Home and Family in *Harry Potter*," in E. E. Heilman (ed.), *Critical Perspectives on Harry Potter* (New York: Routledge, 2003): 187–202, at 190.
27. DH[B]: 240–1.
28. *Ibid.*: 241.
29. *Ibid.*: 254.
30. S. Gupta, *Re-Reading Harry Potter* (New York: Palgrave Macmillan, 2003): 116.
31. K. E. Westman, "Specters of Thatcherism: Contemporary British Culture in J. K. Rowling's Harry Potter Series," in L. A. Whited (ed.), *The Ivory Tower and Harry Potter: Perspectives on a Literary Phenomenon* (Columbia, MO: University of Missouri Press, 2002): 305–28, at 306.
32. Westman: 315.
33. DH[B]: 600.
34. PS[B]: 61.
35. GF[B]: 30.
36. CS[B]: 53.
37. D. De Rosa, "Wizardly Challenges to and Affirmations of the Initiation Paradigm in *Harry Potter*," in E. E. Heilman (ed.), *Critical Perspectives on Harry Potter* (New York: Routledge, 2003): 163–84, at 167.
38. CS[B]: 42.
39. CS[B]: 68.
40. PS[B]: 98.
41. GF[B]: 30.
42. OP[B]: 3.
43. PA[B]: 68.
44. *Ibid.*: 187. See Chapter 10 in this volume for further discussion of this topic.
45. OP[B]: 328.
46. DH[B]: 236.
47. *Ibid.*: 237.
48. *Ibid.*
49. *Ibid.*
50. Daniel: 212.

2

A Fairy-tale Crew?
J. K. Rowling's Characters
under Scrutiny

Anne Klaus

Once upon a time, there was a little boy whose parents had died and who lived with his aunt, his uncle, and their son, but his aunt was a wicked woman who treated him badly. The boy was forced to sleep in the cupboard under the stairs and was harassed by his foster family, until one day, a giant came to take him away and to tell him that he was a wizard....

This summary of the basic concept behind the *Harry Potter* series suggests that J. K. Rowling's work could be tied logically to the plot and the characters of the fairy-tale genre. Scholars such as Jack Zipes or Katherine Grimes have perceived the familiarity of Rowling's series with the characteristic fairy tale, as set forth, for instance, by Vladimir Propp. In *Morphology of the Folk Tale* (1968),[1] the formalist identifies eight dramatis personae of the fairy tale and determines a list of thirty-one core narrative functions that develop in a uniform progression, proposing that they provide a link between all fairy tales.

Yet this chapter puts forward the thesis that, while Rowling may use a fairy-tale framework, her work is more complex than simple fairy tales, partly, of course, because by their very nature, fairy tales are significantly shorter than Rowling's seven-volume series. Plotwise, Rowling certainly meets some criteria of the fairy-tale genre: for instance, the orphan protagonist, the quest structure, and the grand theme of the battle between good and evil. Yet a one-to-one equation of the *Harry Potter* series with a fairy tale would neglect precisely those aspects of Rowling's work that determine its appeal, namely the amalgamation of different narrative traditions.[2]

Not only does the scope of her work fail to stand up to the comparison with the classical fairy tale, neither can her characters be equated with flat and straightforward fairy-tale types as this article will show. The main protagonist, Harry Potter, can by no means be labeled a pure fairy-tale character, and the clear-cut distinction between good and evil, as suggested for fairy-tale characters by Bruno Bettelheim,[3] becomes even more obviously blurred when the focus is cast on his entourage.

The plot

Previous analyses of the connection to fairy tales have focused on the opening scenes of the *Harry Potter* series to argue that they "employ several popular fairy tale conventions."[4] According to Harold Neeman, fairy-tale narratives favor the outsider: the rare, the extreme, such as the only child, the youngest son or daughter, the fool, the orphan.[5] As an orphan child hero, raised and abused by a wicked stepfamily, Harry Potter fits exactly in this range of fairy-tale characters and very much resembles Grimm's "Cinderella" with whom he is frequently compared.[6] Just as the innocent Cinderella has to rest on the hearth among the cinders, the outcast Harry Potter is assigned only the cupboard under the stairs as a sleeping place. In this paradigm, Petunia Dursley is the wicked stepmother who favors her son Dudley over Harry and treats the latter with disdain.[7]

The similarities with the fairy tale genre seem to go beyond the initial setting. Just as many "fairy tale protagonists experience a reversal of fortune thanks to supernatural help,"[8] thus escaping their underdog status, so Harry Potter's life completely alters after his identity as a wizard is uncovered. He is allowed entry into the wizarding community of Hogwarts, which accords with Propp's narrative function of "departure."[9] The insignificant little boy, an unlikely hero, proves to be extraordinary in the course of the story. As Jack Zipes in his *Sticks and Stones* (2001) suggests, "[Harry] is David, Tom Thumb, Jack the Giant Killer, Aladdin, and Horatio Alger all in one, the little guy who proves he's bigger than life"[10] and thus defies the label he had earlier been assigned by his stepfamily.

Harry has to accomplish various tasks on his quest and is equipped with magical objects and abilities, as well as a set of helpers to achieve his goal to fight his archenemy Voldemort (cf. Propp's "receipt of a magical agent"[11]; "guidance"[12]). In line with Zipes's claim in 2001, each of the plots of the first four novels resembles the structure of a conventional fairy tale: a modest little protagonist, typically male, who does not at first realize how talented he is and who departs from his home on a mission […]. Along his way he meets animals or friends who, in return, give him gifts that will help him. Sometimes he meets an old sage or wise woman, who will provide him with support and aid. […] Invariably, he defeats his opponent and either returns home or settles in a new domain with money, wife, and happy prospects.[13]

Zipes, who assigns the label "formulaic"[14] to the *Harry Potter* books, concludes: "If you've read one, you've read them all: the plots are the same."[15] Indeed, as Harry returns to the Dursley family every summer after having finished his school year at Hogwarts, the pattern of departure—trials—return recurs in each volume.

The success of the little hero against a much more powerful enemy, an outcome which is against all odds (cf. Propp's "difficult task"[16]), is equally featured conventionally in fairy tales. Zipes argues that Rowling's novels are predictable in that they provide "happy ends despite the clever turns of phrases and surprising twists in the intricate plots."[17] Rowling "remains within the predictable happy-end school of fairy-tale writers. You know from beginning to end that Harry will triumph over evil."[18]

However, is the issue settled satisfactorily with this statement? It is noteworthy that, like Zipes, the majority of voices that argue in favor of treating the *Harry Potter* series as being in line with fairy-tale conventions were strongest until the publication of the fifth volume.[19] Now that the complete series is published, a one-to-one equation of the *Harry Potter* books with the fairy-tale genre seems much less feasible.

Plotwise, Cedric Diggory's death at the end of the fourth book, *The Goblet of Fire*, has already triggered the concession that "[g]ood does not always win in Harry Potter's world."[20] In so far as Voldemort is defeated in *The Deathly Hallows* (killed not by Harry's hand, but by his own curse), Rowling's final volume clearly follows the fairy-tale tradition (cf. Propp's "exposure,"[21] "punishment"[22]). Furthermore, Harry, like many fairy-tale heroes, makes the noble modest choice by returning the Elder Wand because it caused more harm than it is worth.[23] Rowling even ends her seventh volume with the words "All was well,"[24] an expression that comes strikingly close to the conventional "happily ever after." Nonetheless, as is seen in *The Goblet of Fire*, this overall happy ending at the close of the seventh book is achieved at the expense of numerous heroic characters who sacrifice their lives for the greater good, a loss on a scale that is uncommon in the traditional fairy tale. The depiction of the sorrow and pain these losses cause are equally unparalleled in fairy tales, such as the scene of Harry's numb digging of Dobby's grave.[25]

Furthermore, at least the length and multidimensionality of Rowling's work should make the reader wonder whether an analogy of her series with the fairy tale is persuasive. By dividing her narrative into seven volumes, each of which accords to one year of her protagonist's boarding school life, Rowling proves to borrow not just from the fairy tale alone, but also from the school novel. She thus weaves additional literary strands into her narrative (e.g. the competition between different school houses, sport events, or secret nocturnal ventures), which often serve as a comic relief. The amalgamation of different literary traditions (i.e. fairy tale, mystery novel, school novel) and frequent departures from the main plot result in a multi-layered fabric and do not accord with the fairy tale's traditional linear narrative structure.

Portrayal of characters

In *The Uses of Enchantment*, Bettelheim stresses that "polarization [...] dominates fairy tales. A person is either good or bad, nothing in between,"[26] a statement that is supported almost three decades later by Maria Nikolajeva: "Fairy-tale heroes know no nuances; they are one hundred percent heroic, they never doubt, fear, or despair. In fact, they are seldom individualized."[27] In fairy tales, the characters' motivations, their emotional inner selves and their psychological development are practically ignored. If this were true for Rowling's characters, they would be "types rather than individuals."[28]

Harry Potter as a character

In line with Bettelheim, the protagonist Harry would have to lack ambivalence and authenticity.[29] Fairy tales are plot-oriented rather than character-oriented and, accordingly, do not include elaborate reflections as the "characters' qualities and emotions express themselves through their actions."[30] Maria Nikolajeva has no doubts: "Harry Potter is no exception."[31] And Elaine Ostry supports this view, arguing that Harry is "a static character"[32] "stuck in the role of the fairy-tale hero."[33]

Yet it should not be ignored that Rowling equips her young protagonist "with the same emotions we all know: longing for Mom and Dad, loneliness, insecurity, curiosity about his identity and origin,"[34] sentiments that the traditional fairy-tale hero lacks. Already in *The Philosopher's Stone*, Harry's grief over the detachment from his family becomes obvious when confronted with the Mirror of Erised which shows him "the deepest, most desperate desire of [his heart]': his parents;[35] and Harry "stare[s] hungrily back at them,"[36] illustrating his immense yearning for love, protection and guidance. These feelings are usually absent in fairy tales, which feature "mere figures without a well-defined corporeality, inner, emotional life, or milieu."[37]

Nikolajeva argues that these references to Harry's feelings of fear or loneliness are rather "narrator's statements, not representations of mental states" and that "Rowling does not use any of the more sophisticated narrative techniques for conveying psychological states: free indirect discourse, interior monologue, or psychonarration."[38] If Nikolajeva is right, without these insights Harry would be doomed to remain a rather static and flat character without a complex inner life and psychological credibility. These narrative techniques are, however, though admittedly sprinkled sparingly, not completely absent in Rowling's works. Examples can be found with higher frequency in the last volumes of the series, such as in *The Half-Blood Prince* when Harry weighs the pros and cons of dating Ron's younger sister Ginny Weasley in an interior battle:

> *She's Ron's sister.*
> But she's ditched Dean!
> *She's still Ron's sister.*
> I'm his best mate!
> *That'll make it worse.*
> If I talked to him first –
> *He'd hit you.*
> What if I don't care?
> *He's your best mate!*[39]

In scenes such as this one, Rowling depicts Harry's emotional tumult and offers an insight into the young adult's inner state that hurls him out of the position of a flat type, filling his fairy-tale shell with individuality. Various scholars agree that *Harry Potter* is about emotions and character[40] and that the books "speak volumes to the psychological experience."[41]

Rowling finds additional means to convey the inner states of her characters other than rendering their thoughts through interior monologue. Thomas Kullmann argues that one of the functions of fantasy fiction is to externalize psychological phenomena.[42] The Mirror of Erised is a striking example, as is, for instance, the Sorting

Hat, which assigns each new student a place in one of the four schoolhouses at Hogwarts according to the pupil's traits and values. Magical items in fantasy fiction thus express the characters' inner states. They might also pose a trial for the young protagonists who are tempted to yield to the possibility to abuse their superior abilities, as for instance becomes obvious in Harry Potter's misuse of the curses that he finds in the book of the Half-Blood Prince during his fight against Draco Malfoy.[43] Consequently, complex feelings are by no means absent in Rowling's work but instead are at the reader's disposal in metaphorical form.

It is through these means of externalization of the characters' emotions that one can detect a maturation of Rowling's young protagonist in the course of the series, not only a physical growing up (Mrs. Weasley jokes that it seems as if Stretching Jinxes had been put on him[44]) but also a spiritual maturation. Nikolajeva claims in *Power, Voice and Subjectivity in Literature for Young Readers* that Harry's aging and his outward development are not reflected in an inward ripening; she speaks of Harry's lack of complexity and observes that his development is chronological rather than ethical and that "[i]n the last volume, the seventeen-year-old Harry is not radically different from his eleven-year-old self."[45] Certainly, already in the very first volume Harry's choice of companions reveals a careful consideration and an inner moral compass: he picks his friends based on like-mindedness, regardless of whether these companions will earn him a great reputation. Harry makes the modest choice that affirms his goodness, namely choosing the poor but happy Weasley family and the Muggle-born Hermione Granger over the influential but selfish and materialistic Malfoys. His goodness and selflessness run like a thread through the seven volumes. "In this sense," as Ostry comments, "he resembles effortlessly innocent fairy-tale characters like Snow White."[46]

However, unlike fairy-tale protagonists, Harry shows a growing moral conscience and greater self-reflexivity throughout the series as Whited and Grimes suggest.[47] Harry displays increasingly well-grounded behavior throughout the narrative, observable for example when he rejects the opportunity to kill the traitorous Peter Pettigrew in *The Prisoner of Azkaban*[48] or in *The Goblet of Fire* when he "rescues underwater hostages during the Triwizard Tournament, putting their well-being above his goal of winning the tournament."[49] The biggest leap forward in Harry's spiritual development can be observed in scenes in which Harry reluctantly has to learn that he has to demarcate himself from people he had formerly worshiped or trusted. Thus, for instance, in the last volume, *The Deathly Hallows*, Harry realizes that Dumbledore, to whom he had shown his unquestioned admiration, had put his egoistic aspirations before the well-being of his family in his youth.[50] The disappointment in and the exasperation with the respected headmaster trigger Harry's self-reliance, which makes up an essential part of his maturation. It is the case, then, that at the end of each volume of the series, the respective extraordinary trials have made the hero "a stronger person, one who is wiser to the world's ways"[51] and who is "gradually gaining self-control."[52]

Side characters

Of course, it can be readily maintained that the character of Harry Potter is unquestionably good and that readers sympathize with him as protagonist. At any given point, it can be determined that Harry will succeed in the long run because he hardly ever wavers in the face of temptations, and it is "inconceivable that Harry will eventually go over to the dark side."[53] The more interesting question becomes whether the clear-cut distinction between good and evil becomes blurred as soon as the focus is withdrawn from the hero and, instead, is cast on his entourage. In the following it will be argued that although Rowling maintains the typical fairy-tale opposites between good and evil in terms of outward appearances she presents complex, rounded side characters uncommon for a fairy tale.

Ostry detects the fairy-tale technique of polar opposites between good and evil in Rowling's series, a duality that she suggests is mirrored in the depiction of the characters' outward appearance. She claims that Rowling "engages in the stereotypes of the fairy tale, as traditional European standards of beauty continue to be upheld in her work. Aside from the blonde Draco, her evil characters are dark and often misshapen. Voldemort is the 'Dark Lord', master of the 'Dark Arts', and [...] Dumbledore's first name, Albus, is Latin for 'white'."[54] Rowling's telling names (e.g. "Malfoy" deriving from the French for "bad faith," or "Bellatrix" meaning female warrior) add to the distinctive description of their bearers. Despite their superficial outward similarities with fairy-tale types, however, Rowling's secondary characters exhibit a far more complex inner core, as will be shown.

In traditional fairy tales, the side characters' main function is to further the plot line. Consequently, they seldom show coherence and complexity, but rather embody archetypal figures. Grimes assigns these conventional fairy-tale roles to the various figures of the *Harry Potter* novels. For her, "Vernon Dursley is the fairy tale father from whom the child wants to escape,"[55] "Petunia Dursley is reminiscent of the evil stepmother in folk and fairy tales,"[56] "Rubeus Hagrid represents the fairy tale hunter,"[57] "Molly Weasley is like Mother Holle in German folk tales,"[58] "Sirius Black is like the beast in 'Beauty and the Beast',"[59] and "Voldemort is, of course, the evil fairy tale character, [...] the dragon, the ogre, Bluebeard, the wolf."[60] Although these comparisons are plausible at first sight, they do not seem to capture the characters completely, as Rowling clearly deviates from this pattern and individualizes her cast. Instead of featuring flat "stock characters"[61] without any contradictory traits, Rowling includes three-dimensional personalities in her work that spice up her narrative and constitute a great share of its appeal. The following examples illustrate how Rowling gives life to characters that only at first sight resemble a fairy-tale cast.

As his closest friends, Hermione and Ron should—according to fairy-tale standards—invariably support the hero on his quest and never pursue a goal of their own. Without doubt, the two adolescents repeatedly function as helper figures. However, they prove to have their own problems and follow their own objectives at times as well, a departure from the main plot and the main hero that is uncommon in a fairy tale. Incidences that most prominently individualize Ron Weasley are his moments of envy. Not only the presents that Harry gets but also the increasing attention that he receives throughout the volumes make Ron hanker for becoming less insignificant for his surroundings himself. Scattered snappish commentaries reveal his yearning for some attentiveness and his annoyance with Harry's fame, such as in *The Chamber of Secrets* when Ron, after observing the hype surrounding Harry, remarks: "You'd better hope Creevey doesn't meet Ginny, they'll be starting a Harry Potter fan club."[62] Ron's teasing turns fiercer in *The Half-Blood Prince*, in which the narrator explicitly states that Ron "did not seem to have taken kindly to being ignored by Slughorn" who invites Harry, Hermione, as well as Ron's sister Ginny to his "Slug Club," consisting of those students he regards as extraordinarily talented, aspiring or simply well-connected.[63]

Ron perceives himself as average, lacking Harry's distinctive features and remarkable talents, and has only short moments to savor special attention, for instance when he can boast after the day the wanted Sirius Black enters the boys' dormitory with a big knife and mistakes Ron's bed for Harry's: "Ron had become an instant celebrity. For the first time in his life, people were paying more attention to him than to Harry, and it was clear that Ron was rather enjoying the experience."[64] Ron's fits of jealousy certainly reach a climax in *The Deathly Hallows* in which a voice coming from the Horcrux he is meant to destroy reminds him of his secret grudges: "*Least loved, always, by the mother who craved a daughter... least loved, now, by the girl who prefers your friend... second best, always, eternally overshadowed.*"[65] After some moments of struggle, however, Ron is able to resist the temptation. Without doubt, these passages breathe life into the figure of Ron and transform him from a trite side character to a multifaceted individual. Rowling's reader is invited not only to sympathize with the main protagonist, as would be the case in a typical fairy tale, but is offered a wider range of opportunities of identification in Rowling's work.

Similarly, Hermione Granger does not remain a mere fairy-tale helper figure either. She is "routinely mocked for being a goody-goody,"[66] and the presentation of female pupils as shrieking and giggling characters who struggle to retain their composure seems to undermine their relevance at first glance. However, Hermione "often serves as Harry's and Ron's mom-away-from-home"[67] and excels with her wit and her power of deduction. Her moral sophistication and her rational reasoning reveal themselves in her sensitivity in still not judging Snape as evil after he "apparently" killed Dumbledore in *The Half-Blood Prince* (cf. "'"Evil" is a strong word,' said Hermione quietly"[68]). "By separating Snape's lack of 'nice-ness' from his behavior in a larger conflict between good and evil,"[69] Hermione reaches a degree of moral reasoning that exceeds even that of the hero. Furthermore, it is worth noting that Hermione repeatedly becomes her own agent. She "befriends the underdogs at all costs,"[70] be it by covering Lupin's werewolf identity in *The Prisoner of Azkaban*, assisting Hagrid in defending and eventually saving his pet hippogriff in the same volume, or, most strikingly, founding the Society for the Promotion of Elfish Welfare (S.P.E.W.) in *The Goblet of Fire*.

In fact, fully fleshed characters are spread throughout the series. Damour's assertion that "the children are characters while the adults are caricatures"[71] is certainly wrong with regard to, for example, Dumbledore or Severus Snape. These adults are not at all two-dimensional set pieces, as Mills claims. Dumbledore is not unshakably good just as Snape is not primarily vindictive and cruel. Not even the Dursleys, who seem to embody the classic cold-hearted despised step-family and whom the reader could comfortably label "evil," stay true to the line throughout the seven books. Thus in the very last volume when the Dursley family goes into hiding and says goodbye to Harry, Dudley shows signs of gratefulness that Harry had saved him from the Dementors ("'I don't think you're a waste of space'"[72]). Likewise, Petunia surprises the young protagonist as well as the reader when she slightly wavers before leaving Harry behind.[73] As Harry learns later, his aunt had always been jealous of her younger sister Lily who with her magical abilities had been accepted at Hogwarts, while Petunia's request to join the boarding school had been rejected. Petunia consequently cloaks her jealousy in a strong loathing of all wizards and magic in general. Rowling thus provides the "evil stepmother" with a nuanced motivation that would be impossible in fairy tales.

The protagonist, as well as the readers, has to find out that "nothing in Rowling's series is quite as familiar as it first seems."[74] It turns out that Harry's idealized father James belonged to a group of school bullies in his youth, and the similarly glorified headmaster Albus Dumbledore is removed from his pedestal in the last volume, as mentioned earlier. However, the figure that is the most captivating side character by far is the Potions master, Professor Severus Snape. "Snape is an oily, petty, nasty, vindictive man with a heart of pure malice,"[75] and by all conventional narrative cues, his "nastiness should indicate that he is a villain of the deepest dye."[76] On the contrary, his actions often contradict his alleged villainy. He repeatedly reveals his loyalty to Dumbledore and rescues Harry on several occasions, culminating in his final sacrificial death in the seventh volume. Snape's choice to join "the side of the angels"[77] after a long association with the Death Eaters[78] is a distinct one that defies a black and white moral scheme. As Lisa Andres notes, "while Snape is initially portrayed as the villain of Rowling's series, little by little we come to understand Snape's complex past"[79] that motivated the 2007 unauthorized publication of The Great Snape Debate in which Amy Berner, Orson Scott Card, and Joyce Millman argue whether Snape is really Harry's friend or foe.[80] Summarizing that text, Andres observes that "Snape is teased and tortured at the hands of James Potter and the Marauders; he loses his childhood best friend to his rival; and he is racked with grief over Lily's death—we are shown both sides of Snape's personality."[81] According to Andres, Rowling grounds Snape in the Romantic tradition of pre-Byronic and Byronic heroes, and those readers acquainted with Rowling's clues (e.g. the dark appearance, the brooding manner, the mysterious past, the grief over Lily's death) do not question Snape's heroic nature or where his allegiances lie.[82]

In fact, Rowling's witty use of conventional narrative cues, her manipulation not only of the protagonist's but also of the reader's expectations, lets Snape remain a figure of questionable morality for most of her work.[83] On the one hand, readers encounter Snape bearing the mark of the Death Eaters, favoring Draco Malfoy over Harry Potter, or making the Unbreakable Vow with Narcissa Malfoy.[84] On the other hand, Snape teaches Harry how to shield his mind against Voldemort's intrusion, and he provides Dumbledore with the potion that, "while unable to reverse completely the damage done by the fatal curse of the Peverell ring, prolongs his life."[85] These contradictory hints leave the reader in doubt about his true nature. All along, Rowling plays with the reader's presumptions, such as in the first volume, *The Philosopher's Stone*, in which Harry and the reader are set on the wrong track, assuming that Snape aided Voldemort while, in fact, it was the apparently harmless Professor Quirrell who "mocks Harry. So, by extension, Rowling mocks her reader for being taken in by a particularly sly combination of her own writing and her use of genre conventions."[86] Thus, Rowling's work interrogates narrative conventions as well as simplistic dichotomies such as good and evil, companion and enemy.

Although Rowling's series is set within a bigger framework associated with the fairy tale (orphan protagonist, quest structure, the grand theme of the battle between good and evil), her amalgamation of various literary traditions and the complexity of her characters excel a simple fairy tale. Harry Potter corresponds perhaps most likely to the upright and virtuous fairy-tale hero. Yet, Rowling's side characters reveal nuanced moral profiles, psychological depth and self-determination. Furthermore, dubious moral figures such as Severus Snape are unthinkable in the classic fairy tales such as "Snow White" or "Red Riding Hood" in which sly characters such as the wolf or the envious queen are automatically evil and do not change in the course of the stories. Rowling, however, refrains from the depiction of black and white in favor of presenting shades of grey and the relativity of good and evil. Rowling even consciously plays with the readers' "fairy tale" expectations and undermines conventional literary cues. Consequently, her "Once upon a time"-like beginning and the "And they lived happily ever after"-ending are only a fairy-tale frame for a more multi-layered and multifaceted work.

Notes

1. V. Propp, *Morphology of the Folktale*, trans. L. Scott (Austin, TX: University of Texas Press, 1968).
2. Cf. T. Kullmann, *Englische Kinder- und Jugendliteratur: Eine Einführung* (Berlin: Erich Schmidt Verlag, 2008): 138.
3. B. Bettelheim, *The Uses of Enchantment: The Meaning and Importance of Fairy Tales* (New York: Alfred A. Knopf, 1977): 9.
4. L. Damour, "Harry Potter and the Magical Looking Glass: Reading the Secret Life of the Preadolescent," in G. L. Anatol (ed.), *Reading Harry Potter: Critical Essays* (Westport, CT: Praeger, 2003): 15–24, at 15.

5. H. Neeman, "Classical French Fairy Tales and the Idea of the Outsider," in W. Wright and S. Kaplan (eds.), *The Image of the Outsider in Literature, Media, and Society* (Colorado Springs, CO: Society for the Interdisciplinary Study of Social Imagery, 2002): 400–5, at 400.

6. M. K. Grimes, "Harry Potter: Fairy Tale Prince, Real Boy, and Archetypal Hero," in L. A. Whited (ed.), *The Ivory Tower and Harry Potter: Perspectives on a Literary Phenomenon* (Columbia, MO: University of Missouri Press, 2002): 89–122; X. Gallardo-C. and C.J. Smith, "Cinderfella: J. K. Rowling's Wily Web of Gender," in G. L. Anatol (ed.), *Reading Harry Potter: Critical Essays* (Westport, CT: Praeger, 2003): 191–205.

7. Gallardo-C. and Smith: 192.

8. Neeman: 400.

9. Propp: 39.

10. J. Zipes, *Sticks and Stones: The Troublesome Success of Children's Literature from Slovenly Peter to Harry Potter* (New York: Routledge, 2001): 175.

11. Propp: 43.

12. *Ibid.*: 50.

13. Zipes: 177.

14. *Ibid.*: 171.

15. *Ibid.*: 176.

16. Propp: 60.

17. Zipes: 175.

18. *Ibid.*: 182.

19. See, for example, the compilations of Whited, *The Ivory Tower and Harry Potter* and Anatol, *Reading Harry Potter*.

20. A. Cockrell, "Harry Potter and the Secret Password: Finding our Way in the Magical Genre," in L. A. Whited (ed.), *The Ivory Tower and Harry Potter: Perspectives on a Literary Phenomenon* (Columbia, MO: University of Missouri Press, 2004): 15–26, at 16.

21. Propp: 62.

22. *Ibid.*: 63.

23. DH[B]: 600.

24. *Ibid.*: 607.

25. *Ibid.*: 386–7.

26. Bettelheim: 9.

27. M. Nikolajeva, "*Harry Potter* – A Return to the Romantic Hero," in E. E. Heilman (ed.), *Harry Potter's World: Multidisciplinary Critical Perspectives* (New York: RoutledgeFalmer, 2003): 125–40, at 128; see also M. Nikolajeva, *Power, Voice and Subjectivity in Literature for Young Readers* (New York: Routledge, 2010): 30.

28. Neeman: 400.

29. Bettelheim: 9.

30. Neeman: 400.

31. Nikolajeva (2003): 128.

32. E. Ostry, "Accepting Mudbloods: The Ambivalent Social Vision of J. K. Rowling's Fairy-Tales," in G. L. Anatol (ed.), *Reading Harry Potter: Critical*

Essays (Westport, CT: Praeger, 2003): 89–101, at 97.

33. Ibid.: 98.
34. M. Nikolajeva, The Rhetoric of Characters in Children's Literature (Lanham, MD: Scarecrow Press, 2002): 33.
35. PS[B]: 157.
36. Ibid.: 153.
37. Neeman: 400.
38. Nikolajeva (2003): 134.
39. HP[B]: 482.
40. Cf. C. J. Deavel and D. P. Deavel, "Character, Choice and Harry Potter," Logos: A Journal of Catholic Thought and Culture V(4) (2002): 49–64, at 50.
41. Damour: 22.
42. Kullmann: 164.
43. HP[B]: 489.
44. Ibid.: 82.
45. Nikolajeva (2010): 21.
46. Ostry: 97.
47. L. Whited and M. K. Grimes, "What Would Harry Do? J. K. Rowling and Lawrence Kohlberg's Theories of Moral Development," in L. A. Whited (ed.), The Ivory Tower and Harry Potter: Perspectives on a Literary Phenomenon (Columbia, MO: University of Missouri Press, 2004): 182–208.
48. PA[B]: 199.
49. C. Neal, Wizards, Wardrobes and Wookiees: Navigating Good and Evil in Harry Potter, Narnia and Star Wars (Downers Grove, IL: IVP Books, 2007): 187.
50. DH[B]: 294.
51. Grimes: 105.
52. Neal: 30.
53. Nikolajeva (2002): 32.
54. Ostry: 95.
55. Grimes: 93.
56. Ibid.: 95.
57. Ibid.: 94.
58. Ibid.: 96.
59. Ibid.: 94.
60. Ibid.: 94.
61. Nikolajeva (2002): 129.
62. CS[B]: 77.
63. HP[B]: 220.
64. PA[B]: 199–200.
65. DH[B]: 306, italics in source.
66. V. L. Schanoes, "Cruel Heroes and Treacherous Texts: Educating the Reader in Moral Complexity and Critical Reading in J.K. Rowling's Harry Potter Books," in G. L. Anatol (ed.), Reading Harry Potter: Critical Essays (Westport, CT: Praeger, 2003): 131–45, at 134.
67. Damour: 23.

68. HP[B]: 595.
69. Schanoes: 133.
70. Gallardo-C. and Smith: 201.
71. Damour: 23.
72. DH[B]: 39.
73. *Ibid.*: 40–1.
74. Gallardo-C. and Smith: 203.
75. Schanoes: 132.
76. *Ibid.*
77. *Ibid.*: 134.
78. GF[B]: 531.
79. L. Andres, "'Shut Up in the Caved Trunk of his Body': Locating J. K. Rowling's Severus Snape in the Tradition of the Byronic Hero," MA thesis, North Carolina State University, 2010: 23.
80. A. Berner, O. S. Card and J. Millman, *The Great Snape Debate* (Dallas, TX: BenBella Books, 2007).
81. Andres: 23.
82. *Ibid.*: 11.
83. Schanoes: 132–3.
84. HP[B]: 40–1.
85. Andres: 26.
86. Schanoes: 131.

3

The Way of the Wizarding World: *Harry Potter* and the Magical *Bildungsroman*

Robert T. Tally Jr.

Starting in the late eighteenth century and continuing until roughly the advent of modernism, the *Bildungsroman* was a dominant narrative form in European literature. The *Bildungsroman* offers an entertaining story of a young person's coming of age, moving from innocence to experience, with lost illusions and great expectations, while making his or her way in the world. The word *Bildungsroman* is sometimes translated as novel (in German, *Roman*) of "education" or "formation," but the term *Bildung* suggests something both wider and more formative than mere "learning." It is an education rather broadly conceived to include establishing a self-image (*Bild* can mean "representation" or "image"), maturing physically, emotionally, and intellectually, and of course learning how the world works, thus gaining the ability to make one's own way in the wider world. Although the form is most associated with the nineteenth-century novel, the *Harry Potter* series represents a remarkable updating of the genre for the twenty-first century. In this essay, I argue that the *Harry Potter* books together form a magical *Bildungsroman* well suited to the postmodern condition in the twenty-first century.

The *Bildungsroman*

Historically, the *Bildungsroman* is a narrative form that seems to reveal the anxieties and opportunities of a society undergoing a transformation, as the tale of a young adult's maturation coincides with sweeping social changes as well. In Western literary history, as Franco Moretti has noted,[1] the *Bildungsroman* is both the product and the mirror of a revolutionary period in which traditional societies were giving way to the vicissitudes of modern industrial development. This process eventually leads to literary modernism, in which the developing personality of the individual becomes all the more fragmented and displaced. The social upheavals of the early nineteenth century caused both opportunities and crises, and the young adult becomes a key figure for a society that was fashioning itself into something new.

The *Bildungsroman* thus registers a certain moment of European history, and the form tends to disintegrate once the processes of modernization have saturated social life. The political and industrial revolutions of the late eighteenth century enabled a new way of thinking and writing about personal development, and this confluence of factors also makes *Bildungsroman* possible. The French Revolution, combined with the industrial revolution, had transformed European societies enormously, as older aristocratic social relations no longer had the same power, and commercial relations increased in influence and power. Suddenly, merely having a good "name" was not enough to ensure people's high status in society, and the pursuit of wealth could take them into any number of professions or places. Young adults, who are filled with anxieties but also possess limitless opportunities, become symbolic of the society itself. As Moretti puts it,

> Virtually without notice, in the   dreams and nightmares of the so-called "double-revolution", Europe plunges into modernity, but without possessing a *culture* of modernity. If youth, therefore, achieves its symbolic centrality, and the "great narrative" of the *Bildungsroman* comes into being, this is because Europe has to attach a meaning, not so much to youth, as to *modernity*.[2]

For example, key differences between Johann Wolfgang von Goethe's *Wilhelm Meister's Apprenticeship* (1796) and James Joyce's *The Portrait of the Artist as a Young Man* (1916), the novels that roughly bookend Moretti's study, indicate the trajectory of the form. In Goethe's novel, which is often considered the archetypal *Bildungsroman*, the young protagonist starts off naive in the ways of both love and the world, but through an elaborate series of adventures among theatrical troupes, businessmen, nobles, and commoners, he ends up a mature, well-rounded adult, in a stable marriage and nicely balancing the artistic and the commercial aspects of his life. Wilhelm Meister's "apprenticeship" is really his journey into the world, where he meets people of all social classes, and where he eventually comes to terms with his own identity. Similarly, Joyce's hero, Stephen Dedalus, leaves home to find his place in the world, but in both the style of the novel and the substance of Dedalus's adventures, the modernist *Portrait of the Artist* differs from Goethe's earlier *Bildungsroman*. Notably, Joyce's style presents a kind of running "stream of consciousness" even when it is narrated in the third person; that is, although the narrator is not Dedalus himself, we indirectly see Dedalus's own thoughts and experiences. His *Bildung*, moreover, is far more interior than Wilhelm Meister's. Dedalus's maturity comes from his own intellectual and psychological development, far more so than Meister, whose learning and self-awareness comes primarily from the variety of other people he encounters. In the little over a century between these two novels, we can see how the *Bildungsroman* moves from a symbolic form of the society as a whole to a symbolic form of the isolated individual within a society.

The *Harry Potter* series obviously did not fit within this historical scheme of things, but in its chronicle of a young person's development from childhood to adult maturity, as well as from ignorance and naivety to knowledge and mastery, the seven volumes can be viewed a fitting example of a *Bildungsroman*. The label is really a little anachronistic, but *Harry Potter* offers a kind of *Bildungsroman* well suited to another epoch of anxieties and uncertainties, which is to say, our own epoch. Straddling the millennia, the *Harry Potter* series is like a postmodern *Bildungsroman*, insofar as it takes place in the late twentieth-century world with which its readers are already quite familiar, but the series confronts our own uncertain present by charting a young person's development through a complex world of magic and reality. In this respect, *Harry Potter* moves beyond the narrow interiority of the modernist subject, bringing to the postmodern moment a form closer to the original eighteenth-century genre but supplementing it with a fantastic mode, most visible in the pervasiveness of magic in the series. *Harry Potter*'s "magical" *Bildungsroman* presents literary history with a marvelous variation of the form.

The advent of *Harry Potter* coincides, perhaps not coincidentally, with a world transformed by globalization and by mass media's penetration of the remotest regions of the globe, where the assurances of a previous era no longer hold true. Magic adds greater wonder to the stories, but also provides a strategy for making sense of the world. The magical world of wizards, house-elves, goblins, trolls, dragons, and Dementors constitutes a meta-world, a realm just beyond the senses of most Muggles, but which is intimately related to our own, often terrifyingly *real* world, as is movingly portrayed in "The Other Minister" chapter of *The Half-Blood Prince*. Also, in showing that what some call "fate" is precisely the result of individual choices,

J. K. Rowling reverses the mainstay fantasy conception of destiny. Whether it was Harry's direction to the Sorting Hat, "Not Slytherin!", in *Sorcerer's Stone*[3] or Voldemort's self-fulfilling prophecy in choosing to kill Harry, as Dumbledore explains in *The Order of the Phoenix*,[4] what seemed to be immutable destiny is revealed to be a series of choices. The *Harry Potter* series presents powerful evidence that "the way of the world" is frequently what readers make of it, a valuable lesson for students and teachers alike.

Although each novel forms a complete story in itself, then, the seven books of the *Harry Potter* series constitute an entire *Bildungsroman* for an age transformed. Rowling's magical *Bildungsroman*, much like Goethe's or Dickens's non-magical ones, helps readers to navigate individual paths in this perilously complex social field and gives readers an Everyman hero, both for whom to root and with whom to explore this world.

Harry Potter's *Bildung*

In a rather literal sense, the entire *Harry Potter* series is "about" Harry's *Bildung*, his development from a boy into a man, as well as from a slightly awkward Muggle into a great wizard. It is also, as Rowling so movingly dramatizes, a process of Harry's finding out who and what he is. Readers see this in the ways he learns, bit by bit and hint by hint, about his parents, about his role in a prophecy, and about his relationship to the world. *Harry Potter*, not surprisingly, is an extended story of "Harry Potter," of the formation and definition of this person bearing that name. In this sense, the series fit well within our general understanding of the *Bildungsroman* as a genre.

According to Marianne Hirsch's helpful examination of the genre,[5] the *Bildungsroman* has a number of distinguishing characteristics, all of which seem to fit the *Harry Potter* series quite well. We can address the points of correlation briefly. In Hirsch's model, "The novel of formation is a novel that focuses on one central character [...]. It is the story of a representative individual's *growth and development* within the context of a defined social order."[6] Harry Potter certainly fits the bill. It is "biographical and social," and its plot is "a version of the quest story." In each volume and across the *Harry Potter* series as a whole, Harry engages in a quest while the narrative continues to tell his life story and to present details of the wizarding society. The *Bildungsroman* is principally concerned with "the development of selfhood," ending with the protagonist's "*assessment of himself and his place in society*."[7] In Harry's case, this very much means that part of his "quest" is to discover himself and his place in the larger scheme of things, as readers see this process culminate in his "Chosen One" status in *The Half-Blood Prince* and *The Deathly Hallows*. With respect to narrative voice, "There is always a distance between the perspective of the narrator and that of the protagonist," which enables the reader to witness "errors and the pursuit of false leads" along the way.[8] This space between the narrator and the protagonist is quite usefully maintained in *Harry Potter* by the distance created through the third-person narrative voice, but also by making sure that the reader stays close to Harry at all times.

Interestingly, with only a few exceptions, the entire seven volumes are told in the third person but largely still *from the perspective* of one following Harry around; that is, although the perspective is not Harry's, the narrator "looks over Harry's shoulder," as it were, which allows the reader to see Harry's actions at all times without necessarily being limited to Harry's point of view. The exceptions to this narrative proximity to Harry include the following scenes: the first chapter of *Sorcerer's Stone* ("The Boy Who Lived,"[9] in which Harry appears only at the very end, as a sleeping infant), the first chapter of *The Goblet of Fire* ("The Riddle House"[10]), the first two of *The Half-Blood Prince* ("The Other Minister" and "Spinner's End"[11]), and the first of *The Deathly Hallows* ("The Dark Lord Ascending"[12]). That these all come at the beginning of their respective volumes suggests that they function as prologues, setting the mood as well as giving readers the rare glimpse of a scene to which Harry is not quite privy. The introductory "The Boy Who Lived," in fact, like the Epilogue at the end of *The Deathly Hallows*, is really outside of the main narrative of *Harry Potter* entirely. Hence, other than in these five chapters scattered across the series, the reader is able to follow Harry Potter's own experiences and thoughts, while also maintaining sufficient distance to view him somewhat objectively.

As Hirsch continues her list of the *Bildungsroman*'s attributes, "The novel's other characters fulfill several mixed functions: *educators* serve as mediators and interpreters between the two conflicting forces of self and society; *companions* serve as reflectors of the protagonist, standing for alternative goals and achievements […]; *lovers* provide the opportunity for the education of sentiment."[13] Readers may clearly see these aspects in the "secondary" characters of Dumbledore, Ron and Hermione, and Ginny, among others. Additionally, the *Bildungsroman* is "a *didactic* novel, one which educates the reader by portraying the education of the protagonist."[14] I maintain that much of the enjoyment lies in the reader's joint-educational mission; whether the scene is actually Hogwarts School of Witchcraft and Wizardry or elsewhere, the reader learns right alongside Harry the ways of the wizarding world.

The social hero

The *Ur*-text, as noted above, for any discussion of the *Bildungsroman* is Goethe's tale of Wilhelm Meister's apprenticeship; the German word is *Lehrjahre*, or literally "year of learning", so it is fitting that Harry's story is, more than anything, a narrative of his education, both at Hogwarts and, more generally, in the wizarding world itself. Hogwarts also provides Harry with a utopian space from which he can safely—perhaps, given the mortal dangers he faces so often, this is not the best term for it—explore the wonders of this brave new world of magic. In any case, it is a relatively enclosed setting for Harry to mature and to learn. The various leaps into the wider world, whether attending such events as the Quidditch World Cup or in his quests for Horcruxes later, are still harrowing, of course, but they are not entirely unfamiliar to Harry, thanks to his formal and informal education or apprenticeship.

Other features, as well, link *Harry Potter* to the novel of education or formation. The *Bildungsroman* combines the general and the specific, often in interesting ways. This helps to make its hero—a specific, even remarkable, individual—into a general or representative Everyman. Hence, Harry Potter, with his misleadingly or tellingly pedestrian name, is both the remarkable and unique "Boy Who Lived" or "Chosen One," and just another good guy muddling through. Like Hermione, Ron, Neville, and all the others, Harry struggles not only against the forces of evil, but also against the usual schoolboy problems, such as dealing with bullies, worrying about doing well in class or on the Quidditch field, experiencing the mixed feelings over romantic entanglements, and so on. Throughout the process, the individualized hero becomes a representative figure to which all readers (who are Muggles, by and large) can easily relate. Indeed, although one tends to think of the *Bildungsroman*, and the novel in general, as a profoundly individual form, focused as it is on the development of an individual, it is really much more of a tale in which the individual becomes part of a community or social whole. As Marc Redfield has put it, "the *Bildungsroman* narrates the acculturation of a self—the integration of a particular 'I' into the general subjectivity of a community, and thus, finally, into the universal subjectivity of humanity."[15]

Harry Potter highlights this aspect in a couple of ways: first, by making Harry's development a matter of teamwork, especially in the collaborations with Hermione and Ron, but also in his interactions with various characters throughout the series (e.g., Hagrid, Dobby, Lupin, Moody, Sirius, Dumbledore, Griphook, and others), the series displays how Harry's own *Bildung* is very much a collective effort. And second, by having Harry integrate himself into the wizarding world very gradually, the reader is allowed to discover a broad and nuanced social totality. For example, even in *The Deathly Hallows*, set six or seven years after he enrolls in Hogwarts, Harry is still marveling at things he had never even heard of before, and the reader can still discover novelties while appreciating a vast treasury of knowledge built up along the way. This is very much like the process of education itself.

The complex world cannot easily be processed by an isolated individual, so to see an individual attempting the impossible has some value in itself. To see that individual working with others, who are themselves also largely in the dark and still slogging along trying to figure things out, like the rest of us, is an important lesson. Even Dumbledore, readers come to realize, is ignorant of some things and prone to make mistakes. Indeed, as Rowling makes clear in ways that renders her own pedagogy, if not her storytelling, superior to other fantasists such as C. S. Lewis or J. R. R. Tolkien, what is most "evil" about her great enemy, Voldemort, is not that he is essentially or primordially evil, but that he refuses to acknowledge that his own individual talents, prodigious though they be, are not enough. Voldemort's unwillingness to integrate himself into society is what, in the end, prevents him from both knowing and ruling that society. It is also what makes him *inhuman*, and it is what makes Harry so very human, with all the lovable flaws that accompany that tragic condition.

Harry's distinctly social and frequently circuitous path to gaining knowledge of himself and his world is quite typical. The trajectory of the *Bildungsroman* is not so much linear, such as a rise from a lowly state to an exalted one or from rags to riches, but circular. In his study of the German *Bildungsroman*, starting with *Wilhelm Meister's Apprenticeship* and continuing to Thomas Mann's 1924 novel *The Magic Mountain*, Michael Minden points out that, while the "idea of *Bildung*—the development or formation of a young man—is basically linear," the novels are "in fact circular."[16] Harry's *Bildung* does not simply lead from boyhood to manhood or wizardhood, but it comes full circle, with Harry reenacting the primal confrontation with Voldemort again and again: dueling Professor Quirrell in *The Sorcerer's Stone*, with Tom Riddle and the Basilisk in *The Chamber of Secrets*, with

Wormtail in *The Prisoner of Azkaban*, and with Voldemort in person in *The Goblet of Fire*, *The Order of the Phoenix*, and *The Deathly Hallows*, the final showdown. After all of these episodes, even amid the horror of seeing Cedric Diggory or Sirius Black killed, Harry comes to a greater understanding of his place in the world, even if he is not yet "at home" in it. Quoting Novalis, Minden notes that the movement is "immer nach Hause," that is, always towards home.[17] This is why so many of these tales end in marriage, in the establishment of a home and family, a practice that the *Harry Potter* series continues. Even with such young persons as her protagonists, Rowling could not help to include in her Epilogue (titled "Nineteen Years Later") a scene in which Harry and Ginny, as well as Ron and Hermione, are married and now sending their own children off to Hogwarts, closing the circle of the entire series, while also underscoring the continuity, and endless continuation, of life.[18] The circuitous trajectory from youth to maturity is therefore marked, in *Harry Potter* and in the *Bildungsroman* genre broadly, as a distinctively social experience, and Harry's engagement with others is crucial to his development and ultimate success.

Magic as method

Magic is the critical element of the postmodern *Bildungsroman* in *Harry Potter*, perhaps as opposed to the modern *Bildungsroman* with its emphasis on social or psychological realism. Harry's education requires that he learn the ways of the wizarding world, but also that he learn to use magic effectively. As with traditional tales in which the hero loses innocence and gains experience, Harry discovers more and more about the magical world, how it operates, and how it relates or does not relate to the Muggle world. For the most part, the wizard's world appears to parallel this other one quite neatly. For instance, its own Ministry of Magic stands in for, or alongside, the British parliament and ministries, and so on. There are even parallel histories, as famous wizards include Paracelsus and Cornelius Agrippa who are also well known in Muggle lore, and the ominous rise of Grindelwald in middle Europe clearly coincides with the rise of Hitler and the Second World War. Even the more quotidian aspects of contemporary society, such as the boring jobs, transportation hassles, and tedious regulations find their magical counterparts in the wizarding world.

Additionally, in Harry's world as in ours, individuals constantly need to find ways to make sense of things. Magic is one such way. Magic, like its "real world" analogue technology, can make life easier by solving problems, but it also makes things more complicated, as

Harry discovers over and over again. Muggles' machines fulfill the same functions as wizards' magic does, and readers see Arthur Weasley delighting in this fact: "'*Fascinating!*' he would say as Harry talked him through using a telephone. '*Ingenious*, really, how many ways Muggles have found of getting along without magic'."[19] In fact, the Weasleys prove that relying on magic can be quite the handicap in the Muggle world, as when Ron claims, "'I know how to use a fellytone now',"[20] thus revealing his ignorance. In what is a nice touch, particularly as the realm of magic and wizardry would normally seem so preferable, Rowling shows that wizards are nearly as lost in the non-magical world as Muggles are when faced with inexplicable enchantments.

Rowling's great precursor Tolkien had linked magic and machines as two forms of the same thing: the power to control, for good or ill, the world around us. Explaining his use of "the Machine" or "Magic" in a letter (undated, but probably written in 1951), Tolkien writes that it refers to "all use of external plans or devices (apparatus) instead of developments of the inherent inner powers or talents—or even the use of these talents with the corrupted motive of dominating [...]. The Machine is our more obvious modern form though more closely related to Magic than is usually recognized."[21] Magic, in this case, is another form of technology, of which the *Harry Potter* books are also full.[22]

The magic wand is perhaps the best example of this, since it is a tool that enables one to assume greater control over a given situation. Julia Pond has noted that the wand is a "type of magical object through which fate operates."[23] Furthermore, according to Ollivander, in *The Deathly Hallows*, a wizard's *Bildung* is closely tied to that of his wand. Indeed, for the wizarding world, in which magic is the crucial element—both for understanding the world and for changing it—the magic wand is the principal tool, as well as an important symbol. As Ollivander tells Harry, any wizard worth his salt can "do" magic with any old wand, but the elective affinities between wand and wizard will produce the greatest magic. Harry had learned back in *The Sorcerer's Stone* that "it's really the wand that chooses the wizard, of course,"[24] and this is underscored again later: "'The wand chooses the wizard,' said Ollivander. 'That much has always been clear to those of us who have studied wandlore'."[25] Ollivander then explains that the power formed by the mutual energies of wizard-and-wand progresses according to the mutual development of the wand and its user. Essentially, a wizard's wand has its own *Bildung*, or, rather, the *Bildung* of the wizard is intimately tied to the *Bildung* of the wand. As Ollivander puts it, "'The best results, however, must always come where there is the strongest affinity between wizard and wand. These connections are complex. An initial attraction and then a mutual quest for experience, the wand learning from the wizard, the wizard from the wand'."[26]

This sort of *Bildung* resonates well with the postmodern condition, in which the "grand narratives" of modern thought (as Jean-François Lyotard would have it) no longer function as credible guides to understanding and controlling the forces affecting humanity at its most basic levels.[27] Earlier models for making sense of the social and natural spheres have seemed to many to be inadequate or flat-out deceptive in attempting to answer the perplexing problems of life in the twenty-first century. Yet one cannot really abandon the process of *Bildung* and the desire for understanding merely because the former certainties no longer hold. *Harry Potter*, in fact, provides a wonderful dramatization of the ways that, when confronted with absolute marvels and belief-shattering novelties, we may still press on and even achieve the sort of practical understanding that allows one to lead a happy life even in times of terrifying uncertainty. Describing what he conceded was a rather modernist strategy for overcoming the spatial and political crises of postmodernity, Fredric Jameson called for "an aesthetic of cognitive mapping," a figural or allegorical means of getting a sense of the enormous and unrepresentable totality of a world-system—the alarming vicissitudes of the global financial networks, for example—that can affect us severely, and in ways readers cannot really know by traditional means.[28] Similarly, as a means of representing and making sense of our somewhat bewildering circumstances, magic is a sort of mapmaking activity, providing a plan by which readers can at least provisionally make their way in the world. Magic, when employed by a well-educated wizard, can help make sense of the confusion.

Knowing the world

If magic is a kind of machine, then it is also an educational tool, a means of making sense of, or giving form to, the world we live in. The *Bildungsroman* is an epistemological genre, a form through which the reader may gain knowledge while also following the learning processes of one or more key characters. In this aspect, it is like the gothic novel, and *Harry Potter* certainly draws heavily upon the image repertoire associated with that genre as well. Gothic texts frequently depict a narrative movement from mystery and wonder towards knowledge and understanding. Gothic fiction also places the individual within a confounding and often frightening milieu, which he or she has to transform into a meaningful and coherent order somehow. In Marshall Brown's words, "As their chaotic events unfold, the [gothic] novels return insistently to problems of orientation in time and place, to coherence of experience in a world of magic or mystery, to participation in a community under threat of isolation—in short, to the various continuities of meaning that stabilize a world at risk."[29] In *Harry Potter*, the "world of magic and mystery" overlaps with a more stable world, presenting magic as a perfectly suitable way of dealing with real-world problems. As he makes his way in the wizarding world, Harry's journey becomes an allegorical representation of our own efforts towards a "cognitive mapping" of our world-system.

In a significant, even primal, scene for the entire *Bildungsroman* that is the *Harry Potter* series, Hagrid tries to explain to Harry who he is, what he is, and what "our world" is. Furious at discovering that the Dursleys have not told Harry of his own past, Hagrid growls, "Do you mean ter tell me [...] that this boy—this boy!—knows nothin' abou'—about ANYTHING?" Harry, at first offended, starts to protest that he actually knows a lot of "math and stuff," but Hagrid explains, offhandedly, that he means "About *our* world, I mean. *Your* world. *My* world."[30] Of course, Hagrid means the wizarding world rather than "our world" more generally (i.e., that of the readers), but the scene invites us to explore the world with Harry. After all, the *Harry Potter* series does not really tell us who Harry is or what our world is like, only that these are questions that readers can now seek answers to, quests that readers can embark upon. Rowling's magical *Bildungsroman* invites us to join in Harry's novel of formation or education. It encourages the reader to use his or her imagination, a powerful force in its own right, to become a wizard or witch as well, and, as Hagrid encourages us, each of us can be "a thumpin' good'un, I'd say, once yeh've been trained up a bit."[31]

In exploring the ways of the wizarding world in the *Harry Potter* series, readers gain lasting insights into their own world. As it unfolds in Rowling's work, the magical *Bildungsroman* offers a fascinating reconceptualization of the older genre. This narrative form, like its predecessor, still educates as it entertains, but it also enables a different perspective on the real world. Whereas the older *Bildungsroman* narrated the protagonist's gradual and hard-earned disenchantments and capitulation to the "real world," *Harry Potter*'s fantastic novel of education allows us to understand the enchanting powers of the very real world we occupy.

Notes

1. F. Moretti, *The Way of the World: The* Bildungsroman *in European Culture*, trans. A. Sbragia, 2nd edn (London: Verso, 2000).
2. *Ibid.*: 5, emphasis in original.
3. SS[A]: 121.
4. OP[A]: 842.
5. M. Hirsch, "From Great Expectations to Lost Illusions: The Novel of Formation as a Genre," *Genre* 12(3) (1979): 293–311, see especially 296–8.
6. *Ibid.*: 296, emphasis in original.
7. *Ibid.*: 297, emphasis in original.
8. *Ibid.*
9. SS[A]: 1–17.
10. GF[A]: 1–15.
11. HP[A]: 1–37.
12. DH[A]: 1–12.
13. Hirsch: 298, emphasis in original.
14. *Ibid.*
15. M. Redfield, *Phantom Formations: Aesthetic Ideology and the* Bildungsroman (Ithaca, NY: Cornell University Press, 1996): 38.
16. M. Minden, *The German* Bildungsroman*: Incest and Inheritance* (Cambridge: Cambridge University Press, 1997): 1.
17. *Ibid.*: 1.
18. DH[A]: 753–9.
19. CS[A]: 43.
20. PA[A]: 431.
21. See H. Carpenter (ed.), *The Letters of J.R.R. Tolkien* (Boston, MA: Houghton Mifflin, 2000): 145–6.
22. See E. Teare, "Harry Potter and the Technology of Magic," in L. A. Whited (ed.), *The Ivory Tower and Harry Potter* (Columbia, MO: University of Missouri Press, 2002): 329–42.
23. J. Pond, "Story of the Exceptional: Fate and Free Will in the Harry Potter Series," *Children's Literature* 38 (2010): 181–206, at 189.
24. SS[A]: 82.
25. DH[A]: 494.
26. *Ibid.*
27. F. Lyotard, *The Postmodern Condition*, trans. G. Bennington and B. Massumi (Minneapolis, MN: University of Minnesota Press, 1984): 31–7.
28. F. Jameson, *Postmodernism, or, The Cultural Logic of Late Capitalism* (Durham, NC: Duke University Press, 1990): especially 51–4 and 415–18.
29. M. Brown, *The Gothic Text* (Palo Alto, CA: Stanford University Press, 2005): xiv.
30. SS[A]: 49–50.
31. *Ibid.*: 51.

4

Bewitching, Abject, Uncanny: Other Spaces in the *Harry Potter* Films

Fran Pheasant-Kelly

Following the 2011 release of the final film in the *Harry Potter* series, *The Deathly Hallows: Part 2*,[1] the cinematic adaptations (2001–11) of J. K. Rowling's novels (1997–2007) became the highest grossing franchise ever.[2] The films, inevitably eliciting comparison to their literary sources, display a general fidelity to the novels, although Philip Nel contends that "the attempt to be completely faithful hampers those first two films [while] recognition of the impossibility of being completely faithful liberates the third, fourth, and fifth films."[3] Irrespective of fidelity issues, the different capacities of the visual medium afford certain emphases not available in the novels. For example, Suman Gupta comments that "[a]long with the music the visual effect of the Hogwarts environment provides a sense of continuity that is not wholly due to the descriptions in the books."[4] Gupta further highlights features of the *mise-en-scène* that become more prominent in the films, including the visual impact of colors, costume, and the Gothic settings, as well as a more distinct contiguity between the Muggle and the magic worlds.[5] A marked deviation from the final novel is its two-part cinematic version, while those films made after 2001 display an inflection of their new-millennial contexts not always apparent in the written texts, in particular, in their references to 9/11 and terrorism.

This essay, however, does not intend to analyze the films as adaptations; rather it centers on the visual rendering of the filmic spaces, in particular, their magical, abject, and uncanny qualities, which project their psychological impact and significance. Such settings position the world of wizardry within the generic sphere of fantasy, and are often crucial to motivating each film's plot, since Harry Potter's (Daniel Radcliffe) investigation of them eventually resolves the series'[6] central enigma. In line with the narrative trajectory of many fantasy films, the successful negotiation of the various spaces thus ultimately proves to be a rite of passage.

Initially, however, attention centers on the repressive, confined space that Harry occupies at his foster parents' home. The centrality of space is further apparent in Harry's entry to the world of Hogwarts, which involves transition through a seemingly solid brick wall into a parallel universe. In fact, alongside the external realms of London and Surrey exist the magical, parallel spaces of Diagon Alley, Knockturn Alley, and the Ministry of Magic. Hogwarts itself comprises spaces that invoke unease, fear, or terror. Disgusting, unreal spaces feature prominently, in addition to internal spaces of the psyche, such as memory, nightmares, and thought. Thus, although Hogwarts is a site of schooling, its focus does not lie in the conventional training of social and cultural norms. Rather, it encourages the orchestration of objects in space, and the moral and physical navigation of the self through space. Harry must learn to master different, other spaces in order to prove himself.

This essay also connects certain spaces to the films' post-9/11 contexts. In so doing, it locates the films' commercial accomplishments not only in their literary sources, but also in the generalized success of fantasy film since 9/11. Indeed, *The Philosopher's Stone*[7] and its contemporary, *The Fellowship of the Ring*,[8] heralded an upturn in the fortunes of fantasy film, now the most lucrative genre of the twenty-first century. One obvious explanation for their achievements lay in providing a respite from the 9/11 footage that had saturated the media before their release. Indeed, Kathy Smith suggests that, "in the wake of the realization of events previously confined to disaster movies, the global audience looked for a different kind of fantasy into which to escape, a 'guaranteed' fantasy, the reality of which was securely beyond imagination."[9]

However, the relief implied in Smith's claim seems inconsistent with the *Potter* films' persistent engagement with death. This essay therefore contends that such engagement operates through Barbara Klinger's concept of the "arresting image,"[10] unconsciously mobilizing spectator emotion through associations and memories. In these instances, Klinger describes how "the forward motion of the narrative slows down or temporarily halts, allowing the spectacle to fully capture our attention."[11] She also notes how "[t]he arresting image may have an additionally unusual temporal status, often appearing outside of time in a fantasy or dream-like dimension".[12] Additionally, "[a]rresting images are often generated by juxtaposing incongruous elements"[13] thereby conferring a surreal quality, while the narrative's temporality tends to distort those images.

Such features occur frequently in the films, most obviously, when Harry falls under the psychic influence of his enemy Voldemort (Ralph Fiennes), but also in connection to memory, death, and danger (mediated through bewitched, or magical, uncanny or uncomfortably strange, and abject, or wretched, spaces). The utilization of acute camera angles and extreme perspectives is important in this respect since these choices often enhance the films' magical, wretched, and unfamiliar aspects. Direct movement towards the camera further accentuates threat for the spectator. Alternatively, extreme long shots exaggerate the spectacular nature of conflict and death. These combined effects effectively dissect such scenes from the narratives as arresting images, thereby amplifying their potentially emotional resonances. Additionally, such episodes often deploy imagery directly pertaining to 9/11 and terrorism.

In respect of the novels, Lori Campbell also correlates Harry's quest for identity with the broader socio-political contexts found in the novels, but locates these concerns in a "twentieth-century Great Britain coming to terms with its heroic past."[14] Arguably, the films speak to larger audiences in terms of their post-9/11 associations. Campbell also sees the "other-worlds" of the *Potter* novels as "externalizations of the hero's inner workings."[15] In short, she aligns space with subjectivity and, referring to Honeyman, further notes that the child character may become the vicarious means by which the adult reader (or spectator) accesses the fantasy space.[16]

Visually, the fantasy genre possesses an intrinsic capacity to articulate concerns about terrorism through the "other," here reconfiguring the terrorist as (abject) spectacle in the form of Voldemort and his various incarnations. Moreover, while the films' utilization of magic is attractive to a younger audience, its transformative power, spiritual associations, and conjuring of an afterlife may also unconsciously offer consolation to adult viewers bereaved by the war on terror or 9/11.

The iconography, themes, and narrative structure of the *Potter* films, as fantasies, therefore offer an ideal template on which to map spectator anxieties. In addition, the realm of fantasy, in contrast to real life, enables a sense of resolution, if not necessarily a "happy ending." Indeed, there is already general recognition that traditional fantasy and fairy tales provide consolation, escapism, and recovery,[17] while

Bruno Bettelheim notes that, "[t]he fairy tale [...] confronts the child squarely with the basic human predicaments."[18]

In a similar vein, this essay suggests that the *Potter* films offer safe ways to subconsciously reenact, or work through anxieties for contemporary viewers. Ostensibly, it argues that while narratively and generically tied to the typical fantasy quest (as a means to consolidate subjectivity), the films' fantasy spaces may resonate with contemporary audiences through Klinger's "arresting image."[19] Engaging primarily with Julia Kristeva's study of the abject,[20] Sigmund Freud's notion of the uncanny,[21] and Klinger's concept of the "arresting image,"[22] this essay examines the films' abject and uncanny spaces, their connections with magic, and their meaning for post-9/11 audiences.

Kristeva and the abject

Kristeva's explanation of abjection is relevant to this essay in several respects. Primarily, abjection emerges through compromises to subjectivity; that is, where our subject identity is threatened in some way. The abject has to do with feelings of repulsion. These threats may arise in various ways, but in infancy occur in the child's separation from (initially during childbirth) or rejection of the maternal body in the constitution of subjectivity. Kristeva explains that, "[t]he abject confronts us [...] with our earliest attempts to release the hold of *maternal* entity even before existing outside of her."[23] A major source of contamination is the corpse, for "the corpse, seen without God and outside of science, is the utmost of abjection,"[24] while food revulsion, arising from taboo or polluting sources, figures prominently. Abjection further includes the exclusion of bodily disgust or forms of "difference" that may be racially motivated. Initially, this "mapping of the self's clean and proper body"[25] depends on the mother, a function that the developing subject takes over. A failure to keep the abject at bay may involve incursion of the body's physical border or its social boundaries. Additionally, immoral acts are abject,[26] while a loss of ego through psychological disturbance, and the violation of geographic boundaries may further target identity.[27] Consequently, any transgression that "disturbs identity, system, order" is liable to abjection.[28] Therefore, though we usually associate the abject with physical signs of repulsion, it may also encompass non-somatic, topographical or psychological aspects.

The abject becomes germane to the *Potter* films in several ways: partly, it surfaces at times when Harry undergoes physically repellent and near-death experiences in his progression towards a coherent adult identity. In such cases, the negotiation of such spaces parallels the exclusion of bodily detritus vital to the maintenance of subjectivity. At the same time, these encounters help elucidate Voldemort as a source of evil, and resolve the issue of Harry's identity. In confrontations with Voldemort and his followers, abjection sometimes functions differently, since attention often centers on the maintenance of protective "magical" boundaries as a means of exclusion. These include, for example, Harry's invisibility cloak, the protective shield that Hermione (Emma Watson) summons in *The Deathly Hallows: Part 1*,[29] and the similar shield that Professor McGonagall (Maggie Smith) conjures in *The Deathly Hallows: Part 2*. In other cases, Harry's moral decisions are vital to his development.

More specifically, and corresponding with Kristeva's concept of maternal abjection, Harry is constantly drawn back to his parental world, the film repeatedly flashing back to scenes of him as an infant or as part of a family unit (his reflection in the Mirror of Erised visually encapsulates this desire). The point of separation from his mother was particularly horrific. At the same time, Harry's identity was permanently compromised because Voldemort's attack on him led to the implant of a Horcrux (part of Voldemort's soul) within Harry. Therefore, Harry is unable to divorce himself entirely from the abject until he has fully accepted the death of his parents and rid himself of the contaminating Horcrux.

Subjectivity and the abject

A constant tension exists between Harry's need to attain subjectivity (and take his father's place), and his desire to return to the parental world. For although Harry's identity is distinct in the films' titles, narratively his past is obscure. His quest, while being one of destroying his evil opponent Voldemort, also entails the discovery of his own origins. As John Kornfeld and Laurie Prothro note, "Harry's solitary search for his true family is a search for his own identity; his quest for home and family is the journey all young people take trying to find their place in the world."[30] Ultimately, though intimated in the House Sorting Ceremony, and by Harry's ability to converse with snakes in Parseltongue, viewers realize by the sixth film that Harry's identity relates intimately to that of Voldemort.

The narratives also draw more generally upon instabilities of identity for their various twists and turns. For example, several of the characters' identities change over the course of the eight films, either because they are "Animagi" (shape-shifters) or because of drinking

Polyjuice Potion. Integral to the terror that Voldemort instills is his capacity to assume an amorphous, disembodied form. As Barbara Creed explains, "the monstrous is produced at the border between human and inhuman,"[31] the ability to shape-shift thus invoking abjection in its disruption of bodily boundaries.

Language, magic, and the symbolic

To some extent, attaining subjectivity in the *Potter* world depends on the controlled performance of magic. This connection relates to the abject in its focus on linguistic articulation. Kristeva[32] explains that the abject maternal world, the semiotic *chora*, is one dependent on gestures and sounds rather than structured language. Conversely, the paternal (symbolic) world of the subject possesses order and structure, especially pertaining to language. Language therefore differentiates semiotic and symbolic forms. However, Kristeva maintains that since intonation and gesture are vital for meaning in the symbolic, the semiotic continues to underpin the symbolic. In the general sphere of magic, Marcel Mauss too comments that, "intonation is sometimes more important than the actual words. Gestures are regulated with an equally fine precision"[33] in relation to the *Potter* films; Katherine Fowkes states that, "[t]he magic spells that the characters employ in *Potter* are rooted in ancient language and they demand a performance of voice and gesture suffused with a sense of ritual."[34] In a related way, Kristeva's notion of the semiotic and symbolic is relevant to the chanting of spells in the *Potter* films. Here, the students' conjuring skills not only rest on the successful swish of a wand but also on a mastery of enunciation, for in lectures the students are told, "just swish and flick, and *enunciate*."

Freud and the uncanny

In general, there are alliances between the abject and the uncanny, though the former is mostly associated with feelings of repulsion, and the latter, with sensations of dread. Moreover, the abject poses a persistent threat while the uncanny may be permanently repressed. In the *Potter* films, however, there is a fundamental proximity between the two pertaining to Harry's mother. Freud states that, ordinarily, the traumatic memory of birth is repressed. For Harry, a secondary repression occurs at the time of his mother's murder. Eventually, however, he re-experiences her death through flashbacks, displaying symptoms related to post-traumatic stress disorder. (For some viewers, this element may reflect the real trauma of 9/11.) Apart from the films' abject significations, Harry Potter's world thereby also involves elements of the uncanny.

Freud identifies multiple forms of the uncanny, but in general, describes it as a "theory of the qualities of feeling"[35] whereby sensations of unease are generated by examples such as the ghost, the double, and the automaton. Predominantly, such feelings reflect a fear of death, with Freud commenting that "many people experience the feeling in the highest degree in relation to death and dead bodies, to the return of the dead, and to spirits and ghosts."[36] He also describes the uncanny as "that class of the frightening which leads back to what is known of old and long familiar."[37]

Freud suggests that this combination of strangeness and familiarity resonates most strongly in relation to the mother's body, the original home, which is a "forgotten" place (as a site of trauma) but still familiar. He concludes that, "an uncanny experience occurs either when infantile complexes which have been repressed are once more revived by some impression."[38] In film, these moments often arise in spaces that have visual associations (for example, dark, damp and enclosing) with uterine imagery, such as the cellar. In this respect, the depths of Hogwarts frequently have connotations of the uncanny.

Freud's comment that, "there is a doubling, dividing and interchanging of the self"[39] has relevance to the films' narrative since Harry's quest is in part one of clarifying his origin. The element of "interchanging of the self" is a particularly dominant danger in relation to Voldemort, Pamela Thurschwell explaining that, "this too relates to primitive beliefs about death."[40] Moreover, ghosts and automata, uncanny in the way that they simultaneously acknowledge and repress death, figure prominently in the films, while the revelation of repressed and hidden memories is a significant visual and narrative element. The uncanny is also salient to discourses of magic, since Freud locates the uncanny in animism, a belief system that considers that all living entities possess a soul.[41]

According to Jack Zipes, "the very act of reading, hearing or viewing a fairytale is an uncanny experience in that it separates the reader from the restrictions of reality […] and makes the repressed unfamiliar familiar once again."[42] Zipes goes on to say that during this experience, "there is estrangement or separation from a familiar world inducing an uncanny feeling which can be both frightening and comforting."[43] In a similar vein, this essay contends that the emergence of the uncanny in arresting imagery often mobilizes feelings of both unease and familiarity (in relation to 9/11), arguably enabling a working through of spectator anxiety in relation to contemporaneous concerns.

Abject spaces in the *Potter* films

Over the course of the eight films, the nature of abject space changes, the earliest ones being concerned with physical disgust, and the later ones (whose filming began after 2001) featuring abjection in relation to boundary transgression and terrorist activity (reflecting issues of national security). The final two films especially resonate with images of death and conflict, plus challenges to Harry's identity through increasing psychic disturbance, their darker visual style being politically inflected, and their imagery often resembling 9/11. Scenes of graphic bloodshed and cruelty become more noticeable, with both aspects having abject connotations.

Initially, though, the series opens in an ordinary suburban street where Professors McGonagall and Dumbledore (Richard Harris), together with Hogwart's giant, Hagrid (Robbie Coltrane), leave the infant Harry Potter on the Dursley's doorstep. The film then cuts to Harry at the age of 11, asleep in a cupboard under the stairs, a cramped space that lacks any privacy or comfort. While not obviously abject (in the sense of physical repulsion), there is evidence of the repression of Harry's identity, with the Dursleys' domination of him apparent in consistently low-angle shots of them. Even when Harry acquires his cousin Dudley's (Harry Melling) second bedroom in the second movie, his Uncle Vernon (Richard Griffiths) bars the windows and bolts the doors, Harry's entrapment emphasized by exterior close-ups that look in at him through the bars. The compulsory caging of his pet owl, Hedwig, metaphorically reflects Harry's imprisonment, the use of close-up emphasizing its constriction. When "important" visitors arrive at the Dursley house, Harry ironically comments about hiding in his bedroom, not making any noise while pretending he does not exist.[44] Space therefore relates integrally to Harry's sense of self. In subsequent scenes at Hogwarts, however, his access to and increasingly masterful negotiation of threatening spaces signals a steady transition to adulthood.

Abjection and disgust

As Harry begins to master these threatening spaces, the films' ability to trigger sensations of disgust in the viewer manifests frequently.

Ron Weasley's (Rupert Grint) vomiting of slugs in the second film is a typical example. In relation to these scenes, Lisa Damour argues that, "repulsion is critical to the story line—but much of the time it's just for fun."[45] However, while indicating the fascination of abjection for children, the literal passage through it has implications for adolescence, a time when mastery of the physical body is essential to attaining a coherent adult identity. Consequently, the bathroom tends to be a focal point for scenes of abjection.

The first of these scenes arises in *The Philosopher's Stone* when a giant troll attacks Hermione. Low-key lighting, lightning effects, and dark shadows imply threat while low-angle shots from Harry and Ron's perspective emphasize the troll's enormity. A point-of-view shot from Hermione's perspective first looks down towards the troll's feet and then looks up from an extreme low angle to the troll's head. A cut to long shot of both Hermione and the troll further accentuates the troll's colossal stature. Repeated extreme low-angle shots looking up towards the troll continually convey its scale before Harry jumps onto its head. He then inserts his wand into one of its nostrils and Ron stuns it. As Harry retrieves his wand from the troll's nose, shown in close-up, viscous fluid drips from it, providing an example of abject bodily disgust, its qualities perhaps also having sexual connotations.

Bodily fluids pervade the imagery of the second film, too, which again features the girls' bathroom as an abject space since it is not only haunted by a nihilistic ghost called Moaning Myrtle (Shirley Henderson), but also conceals the entrance to the Chamber of Secrets, an underground labyrinth allegedly home to a monstrous basilisk. The labyrinth itself has connotations of the inner body, while the snake's huge fangs, seen in extreme close-up, drip with saliva and venom. A tracking shot down its entire length emphasizes the enormity of its body, while it glides continually towards the camera, intensifying sensations of danger for the spectator. Having defeated the monster, Harry destroys Tom Riddle's (Christian Coulson) "memory" (found within a diary conjured as a physical space) by jabbing one of the snake's fangs into the bewitched book. Seen in close-up, blood gushes from its blank pages while the psychic space that the book encompasses is further abject because it is a Horcrux.

Some of the most obviously abject spaces are those leading to the site of the Philosopher's Stone. Indeed, Dumbledore signals their foreboding nature when he tells the students to stay away from the third floor in order to avoid dying quite painfully. Dark shadows, low-key lighting and canted angles are ominous, while slow motion and distorted sound effects accentuate the air of terror. Here, a gigantic three-headed dog guards the entrance to the trapdoor through which Harry, Hermione, and Ron must pass. Extreme low camera angles from the trio's point of view heighten the abject aspects of the dog, whose three heads clearly disturb "identity, system, order,"[46] while close-ups of its snapping jaws further amplify its menace.

Returning later, they find the dog asleep. While a close-up of one of its paws fills the frame, the trio's small size in comparison indicates its massive proportions and as they open the trapdoor, a dark shadow engulfs them. At the moment that Harry warns his friends to leave should anything untoward happen to him, an extreme low-angle shot from inside the trapdoor reveals the three-headed hound, its teeth bared, and saliva dripping from its mouth as it looms above both the spectator and the three children. An ensuing medium close-up of Ron reveals a huge pool of saliva dripping down his shoulder before cutting to a high-angle shot from the hound's perspective. This visceral dimension adds to the dog's abject status, sound effects highlighting its viscous nature, and contributing to the "repulsion […] for fun" that Damour identifies.[47]

As the three jump down through the trapdoor to escape the dog, they land on the writhing tendrils of an anthropomorphized plant called Devil's Snare. Close framing and low-key lighting emphasize their anxiety as the plant coils itself rapidly around their bodies, although they escape, falling further downwards. The theme of falling thus recurs frequently, becoming increasingly discernible in the later films. Sound is important too, with the viscous sounds of the plant contributing to its abject status.

Harry's final obstacle to securing the Philosopher's Stone is Professor Quirrell (Ian Hart). Voldemort, who is surviving within Quirrell's body, has subsumed Quirrell's mind. As Quirrell unwraps his turban, he reveals the hidden face of Voldemort—like the three-headed dog, this double-headed body is highly disturbing, exemplifying the uncanny as well as the abject. Conflict between Harry and Quirrell causes Quirrell's body to disintegrate, leading Voldemort to materialize as an arresting image of swirling, anthropomorphized black smoke, his inability to sustain a coherent bodily form consistent with abjection. The reference to complete bodily disintegration and black smoke, absent in the novel, are further relevant to post-9/11 audiences in the way that many bodies were never recovered from the Twin Towers.

The spatial terror escalates throughout the second film, with events leading Ron and Harry to a giant spider's lair in the Dark Forest. Blue-toned lighting and long shots of the boys emphasize their vulnerability as giant tree roots seem to dwarf them. Here, a flesh-eating tarantula named Aragog terrorizes the twosome, with close-ups highlighting the spider's monstrous features and black, glistening eyes. These intercut with high-angle and long shots demonstrating its colossal size in comparison to the two boys. As Ron and Harry are about to leave, the tarantula tells them that fresh meat wandering into the spider's lair is fair game for Aragog's offspring, with the taboo of such consumption (of human flesh) having abject implications.

Abjection, Muggles, and the Nazi regime

The early films thus largely invoke the abject in the context of its fascinating, disgusting and forbidden nature. The later films adopt a more sinister tone, the theme of eating human flesh recurring in *The Deathly Hallows: Part 1* when Voldemort commands Nagini, his pet snake, to devour Charity Burbage (Carolyn Pickles) as punishment for her teaching about Muggles. The term refers to non-magical folk, whom Voldemort and his followers see as "other," conveyed by analogies with the Nazi regime, and reference to the followers' perceived abhorrent mixing of Magic and Muggle blood.[48] Additionally, Harry, Ron, and Hermione notice a sculpture within the Ministry of Magic, which alludes to the persecution of the Jews, a theme reiterated in the Ministry's printed propaganda about Muggles. Such discrimination, especially in its alignment with the Holocaust, is highly abject; Kristeva states "[t]he abjection of Nazi crime reaches its apex when death [...] interferes with what, in my living universe, is supposed to save me from death: childhood, science, among other things."[49]

Abjection, terrorism, and the other

The later films not only lean towards immoral and racist aspects of abjection, but also evoke the other through suggestions of terrorism. Nihilism pervades the fourth film of the series, *The Goblet of Fire*,[50] with its 9/11 resonances emerging in various ways, though the hideous reincarnation of Voldemort conflates multiple abject aspects. The film begins at the Quidditch World Cup, Harry and the Weasley family arriving there by port-key. During the match, Death Eaters ignite the tents, burning them to the ground, with canted angles and rapid editing cutting to a long shot of the smoldering remains. Diegetic silence accompanies this latter image, clearly referencing the 2001 attacks, again a scene absent in the novel. Different from earlier examples, then, this sequence is abject because, as Kristeva states, "Any crime, because it draws attention to the fragility of the law is abject, but premeditated crime, cunning murder, hypocritical revenge are even more so because they heighten the display of such fragility."[51] The scene cuts to Hermione reading a newspaper, the 9/11 connection made explicit in its headline. Seen in close-up, it states, "Terror at the Quidditch World Cup', the combination of words "terror" and "World" familiar territory to a post-9/11 audience. Subsequently at Hogwarts, a new Defense of the Dark Arts teacher, Mad-Eye Moody (Brendan Gleeson), teaches the young apprentices torture and killing curses—in one example, a protracted close-up sees a spider undergoing a torture curse, its screams amplifying its horrific nature. Indeed, the theme of torture becomes increasingly apparent, likely referencing concurrent events at Guantanamo Bay.

Harry's next test of his morality and courage is the Tri-wizard Tournament, the outcome of which leads Harry and fellow student, Cedric (Robert Pattinson) to its final stages. Together the two grasp the cup, unaware that it is a port-key, which transports them to a surreal, low-lit graveyard. Here, the camera pans slowly across the scene to reveal a tombstone bearing the name of Tom Riddle, and then a huge cauldron beneath which a fire spontaneously ignites. In some of the series' most abject scenes, viewers see Wormtail (Timothy Spall), Voldemort's assistant, carrying a hideously emaciated Voldemort in his arms. Wormtail throws Riddle's bones into the cauldron, severs his own hand and adds it to the brew before cutting into Harry's arm; the use of low angles heightening the scene's surreal aspects. With Wormtail's proclamation about the pending return of the Dark Lord, a close-up of Harry's blood dripping from the knife blade into the cauldron becomes a swirling mass from which Voldemort emerges in a scene of monstrous rebirth. The scene is abject, both in its connotations of birth, and Voldemort's physically repugnant appearance, as well as in his symbolization of evil. A long shot reveals him as a slimy, fetal form, with protuberant bones and semi-translucent grey skin, while close-ups accentuate his hairless features and flattened nostrils that render him reptilian in appearance. Moreover, Voldemort lacks a soul, since it remains within the Horcruxes, and he therefore exists in a liminal state. As Kristeva states, "the body without a soul" represents fundamental pollution.[52]

A protracted close-up of Voldemort's insertion of his wand into Wormtail's arm provides a further instance of bodily transgression, and leads to the conjuring of the Death Eaters as black whirls of smoke. After restoring Wormtail's hand, Voldemort turns his attention to Harry, challenging him to a duel. When their wands "connect" in conflict, the materialization of Harry's parents as shimmering, ghostly apparitions not only alleviates the scene's visually abject qualities, but in conjuring a protective shield, also provides a boundary to protect Harry temporarily.

The fifth film, *The Order of the Phoenix*,[53] continues with references to 9/11, its language persistently suggestive of terrorism. These include, for example, "attack without authorization," references to "the war," as well as a theme of recruiting followers to Dumbledore's Army, a group led by Harry to practice and perfect Defense Against the Dark Arts in readiness for Voldemort's attack. When Hermione asks Harry to lead Dumbledore's Army, Harry's response about the horror of nearly dying or watching a friend die also references warfare. In addition, hallucinations increasingly haunt Harry with acute psychic disturbances manifesting themselves as surreal, disjointed flashbacks, narratively reflecting the fact that his body contains one of the Horcruxes, and also suggestive of post-traumatic stress disorder (a condition often associated with warfare, especially the war on terror). These hallucinations constitute a form of abject space in that they indicate Harry's incoherent identity, and compromise his psychic self.[54]

References to torture further surface in the "teaching" techniques of Professor Umbridge (Imelda Staunton) who forces Harry to write lines using a bewitched quill as punishment for questioning her methods. As he writes the words "I must not tell lies," we see in close-up the same words appear on his hand as bleeding, painful wheals, a form of extreme discipline that she utilizes repeatedly.

An increasingly prominent visual element of this film is the shattering of glass from tall edifices, which often takes the form of an arresting image. One example occurs in the sequence where the Weasley twins attack Umbridge with fireworks—the final explosion causes paper fragments and glass to shower out in slow motion from Umbridge's proclamations nailed high on the walls above. There is a silent pause before the proclamations tumble downwards, accompanied by a deep, rumbling sound. A second example arises in the Department of Mysteries where we see from a low-angle perspective the glass-balled "prophecies" tumble downward and shatter in a sequence again including slow motion and disjointed, surreal imagery. The conflict between Voldemort and Dumbledore (Michael Gambon) in the Ministry of Magic features similar low-angle perspectives, disjointed editing, and slow motion as glass and paper shower down from a great height. These scenes may therefore activate unconscious associations with 9/11 in their deployment of arresting imagery.

Abjection and 9/11

The bleaker landscapes of *The Half-Blood Prince*[55] see London landmarks beset by the Death Eaters, as well as rows of empty shops, reflecting a recession-hit London. The somber tone of the film surfaces at the outset, with lightning flashes cutting to a close-up of a still, unfocused eye, establishing a forensic iconography that hints at the darkness to come. A cut to a low-angle shot of distorted reflections of skyscrapers surrounded by black storm clouds onto a glass-fronted building directly references 9/11. Lightning flashes now draw attention skyward where Voldemort's face materializes in the dark clouds, and a swarm of Death Eaters stream down towards London. The theme of infiltration therefore persists, relating to Kristeva's incursion by the other, the differences reflected in abjection. David Sibley's work is relevant here,[56] since he engages directly with Kristevan theory in the context of geographical space, especially concerning the boundary, which he claims has a tendency to abjection. The entry of the Death Eaters into familiar London sights epitomizes the notion of such violation.

A cut to a high-angle shot from the perspective of the Death Eaters adopts a Google-earth aesthetic, revealing London rapidly coming into focus. This precedes a dizzying kinetic negotiation of its streets, and ends in a long shot of a series of explosions that leave bodies scattered on the ground and cause windows to shatter outwards. The Death Eaters' next target is the Millennium Bridge, seen in long shot, which subsequently collapses into the Thames, the camera then pulling back sharply to an overhead long shot to show the Death Eaters retreating skyward. A radio voiceover reporting on the Millennium Bridge disaster leads into the following scene that cuts to a close-up of a newspaper headline stating, "Bridge collapses—death toll rises."

This introduction, distinct from the utopian tendencies of the earlier films, and absent in the novel, locates the film in the real world of the twenty-first century, clearly associating it with terrorism and displaying abjection in connection to premeditated murder, and breaches of national security. Indeed, death dominates this film, from the demise of Aragog, Hagrid's pet tarantula, to the murder of Dumbledore. A theme of loss also emerges in the film's finer details; for example, Horace Slughorn's (Jim Broadbent) recounting of the day that he arose to find his goldfish bowl empty. The gloomy tendencies of the film persist in the scenes of Quidditch, which see the pitch surrounded by stark steel towers rather than festooned with their usual brightly colored team colors. In addition, the *mise-en-scène* is one of darkness and rain, with muted color tones and low-key lighting. References to terrorism occur throughout the film; for example, security is evident as Filch (David Bradley), the caretaker, asks the students for identification when arriving at Hogwarts and searches their belongings for weapons. In the closing scenes, as the Death Eaters cause mayhem, and Harry lies injured on the ground, an extreme low-angle shot of Hogwarts from Harry's perspective, with dark clouds billowing behind it, provides a further example of an arresting image in its semblance to the Twin Towers.

Increasingly, wands and broomsticks become murder weapons or symbols of power. Even Harry resorts to "bad" magic, mastering a curse that almost fatally wounds his adversary Draco Malfoy (Tom Felton). Again, the toilet becomes an abject space as Draco, lying in a pool of water reddening as blood seeps from his wounds, nearly dies until Professor Snape (Alan Rickman) saves him.

The plot of *The Half-Blood Prince* is pivotal since it reveals the existence of the Horcruxes that Harry must destroy in order to kill Voldemort. The Horcruxes, containing part of Voldemort's soul, are inherently abject, part of a fractured subject, and only viable by virtue of murder. One such Horcrux is allegedly located in a distant cavern to which Harry and Dumbledore may gain entry only by the shedding of blood. Dumbledore therefore cuts open his hand and smears blood over the cavern's walls to gain access. The cave is also abject in the hideous, corpse-like figures that emerge from the water to attack Harry and Dumbledore, with Harry temporarily submerged under water. A long shot sees the skeletal hordes attack, while an underwater, low-angle shot looks up through the gloom to see Harry surrounded by thin, writhing arms. Muffled sounds convey the sense of threat before Dumbledore conjures a wall of flames to destroy the monstrous entities.

Indeed, the search for the Horcruxes continually leads Harry into abject spaces. In another example, Harry and Hermione visit Godric's Hollow to search for the graves of Harry's parents. Beguiled by an apparition of Bathilda Bagshot (Hazel Douglas), really a corpse animated by Voldemort, the two, once more, almost become his victims. As Kristeva notes, "[t]he corpse, seen without God and outside of science, is the utmost of abjection. It is death infecting life."[57] Thus, the search for Harry's origins leads him inexorably towards death. Like the abject semiotic and the repressed uncanny, the connection between birth and death lies in their undifferentiated state—both entail existence beyond the self.

The final two parts of *The Deathly Hallows* culminate in scenes of boundary violation (of Hogwarts) and visceral, bloody images of violence, death and wounding, reminding viewers of the recent war on terror, as well as issues relating to national security. *The Deathly Hallows: Part 2* especially conveys a sense of doom, perhaps reflecting a concurrent international pessimism. Its somber *mise-en-scène* comprises muted color tones and dark, heavy skies while the two principal abject spaces, the vaults of Gringotts Bank and the destruction of Hogwarts, each invoke imagery relating to 9/11 and the war on terror. The scene at Gringotts narratively concerns the trio's quest to locate one of the Horcruxes in the vault of Bellatrix Lestrange (Helena Bonham Carter). We see Harry, Hermione, and Ron through a series of rapidly intercutting tracking and panning shots as they enter the vast subterranean caverns of the bank vaults in a motorized carriage. The carriage suddenly upturns and ejects them from it at a great height, extreme overhead shots revealing their falling bodies. Another visual theme of the scene is the threat of burial in Bellatrix's vault as its treasure begins to multiply magically. Both the scenes of falling and burial provide examples of arresting imagery, and likely resonate with contemporary audiences in their reference to the Twin Towers.

Harry's search for a missing diadem containing another of the Horcruxes leads him to the Room of Requirement where once more, imagery of burning edifices and falling bodies conveys associations with 9/11, in particular extreme overhead shots that show bodies falling into the flames. Low-level straight on camera positions also reveal flames billowing towards the spectator (often assuming the form of a dragon), simultaneously enhancing both spectacle and threat for the spectator.

Boundary transgression

The final destruction of Hogwarts has distinct connections with Klinger's notion of arresting imagery through scenes of abject spectacle that correlate closely with challenges to Harry's subjectivity. As Voldemort's forces gather, Professor McGonagall resists their infiltration by conjuring a protective shield around the castle. Essentially, the shield serves as boundary excluding the "terrorist" other, in line with the security themes seen in the preceding films. Despite its invisibility, we are able to visualize this sheath as spectacle because the attack by Voldemort's followers renders streaks of flames around it, conveyed either through a low camera angle and long shot from within Hogwarts or alternatively as an overhead extreme long shot from outside the shield.

Such boundary consciousness and security failure are relevant to contemporary concerns with national security,[58] the protective shield discernible in the final film reflecting post-9/11 anxieties in relation to further "infiltration." Moreover, there are specific allusions to the Twin Towers in the burning Quidditch structures, an extreme long shot rapidly zooming in as they collapse, and flames billow out towards the spectator.

The symbolic interface between good and evil, rendered visually in the shield, is also apparent in conflicts involving wands. We see this in the penultimate showdown between Voldemort and Harry, a long shot revealing a display of vibrant color, conveying conflict as spectacle as their wands issue flames of green, yellow, and orange. A cut to close-up of Voldemort sees the power of Harry's wand begin to overwhelm him, while intercutting long shots repeatedly reveal Nagini sliding towards the camera, conveying additional menace. The whole sequence occurs in slow motion rendering it an example of Klinger's "arresting image."[59] At one point, color fills the frame as spectacle, intercutting with close-ups of Harry's grimly determined expression. Extra-diegetic music builds up to a crescendo as Nagini rises up towards the camera, a close-up revealing its open jaws and razor-sharp teeth as if about to strike the spectator. An edit to a side-on shot then shows Neville Longbottom (Matthew Lewis) raising his sword in slow motion, before decapitating Nagini, blood spraying out towards the spectator as the snake disintegrates into black swirls of smoke.

Longbottom's heroic acts further include a rallying speech to his friends about people such as Remus, Tonks, and Fred who died in the battle, placing emphasis on their deaths not being in vain. These words, as well as his heroic actions, are likely to chime with contemporary audiences, not only in relation to the war on terror, but also more generally.

In the final clash of wands between Harry and Voldemort, extreme high-angle shots reveal them falling over the edge of a tower. The blurring of the background indicates the speed of their descent, while rapid tracking shots follow their flight, Voldemort rendered as a black smoking form before both crash to the ground and reach for their wands. Here the incandescence from their flaming wands dramatically intensifies, the scene then cutting to a long shot of Voldemort, who now appears diminished in the frame. A close-up of his decaying face cuts to an overhead shot to disclose, in slow motion, his complete disintegration before the camera pulls back to reveal Hogwarts silhouetted against a brighter sky. The rays of sunshine beginning to filter through symbolize hope while the death of Voldemort in a film released shortly after the death of Osama bin Laden is inevitably meaningful to some viewers. Additionally, Harry's destruction of Voldemort's wand as a symbol of total power may provide a moral commentary on weapons of mass destruction.

Moreover, as Harry subsequently wanders through the ruins, surveying the dead and wounded, his point of view locates groups talking and smiling. We also see Filch the caretaker sweeping up the rubble. These images offer signs of recovery and are reminiscent of the scenes in Manhattan following 9/11. The subsequent flash-forwards of 19 years further implies optimism and regeneration, and as other films depicting 9/11 have done, relocates traumatic events in the distant past as part of a shared experience with the spectator.

Bewitched and uncanny spaces

In contrast to these scenes of death, disgust, and boundary transgression, the world of Hogwarts also generates fascination and fear in its incarnations of ghosts, anthropomorphism and magic. Inevitably, the rituals and linguistic utterances characterizing the magic of the *Potter* films evoke religious analogies or occult practice. Indeed, Mauss notes that "[m]agic includes [...] a whole group of practices which we seem to compare with those of religion. If we are to find any other rites apart from those which are nominally religious, we shall find them here."[60] However, despite the films' differentiation between "good" and "bad" magic, Emily Griesinger notes that the Potter novels, "have caused a firestorm of controversy among Christian parents and educators for their portrayal of witchcraft and the occult."[61] Certainly, the anthropomorphism evident in the films correlates with animistic beliefs, though arguably there are also scientific connotations in the performance of magic, in particular, the notion of the chemical experiment "gone wrong." For example, we often see Seamus Finnegan's (Devon Murray) performance of wizardry culminating in an explosion that blackens his face. More importantly, as well as offering a point of identification for child viewers, the use of magic is, as Griesinger further notes, "a narrative device in articulating hope."[62] This particular aspect characterizes most fantasy film, and in relation to this essay partly explains the dominance of fantasy since 9/11, and the place that the *Potter* films occupy in the canon.

A particular fascination of the films' magic arises in the way that bewitched spaces exist alongside real spaces. For example, Harry's journey to Hogwarts requires him to pass through a solid brick wall in the "real world" to access the Hogwarts Express on Platform 9¾. The seeming impossibility of the task is emphasized by a point of view shot from Harry's perspective that pans rapidly up and down the wall, accentuating its solidity. Indeed, while he passes effortlessly through in the first year, the subsequent year sees him crash alarmingly into it. Over later years, however, travel becomes increasingly sophisticated and immediate, as Harry learns to "Apparate," and perfects the use of port-keys.

Animism, anthropomorphism, and the uncanny

Magical properties often endow spaces and objects with uncanny effects because of their animistic or sentient features. Freud explains that "we appear to attribute an 'uncanny' quality to impressions that seek to confirm the omnipotence of thoughts and the animistic mode of thinking in general."[63] For animism is, as Freud continues, a primitive belief in the existence of "spiritual beings both benevolent and malignant; and these spirits and demons they regard as the causes of natural phenomena and they believe that not only animals and plants but all the inanimate objects in the world are animated by them."[64] Not only does such evidence of apparently sentient inanimate objects pervade the *Potter* films, but also the central narrative impetus depends on the premise of Voldemort's fragmented soul.

Indeed, as well as Hogwart's spontaneously shifting staircases, the characters that inhabit the portraits hung on the walls move autonomously, and photographs and newspaper images have a third, uncanny dimension, with their characters coming to life in mini-narratives. Moreover, various transport systems seem to have minds of their own, the measure of a student's success frequently depending on control over these animated forms. For example, Neville's lack of broomstick skills, illustrated by point of view shots, rapid camera movements, whip-pans and fast tracking shots as well as extreme high- and low-angle shots, provide a source of humor to his fellow wizards. In contrast, Harry easily learns to maneuver mid-air, his flair for flying subsequently earning him the privileged position of seeker for his house's Quidditch team.

Other enchanted transport systems include the owl postal service, the Floo system, port-keys and portals, the Knight Bus and the vanishing cabinet of *The Half-Blood Prince*. Initially, Harry and Ron have varying degrees of success in utilizing these systems. In *The Chamber of Secrets*, viewers see that Harry's attempt to travel via the Floo system (through fireplaces) accidentally transports him to Knockturn Alley, a shadowy, low-lit place for wizards and witches who are down on their luck. The alley is located one grate further than Harry's destination, according to Mrs. Weasley. After the attempt to pass through the solid wall to Platform 9¾ fails in the second year, Harry and Ron's subsequent journey to Hogwarts in Ron's flying car results in chaos as they crash into the Whomping Willow.

Like Ron's car, the Knight Bus, emergency transport for stranded witches and wizards, is anthropomorphized. Bizarrely decked with a chandelier, and hospital-style beds, the bewitched triple-decker Knight Bus accelerates to hyper-real speeds, and squeezes through small gaps in traffic (long shots suggest that it almost "breathes in"), existing invisibly amid the real world traffic of London. Rapid editing, fast tracking shots, extreme camera angles and a close-up of a fast-talking, disembodied head further contribute to the image as animistic, uncanny spectacle.

Anthropomorphic images begin early in the films. One of the first scenes on arriving at Hogwarts is the Sorting Ceremony. Here, the Sorting Hat, an inanimate object that too has its own identity and is apparently capable of reading minds, further sustains notions of uncanniness in relation to animism. Its role is to assess a student's qualities, and allocate each to one of the four houses of Hogwarts. The Sorting Hat seems indecisive when placed on Harry's head, leading Harry to question further his origins, narratively important in relation to later anxieties about his similarities to Tom Riddle. Other examples of the anthropomorphic uncanny abound—ranging from mandrake roots (seen in close-up) that appear as screaming, hideous infants to Ron's attempt to "transfigure" his pet rat. The resultant squealing, fur-covered goblet that retains a moving rat's tail is seen in close-up to accentuate its living qualities.

Ghosts, automata, and the uncanny

Ghosts and automata constitute another class of the uncanny and for Freud, generate fear through associations with death. Freud notes that uncanny feelings occur in relation to automata when "there is an intellectual uncertainty whether an object is alive or not, and when an inanimate object becomes too much like an animate one."[65] The scene of Wizard's Chess exemplifies this notion of the uncanny. Here, Harry and his two friends find themselves on a giant chessboard, extreme low-angle shots and canted angles amplifying the frightening effects of the gigantic chess pieces as they move autonomously and violently destroy each other.

While the numerous ghosts at Hogwarts, though often emerging unexpectedly, do not generally alarm the students, the materialization of the Dementors en route to Hogwarts in *The Prisoner of Azkaban*[66] generates extreme feelings of dread. In line with Klinger's analysis of the arresting image, the narrative here seems to slow down. Muted color tones, a rainy *mise-en-scène*, canted angles and distorted sound effects amplify unease while the movement of the black spectral forms occurs in slow motion. Close-ups of their long spindly fingers heighten a sense of menace, while their infiltration of the train may have connotations of hijacking for some viewers. Freud argues that "spirits and demons [...] are only projections of man's own emotional impulses. He turns his emotional cathexes into persons, he peoples the world with them and meets his own internal processes again outside himself".[67] Such externalization of Harry's internal battles arguably works in a related way for the spectator, enabling the visualization of the war on terror and rendering visible the otherwise unknown terrorist other.

Repetition, doubling, and time travel

Freud explains that a fear of death may also derive from the double, stating that the double's earlier meanings assured immortality, but has "become the uncanny harbinger of death."[68] Polyjuice Potion and time travel offer opportunities for such repetition and doubling: in *The Deathly Hallows: Part 1*, Harry's friends transform themselves with Polyjuice Potion into seven identical copies of Harry while *The Prisoner of Azkaban* sees Hermione acquire a Time-Turner, a device for time travel. In the latter, the Dementors attack Harry and Sirius Black (Gary Oldman) and initially overwhelm them until a mysterious figure, whom Harry believes to be his father, conjures a "Patronus" spell, forcing the Dementors to retreat. However, in an exact later repetition of the scene, albeit now entirely from Hermione and Harry's perspective as onlookers, Harry learns that the mysterious, powerful figure was himself.

The replication of the scenes from different perspectives and the appearance of each of the characters twice within the same frame generate feelings of déjà vu, both for the spectator and for the characters within the diegesis. In addition, Harry's identification with his father in the "Patronus" scene signals his increasing symbolic power, a significant moment in his transition to adulthood whereby he represses the abject both literally (through repelling the Dementors) and figuratively (he enters the symbolic). Moreover, the Time-Turner enables Harry and Hermione to alter the course of events whereby the Hypogriff (thought to have been executed first time around) escapes. Time travel thus operates as fantasy's mode of dealing with trauma in the way that it enables characters to revisit their past decisions, and change them and perhaps to re-encounter the deceased. It may offer consolation for spectators too. Jacqueline Furby and Claire Hines suggest this, observing that "[a]s fantasy film viewers though, we can travel into the past or to the future, and enjoy a fantasy of freedom from our real world restrictions of movement in time."[69]

Memory and death

In another form of time travel, Harry is able to go back into the psychic space of memory itself. He first does this in *The Chamber of Secrets* by entering the past through Tom Riddle's diary, an apparently blank book that Harry finds in the girls' bathroom. Discovering its ability to converse with him, rendered in close-up as spontaneous written responses appear in the diary, its invisible writer, Tom Riddle, draws Harry back 50 years into Tom's memory. The book's pages suddenly flick open as if caught in a gust of wind, before a blinding flash of light emanates from its pages and fills the screen. Harry disappears from view, leaving the diary on his desk, before there is a cut to a black and white *mise-en-scène*. Narratively, this scene relates to revealing Tom Riddle's past. Visually, the use of monochrome not only indicates that he has travelled back in time, but also signals Hogwarts' strangeness (as uncanny memory).

In *The Half-Blood Prince*, Harry further explores memory through the Pensieve, first summoning Dumbledore's initial encounter with Tom Riddle, using memory signified as psychic space by visual distortion that produces a ghostly effect. Returning a second time, he sees Professor Slughorn in conversation with Riddle, a memory with which Dumbledore believes that Slughorn has tampered. The narrative import of this particular memory lies in its concealed revelations about the Horcruxes. Ultimately, this knowledge relates to Harry's identity, since one of the Horcruxes resides within Harry, thereby explaining the central enigma of the series. In the final film, *The Deathly Hallows: Part 2*, Harry uses the Pensieve to access Snape's memory. Again, these images are conjured as surreal, and in slow motion—though this is a common visual strategy to signify memory, the a-temporality conveys the scene as an arresting image of uncanny space and ghostly incarnation.

Perhaps the films' most uncanny space arises in *The Deathly Hallows: Part 2* when Voldemort first attacks Harry who then seems to enter another dimension, signified by an almost complete blanching of the scene and total diegetic silence. Here, Harry encounters the spirit of Dumbledore in a ghostly incarnation of King's Cross station; these aspects are clearly suggestive of an afterlife. Klinger's notion of the arresting image is salient here, since sound is absent except for their conversation and the image is particularly striking in its incongruent elements—as Harry peers beneath a slab, he sees a disgusting, emaciated entity, its bloody flesh flayed, and mediated as abject spectacle. Dumbledore explains that the abject being is the final Horcrux that had existed within Harry.

As in the original novels, the film adaptations of *Harry Potter* chart the progress of its protagonist towards a coherent subjectivity and his quest to uncover his secret past. Harry also has a mission to defeat Voldemort, leading him into a series of abject, uncanny, and bewitching spaces that each present challenges involving tests of morality, and physical and psychological endurance. Such spaces are highly differentiated, comprising subterranean, mid-air, and underwater realms as well as the psychic spaces of memory, hallucination, and thought.

As a subject in process, Harry displays a control of spaces by the articulation of his wand, and the use of advanced magic, excelling in the mastery of flight. His socio-cultural and psychosexual development is thus not discernible by conventional methods of schooling and social interaction, but by his negotiation and command of bewitching, abject, or uncanny spaces. This negotiation often results in instances of spectacular arresting imagery that may mobilize spectator emotion through associations or memories pertaining to 9/11. In fact, at times, the films contain direct references to 9/11, including falling bodies, smoke, and shattering glass, recalling imagery of the Twin Towers' collapse.

The films' rendering of memory as a physical space has uncanny connotations in its capacity for enabling repetition and revelation of hidden traumatic pasts, while the visualization of psychic space, often indicating Harry's slowly fracturing identity, is especially illustrative of Klinger's notion of the arresting image. In this way, Harry's quest not only culminates in a coherent subjectivity through the destruction of evil, but may also unconsciously provide relief, hope, or a sense of resolution for some spectators. In addition, the *Potter* films may offer solace for those bereaved by warfare and acts of terrorism in their suggestions of an afterlife.

Jack Zipes claims that, "Fairytale films [...] are concerned with profound human struggles and seek to provide a glimpse of light and hope despite the darkness that surrounds their very creation and production."[70] The final scenes of the series inevitably seek to deliver such hope, portraying recovery and regeneration, while the utilization of magic enables death to be a transient state from which one can return.

Notes

1. *Harry Potter and the Deathly Hallows: Part Two* (2011) Directed by David Yates. UK/USA.
2. See http://boxofficemojo.com/news/?id=3217&p=.htm (accessed December 25, 2011).
3. P. Nel, "Lost in Translation? Harry Potter, from Page to Screen," in E. Heilman (ed.), *Critical Perspectives on Harry Potter* (London and New York: Routledge, 2003): 275–90 at 276.
4. S. Gupta, *Re-Reading Harry Potter* (New York: Palgrave Macmillan, 2009): 146.
5. *Ibid.*
6. Unless otherwise stated, all reference to the *Potter* series refer to the film versions.
7. *Harry Potter and the Philosopher's Stone* (2001) Directed by Chris Columbus. UK/USA.
8. *The Fellowship of the Ring* (2001) Directed by Peter Jackson. UK/USA.
9. K. Smith, "Reframing Fantasy: September 11 and the Global Audience," in G. King (ed.), *The Spectacle of the Real* (Bristol and Portland: Intellect Publishing, 2005): 59–70, at 69–70.
10. B. Klinger, "The Art Film, Affect and the Female Viewer: *The Piano* Revisited," *Screen* 47(1) (2006): 19–41, at 24.
11. *Ibid.*
12. *Ibid.*: 24.
13. *Ibid.*: 30.
14. L. Campbell, *Portals of Power: Magical Agency and Transformation in Literary Fantasy* (Jefferson and London: McFarland Press, 2010): 18.
15. *Ibid.*: 6.
16. In Campbell: 14.
17. J. Zipes, *Breaking the Magic Spell: Radical Theories of Folk and Fairy Tales* (Lexington: University of Kentucky Press, 2002): 162.
18. B. Bettelheim, *The Uses of Enchantment: The Meaning and Importance of Fairy Tales* (London and New York: Penguin Books, 1991): 8.
19. Klinger: 24.

20. J. Kristeva, *Powers of Horror*, trans. L. Roudiez (New York: Columbia University Press, 1982).

21. S. Freud, *The Standard Edition of the Complete Psychological Works: An Infantile Neurosis and Other Works*, 17, trans. J. Strachey (London: Hogarth Press, 1955a).

22. Klinger: 24.

23. Kristeva: 13, original emphasis.

24. *Ibid.*: 4.

25. *Ibid.*: 72.

26. *Ibid.*: 4.

27. D. Sibley, *Geographies of Exclusion: Society and Difference in the West* (London and New York: Routledge, 1995).

28. Kristeva: 4.

29. *Harry Potter and the Deathly Hallows: Part One* (2010) Directed by David Yates. UK/USA.

30. J. Kornfeld and L. Prothro, "Comedy, Quest, and Community," in E. Heilman (ed.), *Critical Perspectives on Harry Potter*, 2nd edn (New York and London: Routledge, 2009): 121–37, at 135.

31. B. Creed, *The Monstrous-Feminine: Film, Feminism, Psychoanalysis* (London and New York: Routledge, 1993): 11.

32. J. Kristeva, *Revolution in Poetic Language*, trans. M. Waller (New York: Columbia University Press, 1984).

33. M. Mauss, *A General Theory of Magic* (London and New York: Routledge, 1991): 72.

34. K. Fowkes, *The Fantasy Film* (Oxford and Malden: Wiley-Blackwell, 2010): 166.

35. Freud (1955a): 219.

36. *Ibid.*: 241.

37. *Ibid.*: 219.

38. *Ibid.*: 249.

39. *Ibid.*: 234.

40. P. Thurschwell, *Sigmund Freud* (London and New York: Routledge, 2000): 118.

41. S. Freud, *The Standard Edition of the Complete Psychological Works: Totem and Taboo and Other Works*, 13, trans. J. Strachey (London: Hogarth Press, 1955b): 76.

42. J. Zipes, *The Enchanted Screen: The Unknown History of Fairy-tale Films* (London and New York: Routledge, 2011): 2.

43. Zipes (2011): 3.

44. *Harry Potter and the Chamber of Secrets* (2002) Directed by Chris Columbus. UK/USA/Germany.

45. L. Damour, "Harry Potter and the Magical Looking Glass: Reading the Secret Life of the Preadolescent," in G. L. Anatol (ed.), *Reading Harry Potter: Critical Essays* (Westport, CT: Praeger, 2003): 15–24, at 19.

46. Kristeva: 4.

47. Damour: 19.
48. *The Deathly Hallows: Part 1.*
49. Kristeva: 4.
50. *Harry Potter and the Goblet of Fire* (2005) Directed by Mike Newell. UK/USA.
51. Kristeva: 4.
52. *Ibid.*: 10.
53. *Harry Potter and the Order of the Phoenix* (2007) Directed by David Yates. UK/USA.
54. Kristeva: 46.
55. *Harry Potter and the Half-Blood Prince* (2009) Directed by David Yates. UK/USA.
56. Sibley, *op. cit.*
57. Kristeva: 4.
58. See F. Debrix, "Discourses of War, Geographies of Abjection: Reading Contemporary American Ideologies of Terror," *Third World Quarterly* 26(7) (2005): 1157–72; C. Weber, *Imagining America at War: Morality, Politics, and Film* (London and New York: Routledge, 2006).
59. Klinger: 24.
60. Mauss: 11.
61. E. Griesinger, "Harry Potter and the 'Deeper Magic': Narrating Hope in Children's Literature," *Christianity and Literature* 51(3) (2002): 455–80, at 456.
62. *Ibid.*: 458.
63. Freud (1955b): 86.
64. *Ibid.*: 76.
65. Freud (1955a): 233.
66. *Harry Potter and the Prisoner of Azkaban* (2004) Directed by Alfonso Cuarón. UK/USA.
67. Freud (1955b): 92.
68. Freud (1955a): 235.
69. J. Furby and C. Hines, *Fantasy* (London and New York: Routledge, 2011): 151.
70. Zipes (2011): 350.

5

Free Will and Determinism: A "Compatibilist" Reading of J. K. Rowling's *Harry Potter* Series

Charlotte M. Fouque

Great minds have debated the issue of free will and determinism for centuries; in the process, these concepts have been applied to science, religion, philosophy, and consequently literature. The basic definition of determinism is that "Every event has a cause."[1] Hard determinists and libertarians argue that free will and determinism are exclusive of each other: "if an action is determined, then the person was not performing the action of his own free will."[2] This view is considered quite radical; therefore, a more moderate theory of compatibility has arisen which suggests that freedom and thus moral responsibility are compatible with the doctrine of causal determinism: people are free to make choices concurrently with the belief that "all events (including human behavior) are the results of chains of necessitating causes that can be traced indefinitely into the past."[3] Compatibility, then, necessitates the understanding that choices are "events that do not necessarily have antecedent causes."[4]

Scholars have taken on this debate in the context of J. K. Rowling's *Harry Potter* series. In this fantasy world, certain magical objects such as the Sorting Hat, which is essentially an instrument of fate, are indicative of determinism and add significantly to the literary qualities of the series. Upon their arrival at Hogwarts School of Witchcraft and Wizardry, with the aid of the Sorting Hat, the children are sorted into one of four houses as soon as they arrive, effectively sealing their destinies. The branch of magic known as Divination and the importance of prophecy in the plot reinforce a fatalistic outlook. Finally, the main characters' ancestries almost invariably hold such a supreme importance over their choices that their free will must come into question. While they do make choices, the characters of the *Harry Potter* books are still ruled by the determinism that pervades their world.

The Sorting Hat

The Sorting Hat, enchanted by the founders to perpetuate the sorting process after they are gone, is placed on the students' heads as soon as they arrive at Hogwarts at the age of eleven, and it determines where the students belong. Each of the four houses to which the students are attached is defined by the characteristics of its founder. The Sorting Hat ascertains which students embody those traits, and then fits them magically with their family away from home. Once placed, the student is expected to live up to the ideals of the house, just as one is bound to a family code. The brave and courageous go to Gryffindor, the most studious are in Ravenclaw, the hard workers belong in Hufflepuff, and Slytherin only accepts the most cunning and ambitious.

A person's inner nature is laid bare to the Sorting Hat. It claims, in one of its annual songs, that "*There's nothing hidden in your head / The Sorting Hat can't see, / So try me on and I will tell you / Where you ought to be.*"[5] However, sorting is problematic as the rivalry between houses, which is encouraged at an early age, is not restricted to schoolchildren and Hogwarts, but extends to the rest of the wizarding world. Wizard children are shaped by their experiences in their house during their most formative years and therefore grow into adults who uphold the views and values generally associated with that house. In one of its later songs, the Hat expresses concern over its role in perpetuating the divide between students: "*Though condemned I am to split you / Still I worry that it's wrong, / Though I must fulfil my duty / And must quarter every year / Still I wonder whether Sorting / May not bring the end I fear.*"[6] Although the Hat is bound to do that for which it was created, it perceives the problems that could arise from its duty, which include lifelong rivalries due to the house system.

Because of the founders' views, each house denotes a specific character, and Slytherin is the subject of seemingly justified widespread wariness. As the groundskeeper Hagrid says to Harry when they first meet, "There's not a single witch or wizard who went bad who wasn't in Slytherin."[7] While this later proves not to be entirely true, most of the Slytherin students are portrayed at the outset as dark wizards in training. As the conflicts become more serious throughout the series, the Slytherins evolve from unkind and bullying children into young supporters of Voldemort, the series' villain and Harry Potter's nemesis, incidentally a Slytherin himself when he was at Hogwarts. When Dumbledore toasts Harry for his valor in facing Voldemort at the end of *The Goblet of Fire*, many Slytherins "remained defiantly in their seats, their goblets untouched."[8] In the next installment, *The Order of the Phoenix*, they join Professor Umbridge's reviled Inquisitorial Squad, and their sadistic tendencies are fully developed by *The Deathly Hallows*, where they are seen practicing the Dark Arts, including the Cruciatus Curse that inflicts unbearable pain upon its victim.[9] At the climax of the battle between good and evil, when the Slytherins are given the choice to stay at Hogwarts and fight Voldemort, a true test of free will, every single one of them leaves. In so doing they declare their support for the Dark Lord, and sustain the character of their house.[10] Being sorted into Slytherin typecasts those children and shapes their futures negatively, justifying Dumbledore's comment later in the series that the sorting process occurs too early in the development of witches and wizards.

Free will asserts itself

When Harry Potter arrives at Hogwarts in his first year, he has no knowledge of the Hogwarts houses because he was raised by his aunt and uncle, who are Muggles, or non-magical people. He approaches the school of magic with no preconceived notions about the four houses until he experiences an instant dislike for the arrogant Draco Malfoy, who himself hopes to be sorted into Slytherin.[11] Harry subsequently pleads the Sorting Hat not to place him in Slytherin, and the Hat obliges (after some doubt) by placing him in Gryffindor.[12] This is the first instance of Harry asserting his will and making a choice on his own.

However, when Harry discovers that he is a Parselmouth (someone who possesses the ability to speak to snakes), he begins to worry that he might be the fabled heir of Salazar Slytherin who had the same skill. According to legend, Slytherin's heir is destined to open the Chamber of Secrets, releasing a monster. Remembering that the Sorting Hat had been inclined to place him in Slytherin rather than Gryffindor, Harry seeks reassurance from the wise headmaster Albus Dumbledore, who reminds him that he is in Gryffindor because that is what he asked for. Dumbledore tells Harry "It is our choices [...] that show what we truly are, far more than our abilities,"[13] a sentiment that Dumbledore echoes time and again.

The role of determinism

In the deterministic world of *Harry Potter*, Dumbledore remains always a proponent of free will, and, as "the constant voice of wisdom, spends much of his time refuting [...] fatalistic views of the person."[14] Causal determinism reigns supreme, however, as a child is almost always sorted into the same house as their parents and siblings. Therefore, Harry may have been predetermined to make his choice of house due partly to his lineage, as both of his parents were placed in Gryffindor, and his father's father as well.[15]

In this world, prime importance is placed on bloodlines, and sorting is one of the many elements influenced by this fact. Children of wizards are generally born with magical abilities, while those anomalous few who are born without powers are called Squibs and are the subject of prejudice. When Hagrid announces to Harry that he is a wizard, he adds, "With a mum an' dad like yours, what else would yeh be?"[16] The reader is always reminded how similar Harry is to his parents, and that he is a direct heir to their virtues. He has inherited his father's prowess at the game of Quidditch as well as his physical attributes, right down to the messy hair and glasses, and the emerald green eyes of his mother. Harry is clearly an exemplar of his lineage.

Just as some children of wizards are born powerless, so too are there wizards born of Muggles. The widespread prejudice against these Muggle-borns is central to the story. Draco Malfoy introduces the term "Mudblood" as an insult to Hermione Granger, a daughter of Muggles, who has proven herself to be the most talented witch in their class. This prejudice stems from a refusal to accept that Muggles could produce children as magical as wizard parents might produce. Some pure-blood families have gone to extremes to preserve the status of purity: the family motto of the House of Black is "Toujours Pur,"[17] or "always pure," and they have rejected members who have disagreed with that point of view or (even worse) married into half-blood families. However, as Ron points out, "Most wizards these days are half-blood anyway."[18] The wizarding community would not have survived without marrying Muggles.

The idea of "dirty blood" is an allegorical one, and to stress the point, Rowling has made sure that those who discriminate on the grounds of blood purity are unfailingly proven to be villainous. Indeed, the foremost villains are notable adherents to the pure-blood philosophy: Salazar Slytherin held that only pure-blood children were entitled to study magic at Hogwarts, and for this radical belief he was forced to leave the school. He walled up a monster in a secret chamber of the castle that could only be opened by his heir.[19] This heir of Slytherin, Lord Voldemort, himself a half-blood,[20] nevertheless proceeds to open the chamber, unleashing "the horror within, [using] it to purge the school of all who were unworthy to study magic."[21] All the students in Slytherin house likewise follow in Slytherin's footsteps, and the password for their common room is "pure-blood."[22] It is a basic assumption in this fictional world that good people have good children and that bad people have bad children, with few exceptions. Like the Black family, all the Malfoys are said to be, "rotten ter the core,"[23] and the children of Voldemort's henchmen, the Death Eaters, are all Slytherins as a matter of course. Lord Voldemort's own ancestry also shows this to be true. His father was a Muggle, but his mother came from a long line of Muggle-hating inbred pure-bloods, the Gaunts. They trace their line straight back to Salazar Slytherin, who is himself descended from the Peverells.

Destiny's role and choices made

It would be easy to assert, as Dumbledore does several times, that "Despite their similarities, Harry and Voldemort's choices set them decisively apart."[24] However, the importance of the role of bloodlines in the outcome of those characters' choices becomes clear in the final installment, *The Deathly Hallows*, when it is revealed that Harry Potter is also descended from the Peverells. According to legend, the three Peverell brothers acquired or fabricated three hallows that together would conquer death. These were an unbeatable wand, a resurrection stone, and an invisibility cloak. One of the brothers, Ignotus, appropriates the cloak and is portrayed as the wisest by his decision. It is no coincidence that he is Harry's ancestor. Cadmus, the brother who chooses the stone is power-hungry and foolish, and he is Voldemort's ancestor. As descendants of two brothers with such opposing values, Harry and Voldemort are related by blood, yet fated to be enemies. Their destinies have been entangled for centuries, and the outcome of their relationship is predetermined.

Destiny is perhaps the most important deterministic element in the story. Aside from being descended from the same familial line, Harry Potter and Voldemort are inextricably linked to each other, even by prophecy. Divination, which is taught at Hogwarts, is repeatedly referred to as an "imprecise branch of magic"[25] by the more pragmatic characters. However, Professor Trelawney, the Divination

Teacher, speaks two very real prophecies in her lifetime, one of which is the catalyst for the entire plot. She predicts that "The one with the power to vanquish the Dark lord" will be born, that "the Dark Lord will mark him as his equal," and that "either must die at the hand of the other for neither can live while the other survives."[26] Voldemort only hears the first part, and manages to fulfill the prophecy when he attempts to kill Harry as a baby. However, the Killing Curse he casts on Harry fails and endows the child with the ability to speak to snakes and embeds a piece of Voldemort's soul into Harry, further twining them together.

This event, as it was foretold, marks Harry Potter as the "Chosen One,"[27] destined to either vanquish Voldemort or die at his hand. When Harry comes to the realization that he must sacrifice himself in order to save his world from Voldemort, he is suddenly faced with the determinism of his life: "Now he saw that his lifespan had always been determined by how long it took to eliminate all the Horcruxes. [...] How neat, how elegant, not to waste any more lives, but to give the dangerous task to the boy who had already been marked for slaughter."[28] If Voldemort had only heard the prophecy in its entirety, he would have been aware of the danger. His actions, meant to prevent death at Harry's hands, ultimately cause exactly that, in the perfect execution of a self-fulfilling prophecy.

A further fateful connection between Harry and Voldemort is to be found in their wands. According to Ollivander the wand-maker, "it's really the wand that chooses the wizard."[29] He thinks it curious that Harry should be "destined" to be chosen by the one wand that contains the same phoenix feather core as the wand that chose Voldemort. These two wands are referred to as brothers, but Harry takes a tolerant stance: "He was very fond of his wand, and as far as he was concerned its relationship to Voldemort's wand was something it couldn't help—rather as he couldn't help being related to Aunt Petunia."[30] The connection shared by the two wands echoes the connection between the two wizards. Just as the feather wand cores originate from the same phoenix, Harry and Voldemort originate from the same bloodline. At the end of *The Goblet of Fire*, Voldemort ritualistically absorbs some of Harry's blood, but, as Dumbledore explains in *The Deathly Hallows*, Harry's wand "imbibed some of the power and qualities of Voldemort's wand that night, which is to say that it contained a little of Voldemort himself."[31] Since the wands are so closely related, and since they independently choose the wizard, Harry and Voldemort's destinies are ever more tightly wound together.

Both Harry and Voldemort exercise free will within this predetermined structure. Harry requests that the Sorting Hat not place him in Slytherin, and Dumbledore insists on several occasions that Harry is free to make his own choices. As one critic points out, however, it would be simplistic to assume that the universe lacks causation because these examples of free choice exist: "For example [...] it is not clear whether Harry's [...] wish or desire is not also a link in the causal chain of the Sorting Hat's decision-making process, thereby becoming one of several causal influences on the Sorting Hat. It is even possible that these desires are the effects of previous events."[32] Harry's ancestry, his parentage, and his prophesied opposition to the Dark Lord help determine the choices that he makes. Voldemort exercises his free will in attempting to vanquish death by securing pieces of his soul in Horcruxes and by his choice to eliminate Harry. He was also destined to attempt to cheat death like his ancestor Cadmus Peverell. Despite Voldemort's half-blood status, his hatred of Muggles is ingrained in his heredity, descending straight from Slytherin himself. In a compatibilist frame, Harry and Voldemort's choices as well as their enmity are indeed predetermined.

Ancestry, magical wands, prophecies, and the sorting system at Hogwarts contribute to this general determinism that pervades the series. Rowling makes it clear that the *Harry Potter* world will continue to be deterministic even after the end of the books. In the Epilogue of *The Deathly Hallows*, which takes place 19 years later, Ron perpetuates the old rivalry and prejudices associated with houses and blood purity. He tells his son Hugo, "If you're not in Gryffindor, we'll disinherit you,"[33] and he warns his daughter Rose about Draco Malfoy's son Scorpius: "Make sure you beat him in every test [...] don't get too friendly with him [...] Granddad Weasley would never forgive you if you married a pure-blood."[34] When Harry Potter's son Albus worries about being Sorted into Slytherin, Harry reassures him that there is nothing wrong with it, and that he will be able to choose Gryffindor over Slytherin if he wants.[35] In the end, young Albus Potter, like his father Harry, does have that choice, but he is unaware that he exists in a deterministic universe and that his choices are consequently guided by external forces. The uneven balance between free will and determinism then perpetuates itself into the next generation of characters, and will affect them like it has affected all the major characters of the series.

Notes

1. B. Berofsky (ed.), *Free Will and Determinism* (New York: Harper & Row, 1966): 4.
2. *Ibid.*: 8.

3. J. M. Fischer, *Four Views on Free Will* (Malden, MA: Blackwell, 2007): 44.
4. P. Donaher and J. M. Okapal, "Causation, Prophetic Visions, and the Free Will Question in *Harry Potter*," in G. L. Anatol (ed.), *Reading Harry Potter Again* (Santa Barbara, CA: Praeger, 2009): 47-62, 53.
5. PS[B]: 88.
6. OP[B]: 186.
7. PS[B]: 61–2.
8. GF[B]: 627.
9. DH[B]: 462.
10. *Ibid.*: 491.
11. PS[B]: 60.
12. *Ibid.*: 91.
13. CS[B]: 245.
14. D. Deavel and C. Deavel, "A Skewed Reflection: The Nature of Evil," in D. Baggett (ed.), *Harry Potter and Philosophy* (Chicago: Open Court, 2004): 132-47, 143.
15. DH[B]: 539.
16. PS[B]: 42.
17. OP[B]: 103.
18. CS[B]: 89.
19. *Ibid.*: 231.
20. See Tess Stockslager's essay, "What it Means to Be a Half-Blood: Integrity versus Fragmentation in Biracial Identity," Chapter 9 in this book.
21. CS[B]: 114.
22. *Ibid.*: 165.
23. *Ibid.*: 51.
24. Deavel and Deavel: 144.
25. PS[B]: 190; PA[B]: 84.
26. OP[B]: 741.
27. HP[B]: 43.
28. DH[B]: 555.
29. PS[B]: 63.
30. GF[B]: 272.
31. DH[B]: 570.
32. Donaher and Okapal: 50.
33. DH[B]: 604.
34. *Ibid.*: 605.
35. *Ibid.*: 607.

6

Dumbledore's Ethos of Love in *Harry Potter*

Lykke Guanio-Uluru

An "ancient quarrel" is still occurring between poets and philosophers that amounts to a comprehensive clash between world views. It goes back at least to Ancient Greece and Plato's claim in *Republic* that poetry has a pervasive and often harmful effect on society. According to Plato, this discord occurs because poets invent rhetorical figures to please or sway their audience—in contrast to philosophers who, more wholesomely, aim to disclose the truth.[1]

During the Middle Ages, literature was assigned worth in terms of being the pedagogical sugar-coating that made the soul medicine of Christian morality go down with the general public. However, with Romanticism in the eighteenth century, a distinct shift in the moral status of literature evolved as imagination came to be considered intrinsically ethical.[2] All of this review goes to show that, historically, a strong belief exists in the influence—for better or worse—that literature may exert on the reader's morality. In Britain, for instance, this belief led to the policy of using literature as a means both to "civilize the natives" in colonial India, and to instill and restore humanitarian values in the British people after World War I.[3] This traditional emphasis on the ethical powers of literature has its counter-current in literary criticism of recent decades that tends to regard literature as existing in a space outside of moral considerations as "art for art's sake."

The long-standing tension between the discourse fields of literature and moral philosophy may go a long way in explaining why academic debate on the ethical propositions of J. K. Rowling's vastly popular *Harry Potter* series has been scant so far. C. M. Lavoie has written on lies,[4] Maria Nicolajeva on the subversion of adult norms,[5] N. Sheltrown on the Potter world as a morality tale,[6] and Ron W. Cooley on rule-breaking[7]; but none of these authors draws explicitly on ethical theory in their work on *Harry Potter*. This lacuna seems all the more surprising as a better understanding of the ethical dimension of the series would be a vital supplement and corrective to the religiously inspired controversies that it has provoked.

Karin E. Westman has dealt eloquently with the obsessive side of love as it is expressed in the *Harry Potter* novels.[8] The present essay focuses on love as an ethical and philosophical concept. It is my view that, in relation to the concept of love thus understood, Rowling has created in the *Harry Potter* series a type of hybrid ethics that contains elements from both New Testament Christian ethics and the long tradition of secular philosophy also underpinning Western democracies. More specifically, I will be arguing below that if love demands openness, then Dumbledore's way of furthering his plan undercuts his own insistence on the supreme power of love. This behavior is best understood with reference to the ethical theory of consequentialism, whereas Dumbledore's ethical shortcomings are clarified with reference to Kant's distinction between price and dignity. Further underscoring the ethical complexity of the concept of love in *Harry Potter* is also the strong undercurrent of religious symbolism in the series, which opens up the possibility of a Christian allegorical reading of the books. This "hybrid" ethical blend is further tempered by the typical postmodern critical self-reflection and the present-day demand for a sense of personal freedom through an active sense of choice.

Nussbaum and love's knowledge

A contemporary philosopher who has sought to bridge the "ancient quarrel" between literature and moral philosophy is Martha Nussbaum. In several essays collected in *Love's Knowledge*,[9] she argues that literature ought to be incorporated into moral philosophy, as its formal features enable it, in contrast to analytical philosophy, to deal adequately with emotions. Rowling seems to sanction this view of the moral importance of emotion in the sense that she has cast her main villain as a psychopath unable to care for or about others. In the *Harry Potter* series, ethical questions regarding power, authority, tolerance, death, and trust—reflected through the concept of love—are all crystallized in relation to the character of Albus Dumbledore, who is initially set up as the pillar of normative authority in the series. As his ethical reputation is deconstructed in *The Deathly Hallows*, this action prompts a secondary and potentially subversive reading of all normative parameters in the books, especially relative to Dumbledore's credo that love is the strongest force there is. In seeking to pin down exactly what Dumbledore's concept of love involves, it is useful to draw on Nussbaum, who has analyzed love in a literary-philosophical context, and J. David Velleman, who regards love in relation to a Kantian understanding of respect. Both of these approaches shed light on the concept of love as it is developed in *Harry Potter*.

In *Love's Knowledge*, Nussbaum is concerned with the love that expresses itself as a relationship with a particular, irreplaceable person. In exploring the concept of love through close reading of the novels of Henry James and Charles Dickens, she finds that her views on love refine through three stages. The first stage is marked by the belief that the Aristotelian ethical stance can encompass every constituent of a good human life, love included. During the second stage, she experiences a gulf between love and ethical attention, in the sense that the intensely private attention demanded by erotic or romantic love is at odds with the ethical viewpoint of valuing all people the same.

After modifying her ethical beliefs, Nussbaum experiences romantic love differently, and the tension in stage two is resolved in a third stage during which she contemplates what she terms non-judgmental love: "I suggest that the non-judgmental love of particulars characteristic of the best and most humane ethical stance contains within itself a susceptibility to love, and to a love that leads the lover at times beyond the ethical stance into a world in which ethical judgment does not take place."[10] In other words, in loving a particular person in a non-judgmental way, one is susceptible to seeing the other in a way that suspends the usual habit of ethically judging that person's behavior. Here, love and ethical concern "support and inform one another," in the sense that "each one is less good, less complete without the other."[11] With this explanation, Nussbaum means to describe a morality of sympathy, inspired by Roman Stoic ideas of mercy, which she sees as elaborated in Christian ethics. It is especially Nussbaum's descriptions of the second and—in relation to Voldemort—third stages that are useful in analyzing the concept of love in *Harry Potter*.

Authority versus ethical credibility

In *Harry Potter*, the character of Albus Dumbledore functions as the center of ethical authority. Because the whole series (with the notable exceptions of the first chapter of the first and the seventh books) is narrated in close alignment with Harry's perspective, the reader perceives Dumbledore mainly through Harry's eyes. As Harry matures, his psychological observations become more complex, presenting the reader with a relational world of steadily increasing sophistication. Consequently, what the reader "knows" about Dumbledore is what Harry thinks and knows at any given age, based on the impressions he forms of a man he greatly admires.

Through his position as a substitute father figure for Harry, his role as headmaster and his high standing within the wizard community, Dumbledore is a seemingly universally admired mentor figure. He is sought out for advice and guidance by Hogwarts students and staff alike, as well as by various ministers of magic. In addition, he is the head of both the Wizengamot court and of the anti-Voldemort resistance movement, the Order of the Phoenix. According to Farah Mendlesohn, who has developed a system of classification for fantasy texts, such a "patriarchal" notion of authority is typical of most quest fantasies, as is the notion that there is only one correct version of the world to which any morally just person ought to conform.[12] Her description seems to fit the first six *Harry Potter* books, but in the last volume, things become more complicated. As the story progresses, a gap opens up between Dumbledore's words and his actions. This split undermines Dumbledore's reliability, creating an interpretive plurality within the narrative that reverberates back through the previous books. Ethical plurality is also achieved through the introduction of several overlapping narrative schemata. These layers allow the author to operate with plural aims within the text, yet still achieve a sense of cohesion.

More specifically, Dumbledore's ethical reputation is challenged after his death by several critical voices. This deconstruction of Dumbledore as the stable ethical center of the Potter universe forces the reader to reinterpret the ethical implications of the whole story. Cleverly, even as subverting the authority of Dumbledore opens up the moral discourse, his position is simultaneously validated through its eventual success. The result helps secure a satisfactory sense of closure in all the several narrative schemata that have been set up: there is the fairy tale and romance resolution of happy marriage, the crime resolution in which the villain is found out and "arrested," a suspense resolution in which the mystery is solved and all the clues come together, the quest resolution of a mission successfully accomplished, and finally the moral resolution of Harry's "right choice" in denouncing the Hallows, following through with Dumbledore's plan of destroying the Horcruxes and in accepting death without resistance.

Acting as the mentor, it is Dumbledore who points out to Harry both the fear of death that drives Voldemort and the possible means of defeating him through destroying his Horcruxes. It is also Dumbledore who, through his guidance, prepares Harry for his search for these Horcruxes and for his own final surrender to death as a love sacrifice. In these ways, Dumbledore both forges Harry's sense of destiny and helps him prepare for its fulfillment. He is thus an agent for Harry's moral growth, guiding him from his first vindictive rage through to his selfless choice of surrendering to Voldemort in order to protect his friends.

Dumbledore is also the catalyst for Snape's conversion from Death Eater to double agent, working seemingly for both Voldemort and for the Order of the Phoenix; the reader is long left to wonder where his real allegiance lies. Snape depends on Dumbledore's protection in the aftermath of Voldemort's first demise and avoids being sent to Azkaban because Dumbledore vouches for him. His allegiance is also secured by his reliance on Dumbledore to hide his most shameful secret: his love for Harry's mother Lily. This love is what prompts Snape's unceasing but secret work to keep Harry safe—despite an instant personal dislike that arises between them. In this sense, Snape puts one in mind of Kant's reluctant philanthropist: only the person who drags himself, almost in spite of himself, to do his duty for the sake of duty alone acts with moral worth.[13] Though Snape ultimately is motivated by love, it is Dumbledore who points out to him that his love carries with it an obligation to protect Harry and thus to honor Lily's own sacrifice. Upon Snape's death, late in the last book, Harry, and thereby the reader, learns of the degree of secrecy and manipulation that lies behind Dumbledore's moral influence on both Harry and Snape, and of the sense of betrayal they both experience. This sense of betrayal is closely linked to their private interpretations of Dumbledore's frequent references to the power of love.

Dumbledore's love for Harry

In analyzing the concept of love in the *Harry Potter* series, it becomes apparent that the implied author is grappling with a philosophical question similar to that encountered in Nussbaum's second stage; the apparent conflict between the partiality and obligations that go with personal love relationships on the one hand and the universalizing requirements of morality on the other. The technical term of implied author is indispensible to the rhetorical theory of narrative, which underpins my own reading of the series. The term was coined by Wayne C. Booth[14] and is described by him as an ethical mask worn by the real author when writing literature,[15] and by J. Phelan as "an actual or purported subset of the real author's capacities, traits, attitudes, beliefs, values."[16] It is indispensible here because it makes a distinction between the rhetorical intent of the flesh-and-blood author (Rowling) and the rhetorical intent that is discernible through a textual analysis of the text as it stands. Hence, a rhetorical reading attributes power to the reader in discerning textual intent, which is why subsequent extratextual information becomes less relevant.

Prior to his death, Dumbledore acknowledges that he has been partial to Harry in order to protect Harry's life at the potential expense of other lives, and he judges himself for what he sees as a flaw that needs defending. It is clear that Dumbledore *does* value Harry as special. This is why he has kept him in the dark about certain things, he explains, because he wanted to save Harry from pain and worry:

> "I cared about you too much," said Dumbledore simply. "I cared more for your happiness than your knowing the truth, more for your peace of mind than my plan, more for your life than the lives that might be lost if the plan failed. In other words, I acted exactly as Voldemort expects we fools who love to act.
>
> Is there a defence? I defy anyone who has watched you as I have— and I have watched you more closely than you can have imagined—not to want to save you more pain than you had already suffered. What did I care if numbers of nameless and faceless people and creatures were slaughtered in the vague future, if in the here and now you were alive, and well, and happy? I never dreamed that I would have such a person on my hands."[17]

This passage in which Dumbledore expresses his love for Harry highlights the distinction between personal affection and the moral demand that all lives have the same value. Here is precisely that tension between favoring someone in particular versus the impartiality that Dumbledore thinks ought to guide his actions. In this passage, Dumbledore seems to regard his feelings towards Harry as a moral shortcoming. (Rowling's extra-textual revelation during a talk in New York's Carnegie Hall that Dumbledore is gay raises further issues in the analysis of love in *Harry Potter*,[18] which will not be inquired into here,[19] nor will the further extra-textual revelations Rowling makes on Pottermore.[20])

Dumbledore's secrets and lies

In the passage quoted above, Dumbledore stresses that he has been intently watching Harry. As a result, this close attention has led him to love and appreciate Harry as truly unique. This view of careful attention as a precondition for love is one that is shared by both Nussbaum and Velleman. Notably, the way that Dumbledore accomplishes his "great plan" is by deliberately and carefully hiding aspects of it from Harry—as well as from Snape. This secrecy implies a reliance on a force opposed to the openness and possibility for true perception that is the hallmark of love—at least in reciprocal relationships. As a result, there is an implicit questioning of Dumbledore's ability to love others *as equals*. His own brother, Aberforth, warns Harry that people whom Dumbledore cared about "ended up worse than if he had left them well alone,"[21] and tells Harry that Dumbledore was always talented with secrets and lies. Thus, if love demands openness, the very way that Dumbledore furthers his own plan seems to undercut his own insistence on the supreme power of love.

When Harry and the reader are made privy to Snape's memories after his death, it becomes evident how skilled Dumbledore has been at lying through omission, and his trustworthiness receives another blow. However, once again, because the information that discredits Dumbledore arrives in the form of Snape's memories, the reader cannot be sure how to judge it. Snape's memories turn Snape into a hero and Dumbledore into a calculating manipulator—but that is Snape's version of the story. Still, these shifts in perspective cast doubt on Dumbledore's moral supremacy and the text is left with an unstable moral center. In this sense, Dumbledore's moral fall has a domino-effect that deconstructs the reader's previous interpretations: one is encouraged to reconsider the whole text in light of both the "new" Dumbledore and the "new" Professor Snape. Harry partly performs this re-reading through his psychological agonizing over Dumbledore in the course of *The Deathly Hallows*. When he makes the *choice* to continue to trust Dumbledore, his decision makes possible a "stabilized" moral reading of the text, that is, one that validates Dumbledore. Such a reading is supported by the last chapter, in which a post-war scenario of wizard children going to Hogwarts from Platform 9¾ suggests that the world is "back to normal."

Love as suffering: allusions to Christ

In line with the constant interpretive ambiguity set up by the implied author, the most succinct definition of love provided in *Harry Potter* is

Dumbledore's description of love as a mysterious and powerful force that cannot be fully apprehended:

> "There is a room in the Department of Mysteries," interrupted Dumbledore, "that is kept locked at all times. It contains a force that is at once more wonderful and more terrible than death, than human intelligence, than the forces of nature. It is also, perhaps, the most mysterious of the many subjects for study that reside there. It is the power held within that room that you possess in such quantities and which Voldemort has not at all. [...] In the end, it mattered not that you could not close your mind. It was your heart that saved you."[22]

This description of love as something more and other than human intelligence emphasizes the spiritual dimension of love. Notably Dumbledore describes love here as both wonderful and *terrible*. The terrible element of love is linked to Dumbledore's notion that love includes and sometimes demands suffering. This element of suffering is vividly present in the cave scene, in which Harry—due to his allegiance with Dumbledore—is forced to keep pouring Voldemort's potion into Dumbledore's mouth in order to secure one of the Horcruxes, even though the potion is evidently tormenting his headmaster. Empathic ability is a general trait with Harry (it is a way in which he occasionally models compassion), and here his suffering is made worse due to his deep love for Dumbledore.

The most culturally salient emblem of a love that demands suffering is that of Christ dying on the cross. Thus the scene in the cave is one element in the associative link that is forged between the morality of the *Harry Potter* series and New Testament Christian ethics, especially since it occurs before Dumbledore's normative authority is deconstructed. The spiritual and transcendent understanding of love found in *Harry Potter* is underscored by such an allegorical reading of the series. In the course of the first six books, Dumbledore is elevated (by the youthful Harry) to the position of a supreme all-knowing God. This reading is supported by the profusion of Christian religious symbolism that permeates the text: evil in the shape of the snake, the temptation that must be overcome, death as a sacrificial act "for the greater good" in the manner of Christ. In such a reading, Dumbledore becomes God, sacrificing his "son" to save wizardkind from the evil Voldemort, who rebels against the proper moral order of the universe in his quest for immortality. The twist to this allegorical element in *Harry Potter* is the self-reflection on the part of divine authority when "God," in the shape of Dumbledore, admits to his own selfishness and hunger for power and glory, and he is finally forced to ask: "Was I better, ultimately, than Voldemort?"—to which Harry's reply is "Of course—how can you ask that? You never killed if you could avoid it?"[23] In this way, the supreme power questions itself, but is at the same time validated by the hero, who by his choices serves to validate the moral order that this power has set up and represents.

If read as a Christian allegory, the text potentially also carries an element of blasphemy: After all, the superior power that Harry rages against, doubts, and then finally resigns to, trusts and whose will he tries to divine—is all along Dumbledore (who later deeply regrets what he considers his own morally flawed behavior). Going against such an allegorical reading of the text is the emphasis throughout that Harry has a free choice in terms of following Dumbledore's lead or not. This underlining of personal choice blunts the edge of moral destiny, obligation and duty that are typical elements of the quest fantasy. The element of choice is also stressed in relation to the proto-typical quest-fantasy prophecy, which is revealed to contain several levels of ambiguity and is reinterpreted several times for Harry by Dumbledore.

Although the implied author, not least by frequently adopting Harry's perspective, actively questions the nature, conflicts and limits of love as a moral emotion in the seventh volume especially, Harry as a character demonstrates a profound belief in the power of love. He does so first through his own personal bonds and relationships, and ultimately though the sacrificial act he commits when he surrenders to Voldemort. Harry's life and choices seem to bridge the conflict between personal love and the universalizing requirements of morality in the sense that his sacrifice for the common good requires his own *sanction* in order for the power of love to function fully. It is his *willingness* to die that saves his life. Because of this willingness, the sacrifice signals spiritual growth for Harry: at the end of the last volume, Dumbledore concludes that Harry has outgrown him morally and is "the better man."[24]

Love "for the greater good"

A major aspect of Harry's re-evaluation of Dumbledore in *Deathly Hallows* is his attempt to come to terms with Dumbledore's secretive behavior relative to his headmaster's professed love for him. At seventeen, on the run from Voldemort and struggling to fulfill Dumbledore's "great plan" of destroying Voldemort's remaining Horcruxes, Harry learns that when Dumbledore was his age, he made friends with one of the most evil wizards of all time, Grindelwald, and coined the slogan "for the greater good" as an excuse for advocating wizard rule over Muggles. Grindelwald even later used Dumbledore's slogan to justify a number of atrocities. When Harry discovers that Dumbledore has guided him by concealing such vital aspects of the truth, his faith in and respect for Dumbledore is shaken. Dumbledore's slogan "for the greater good" is closely associated with the ethical theory of *consequentialism*, which holds that an action can only be judged on the basis of its outcome. The essence of the theory is popularly expressed with the aphorism: "the ends justify the means."[25] By the force of Dumbledore's normative position, consequentialism becomes a strong facet of the ethical argument in the *Harry Potter* series, though one that the implied author of the text renders ambiguous. The ambiguity arises both because Dumbledore's authority ultimately is questioned, but also because the first time the reader learns about Dumbledore's slogan is in the context of his friendship with an evil wizard. Hence, in the text this concept is associated with ideas of supremacy rule grounded in racism. (The slogan also brings to mind the Philosopher Kings—the ruling elite portrayed in Plato's *Republic*[26]; thus there seems to be an implicit critique of Plato's ideal state embedded in *The Deathly Hallows*.)

Dumbledore distances himself from such ideas throughout all of his adult life, and he regrets his involvement with ideas of "the greater good" in his afterlife when meeting with Harry in "King's Cross." His stance seems to indicate that the implied author of the series denounces consequentialism as bad moral strategy and warns that it can easily be used as a rhetorical disguise for seeking personal gain, in the way that Grindelwald uses Dumbledore's slogan to justify his own power games. Later, however, the same slogan is used by Harry to defend Dumbledore against accusations that he was unable to love: "'Because,' said Harry, before Hermione could answer, 'sometimes you've *got* to think about more than your own safety! Sometimes you've *got* to think about the greater good! This is war!'"[27] The way the term is used by Harry here, it implies looking further than one's personal safety in order to stand up for important common values. In war, this approach is justified, Harry says, defending Dumbledore's consequentialist calculations. The problem—and the difference—is that whereas Harry sacrifices *himself*, Dumbledore is prepared to sacrifice *another* "for the greater good."

When it is revealed that Dumbledore's "great plan" all along is directed toward the sacrifice of Harry to Voldemort—as Harry unknowingly became a Horcrux at the age of one and thus has to die to rid the wizard world of evil—it highlights the relative, rather than absolute, value placed by consequentialist ethical theories on the moral worth of one individual's life, and this becomes an issue in the text. There is an ethical dimension regarding respect for persons that is absent in Dumbledore's treatment of both Snape and Harry, which is put more clearly into perspective by Velleman's Kantian interpretation of the concept of love below.

Velleman and love as moral emotion

In his essay "Love as Moral Emotion," J. D. Velleman juxtaposes love with Kantian respect in order to illuminate both concepts, and he holds that the alleged conflict between love and morality depends on a conceptual error, as love is a moral emotion and hence cannot be opposed to love itself.[28] Arguing for the impartiality of love by comparing it to Kant's conception of respect for persons, Velleman claims that, since Freud, numerous philosophers have conceived of love as a drive, and hence made the other person instrumental to satisfying an inner "itch" of some kind. He points to Kant's distinction between price and dignity to show that, when someone is valued as a person, this constitutes a respect for that person's dignity. "Dignity" involves valuing persons as ends in themselves, as irreplaceable, and is opposed to the concept of "price" through which a value may be fixed and, hence, replaced by a comparable value. Velleman's Kantian terminology allows one to diagnose Dumbledore's treatment of Harry, and also of Snape, as one of seeing them as a means to an end. Thus in spite of his professed love for Harry, Dumbledore treats Harry as a price that may be balanced against the lives of others whose lives each have equal value. He thus denies, in Kantian terms, Harry's dignity by which he is irreplaceable. In this way, Harry becomes the victim of Dumbledore's consequentialist calculation: sacrifice the one in order to save the many.

In Velleman's view, loving some but not others *does* mean that we value them differently, but not that they have a different value. His bottom line is that the love we experience through personal relationships is a form of moral education that teaches us about the absurdity of weighing people's value against each other—something that Dumbledore perhaps ought to have learned through his personal love for Harry. Velleman renounces Nussbaum's idea that love can be "beyond the ethical" and casts doubt on the validity of treating people as means to an end, even if doing so serves "the greater good." In other words, his conception of love runs against both consequentialist thought and transcendent ideas about love. Hence applying his ideas to a reading of the *Harry Potter* series highlights both these aspects of the text.

New Testament Christian ethics: love as self-sacrifice and compassion

The kind of love that is presented in the *Harry Potter* series as morally superior is the love that ultimately leads to self-sacrifice. It is the most steadily reinforced argument for what love is, and in this respect, the text's moral message is firmly in line with Christian thought. This motif is established early on, as Lily sacrifices her own life in order to protect her baby son Harry from Voldemort. The power of this sacrifice is what keeps Harry safe for the next 17 years. The ethically ambiguous Professor Snape also lives (and dies) to protect Harry in order to honor his own love for Lily. This love sacrifice by Snape effectively changes Harry's long-standing loathing for Snape into deep respect and recognition. Thus, indirectly it demonstrates the transformative power and mysterious force previously attributed to love by Dumbledore. Harry duplicates Lily's sacrifice as he dies to save his own friends from Voldemort: like him, they are safe from harm in the final struggle, protected by the force field of sacrificial love. Both Harry's and Snape's sacrifices for love are catalyzed by Dumbledore, allowing Dumbledore to sacrifice his moral charges rather than himself "for the greater good." (Dumbledore's own fatal wound—which caused him to pressure a reluctant Snape to perform euthanasia on him to avoid being captured by Voldemort's followers—was after all sustained when Dumbledore, in his desire to possess the Hallows, forgot that Marvolo's ring was a Horcrux and put it on.) Thus, the implied author of the *Harry Potter* series seems to be arguing for the Christian notion of self-sacrifice, while at the same time to sanction, through Harry's acceptance of these sacrifices, Dumbledore's consequentialist calculations. Despite his regret, there remains a certain ethical uneasiness about Dumbledore's ethos concerning his degree of secrecy and manipulation from a position of both social and moral authority.

The emphasis on love throughout the text creates further ethical uneasiness in relation to the treatment of Voldemort. This position raises several interesting questions, all of which cannot be pursued fully here: If Dumbledore truly believes that love is the strongest force there is, then why does he have to kill Voldemort and even Voldemort's soul fragments? Ought he not to try to further his healing instead? Is it the mysterious force of love that causes Voldemort's curse to rebound and kill him? Or does love only affect those who are able to love?

In *The Deathly Hallows*, both Harry and the reader learn—through Hermione's answer to Ron's question about whether there is any way of putting one's soul back together again—that the only thing that can reverse a Horcrux is remorse: "to really feel what you've done."[29] The pain of this remorse is so intense that "it can destroy you," Hermione says. "I can't see Voldemort attempting it, somehow, can you?"[30] If there is any compassion in the love of Dumbledore or Harry towards Voldemort (which one would expect considering the frequent allusion to New Testament Christian ethics), then there is certainly a "flaw in the plan." In any case, there is a logical flaw—and perhaps even a moral one—as Harry, after first having destroyed all of Voldemort's soul fragments, still urges him during their final confrontation to "try for some remorse, Riddle…"[31] Surely, the point for redemption must be gone, as Voldemort's soul mostly is as well. So what kind of love is it that conquers Voldemort by removing his only chance of becoming whole? This type of love may serve the greater good, but it is certainly not compassionate. It does at least not seem to come from a place of mercy or non-judgment, which according to Nussbaum characterizes "the most humane ethical stance."[32]

Conclusion: the hybrid ethics of *Harry Potter*

I have argued that, because Dumbledore is established as the central source of normative authority in the first six books, the questioning of his moral integrity taking place in *The Deathly Hallows* has consequences for the ethical perspective of the whole series. In addition, because Dumbledore's most frequently affirmed credo is that love is such a powerful force, this concept acts as a prism through which many issues are reflected. Therefore, an analysis of the various ethical nuances of the concept of love, as it is played out in the series, is useful for understanding the values transmitted by the work as a whole.

By seemingly advocating the Christian ideal of love as self-sacrifice through the use of religious symbolism, while at the same time rolling this into a different conception of love, that of love and morality as served by consequentialist calculation, Rowling is able to cater to both readers with a Christian moral sensibility and readers with a more secular ethical bent. At the same time, in a manner typical of postmodern critical self-reflection, the consequentialist element of the text is undercut by an implied critique of Dumbledore's use of both Harry and Snape—but not of their destruction of Voldemort's soul fragments. Hence, in terms of love as compassion or Stoic mercy, this blend leaves a slightly bitter aftertaste, ethically speaking. The destruction of evil is a trope of the quest fantasy, so it seems that form has had a final word over ethics in this case.

Notes

1. C. Griswold (2008) *Plato on Rhetoric and Poetry*, http://plato.stanford. edu/entries/plato-rhetoric/ (accessed December 8, 2010).
2. A. Locatelli, "Literature's Versions of its own Transmission of Values," in A. Errll, H. Grabes, and A. Nünning (eds.), *Ethics in Culture: The Dissemination of Values through Literature and Other Media* (Berlin and New York: Walter de Gruyter, 2008): 19–34.
3. R. Eaglestone, *Doing English: A Guide for Literature Students*, 3rd edn (Abingdon and New York: Routledge, 2009): 11.
4. C. M. Lavoie, "The Good, the Bad, and the Ugly: Lies in Harry Potter," in G. L. Anatol (ed.), *Reading Harry Potter Again: New Critical Essays* (Oxford: ABC Clio, 2009): 77–90.
5. M. Nicolajeva, "Harry Potter and the Secrets of Children's Literature," in E. E. Heilman (ed.), *Critical Perspectives on Harry Potter* (Abingdon and New York: Routledge, 2009): 225–42.
6. N. Sheltrown, "Harry Potter's World as a Morality Tale of Technology and Media," in E. E. Heilman (ed.), *Critical Perspectives on Harry Potter* (Abingdon and New York: Routledge, 2003): 47–64.
7. R. W. Cooley, "Harry Potter and the Temporal Prime Directive: Time Travel, Rule-breaking, and Misapprehension in *Harry Potter and the Prisoner of Azkaban*," in C. W. Hallett (ed.), *Scholarly Studies in Harry Potter: Applying Academic Methods to a Popular Text* (Lewiston, NY: Edward Mellen Press, 2005): 29–42.
8. K. E. Westman, "Specters of Thatcherism: Contemporary British Culture in J. K. Rowling's Harry Potter Series," in L. A. Whited (ed.), *The Ivory Tower and Harry Potter: Perspectives on a Literary Phenomenon* (Columbia, MO: University of Missouri Press, 2008): 305–28.
9. M. C. Nussbaum, *Love's Knowledge, Essays on Philosophy and Literature* (Oxford: Oxford University Press, 1990).
10. Nussbaum: 52.
11. Nussbaum: 53.
12. F. Mendlesohn, *Rhetorics of Fantasy* (Middletown, CT: Wesleyan University Press, 2008).
13. B. Herman, "On the Value of Acting from the Motive of Duty," *The Philosophy Review* 90(3) (1981): 359–83.
14. W. C. Booth, *The Company We Keep: An Ethics of Fiction* (Berkeley, CA: University of California Press, 1988).
15. W. C. Booth, "Resurrection of the Implied Author: Why Bother?" in

J. Phelan and P. J. Rabinowitz (eds.), *A Companion to Narrative Theory* (Oxford: Blackwell, 2008): 75–88.

16. J. Phelan, *Experiencing Fiction: Judgments, Progressions, and the Rhetorical Theory of Narrative* (Columbus, OH: Ohio State University Press, 2007): 45.

17. OP[B]: 739.

18. See Jim Daems' essay "'I Knew a Girl Once, whose Hair…': Dumbledore and the Closet," Chapter 12 in this volume.

19. BBC News (2007), "J. K. Rowling Outs Dumbledore as Gay," http://news.bbc.co.uk/2/hi/7053982.stm (accessed December 8, 2010).

20. http://www.pottermore.com/

21. DH[B]: 452.

22. OP[B]: 743

23. DH[B]: 571.

24. *Ibid.*

25. See, for example, S. Scheffler, *Consequentialism and its Critics* (Oxford: Oxford University Press, 1988).

26. Plato, *Republic*, ed. R. Waterfield (Oxford and New York: Oxford University Press, 1993): 190–225.

27. DH[B]: 458.

28. J. D. Velleman, "Love as Moral Emotion," *Ethics* 109(2) (1999): 338–74.

29. DH[B]: 89.

30. *Ibid.*

31. *Ibid.*: 594.

32. Nussbaum: 52.

7

Harry Potter and the Origins of the Occult

Em McAvan

In the 2001 documentary *Hell House*,[1] a Dallas Pentecostal church creates a multimedia presentation designed to scare its patrons away from the temptations of hell. Among the sins enumerated by the performance (abortion, homosexuality, drugs, incest, suicide) is the occult. Two of the church's scriptwriters work on a scene that situates *Harry Potter* within a continuum of the occult, writing a "demon's" monologue by accusing the series of encouraging an interest in the occult, including playing with Ouija boards and becoming involved in role-playing involving magic. As with all of the other plot lines in *Hell House*, the occult inevitably leads to eternal damnation in hell. *Harry Potter* clearly represents the beginning point of a contemporary trajectory towards the occult imagined by the Dallas church's writers and performers.

However, the inclusion of *Harry Potter* as a sinful "temptation" towards the occult is far from an accidental or isolated response to the success of the series in the Bible Belt. J. K. Rowling's series has faced numerous criticisms from religious leaders across the globe—evangelical, Anglican, Catholic and even Muslim, though it has primarily centered on the loose movement of evangelical and fundamentalist Protestants in the United States known as the Christian or Religious Right. Sociologist Danielle Souillere has documented the astounding amount of material devoted to the series by the Christian Right in the United States over the last decade.[2] At times this rhetoric has been extreme, as when Pastor Joseph Chambers, of the Paw Creek Ministries in North Carolina ties the occult to Rapture theology on his website:

> Without question I believe the *Harry Potter* series is a creation of hell helping prepare the younger generation to welcome the Biblical

prophecies of demons and devils led by Lucifer himself. Infallible Scripture, the Holy Bible, has outlined the end time scenario and the *Harry Potter* script sounds exactly like the devil's part.[3]

Interestingly, the fierce reaction to *Harry Potter* in fundamentalist and evangelical circles has tended to set the terms of the debates around the legitimacy of reading or watching *Harry Potter*, even for more moderate Christians. Popular apologias for the series such as Connie Neal's *What's a Christian to Do with Harry Potter?*[4]; J. Killinger's *God, The Devil and Harry Potter: A Christian Minister's Defense of the Beloved Novels*[5]; and Gina Burkart's *A Parent's Guide to Harry Potter*[6] tend to begin by acknowledging some legitimacy to the opposition to *Harry Potter*. Burkart admits that "there are areas of concern in the books—in particular Rowling's use of witchcraft and violence."[7] Authors such as Neal and Burkart, in response to this concern, are careful to delineate a properly Christian pedagogical response to the series, underlining Rowling's few explicit references to Christianity (for instance, the reference to 1 Corinthians 15:26 on James and Lily Potter's gravestone in *The Deathly Hallows*). Similarly, chapter titles such as "discussing fantasy with children" and "morals not magic" attempt to ward off the specter of the unreal through a strategy of containment and restatement of orthodox morality. Burkart suggests that the "concerns about a child's ability to discern reality and fantasy" are simply "good common sense."[8] In an argument determined by competing (partial) readings of text and Scripture, both sides participate in the long Christian history of heresiography and apologia.

Nevertheless, to engage in a defense of *Harry Potter*, while necessary in some religious communities, is in some ways to miss the point, obscuring the vital question of what it is that the discourse directed at *Harry Potter* as occult does, from where it emerges and to what purpose. Critics must analyze the roots of the evangelical Protestant criticisms that have been directed at the books from churches in the United States such as the one in Dallas seen in *Hell House*. Such an analysis will show the ways in which "religious discourse in its many hybrid forms serves as a flexible American paradigm of personal *and* civil identity."[9] Why would the common trope of magic in children's literature become a source of cultural anxiety particularly centered on *Harry Potter*? From where does this accusation of "the occult" emerge? What tensions within religious communities does its mobilization resolve?

The occult?

As numerous writers have noted, religious anxiety about the fantastic or supernatural is nothing new in the United States. At the beginning of the decade, concerned religious leaders denounced the Japanese television series *Pokemon* as evil. In the 1970s and 80s, the religious Right put forth similar kinds of rhetoric about the role-playing game *Dungeons & Dragons* and heavy metal music. As Souillere points out, "that the *Harry Potter* series is an integral part of popular culture marketed primarily to children and youth, which ostensibly deals with themes perceived to be associated with the occult (magic, witchcraft, wizardry), makes it ripe for a moral panic generated and fueled by members of the Christian Right."[10] Similarly popular series such as J. R. R. Tolkien's *Lord of the Rings* consumed primarily by adults have by and large escaped the moral hysteria directed at *Harry Potter*. The perceived vulnerability of children and teens marks the precondition for any text designated as part of the putative occult.

However, to understand this phenomenon further, critics must understand the evangelical Protestant movements themselves. British historian David Bebbington has influentially outlined four criteria by which critics can understand evangelical faith and practice.[11] First, he argues that evangelicals are motivated by "conversism," the belief that lives have been or should be changed by the faith being practiced. "Jesus saves" succinctly captures the kinds of conversism endemic to evangelical communities. Second, Bebbington isolates evangelical "activism" that grows *from* these personal changes into a concern for remaking the public sphere in the image of evangelical belief. Third, evangelicals are noted for their "biblicism," which is a strong belief in the (Christian) Bible as the source of ultimate truth. This feature leads to the uniquely evangelical disavowal of the history of Christian hermeneutics, instead seeing the believers' interpretation as largely founded in an unmediated relation to the Bible. Last, there is "crucicentrism," the theological focus on the death and resurrection of Christ on the Cross. Common phrases in the Bible Belt such as "washed in the blood of the Lamb" point graphically to the redemptive nature of Christ's sacrifice. All of these facets are a factor in the development of a discourse of the occult, though the very discourse too itself is under erasure, a largely unreflexive disavowed history of interpretation and American cultural practice that leads back to the country's origins in the New England colonies.

Therefore, if one reads evangelical criticisms of *Harry Potter* such as Chambers',[12] though they depend heavily on extra-textual interpretations and practices derived from the Puritans onwards, the *only* textual evidence given is biblically based. The biblical justifications themselves for this glossing of the fantastic as occult are fairly unambiguous if read literally. Deuteronomy 18:10-12 (KJV) puts it this way:

> There shall not be found among you any one that maketh his son or his daughter to pass through the fire, or that useth divination, or an observer of times, or an enchanter, or a witch. Or a charmer, or a consulter with familiar spirits, or a wizard, or a necromancer. For all that do these things are an abomination unto the LORD: and because of these abominations the LORD thy God doth drive them out from before thee.

Exodus puts it even more bluntly: "thou shalt not suffer a witch to live" (Exodus 22:18 KJV). To Christians inclined on reading the Bible literally, the evidence seems clear: there is to be no tolerance for witchcraft.

This literalism extends to the evangelical reading of *Harry Potter*, which takes the most surface of readings of the representation of magic in the series. For many, the *Harry Potter* series seem to fit the model of witchcraft or wizardry described in Deuteronomy. Rowling has indeed created an enchanted (in the Weberian sense) world, a supernatural realm inhabited by capricious spirits, giant spiders, pixies, Dementors, unicorns and other fantastic creatures. At the wizarding school Hogwarts, students study magic, flourishing wands and chanting incantations of mostly Latin linguistic origin such as *Expelliarmus* (a disarming charm) and *Expecto Patronum* (a protection spell). Similarly, potions are used throughout for purposes mundane and profound, from the joke potions of Fred and George Weasley to Madam Pomfrey's healing potions in the Hogwarts infirmary to the Polyjuice Potion that causes complete appearance transformation for an hour in *The Chamber of Secrets*. Harry's owl Hedwig and Ron's rat Scabbers may be considered familiars of a kind. Ghosts too walk the halls (and walls) of Hogwarts, with the Fat Lady in the Painting, Moaning Myrtle and Nearly Headless Nick recurring elements in the narrative, while the classical image of witchcraft is invoked with students flying on broomsticks in the lacrosse-esque sport Quidditch. Last, and by no means least, the dark wizard Voldemort is more necromancer than traditional wizard, sharing Professor Quirrell's body, breathing life into his old notebook in *The Chamber of Secrets*, and dividing his soul with the Horcruxes that make up the quest in the final two books of the series. To the superficial evangelical reading, it is these elements alone that are enough to determine that the text is occult.

Writers such as Neal and Burkart engaging in Christian apologetics, however, set the magical element aside and read the text looking for a clear moral framework. Rowling instructs her readers in the value of friendship, love, loyalty and bravery time and again. Indeed, the text can hardly be seen as an unmitigated affirmation of the supernatural, for Rowling starkly condemns the necromancy of Voldemort. This exchange between Dumbledore and Voldemort in *The Order of the Phoenix* makes Rowling's position on Voldemort's unnaturally extended life plain:

> "You do not seek to kill me, Dumbledore?" called Voldemort, his scarlet eyes narrowed over the top of the shield. "Above such brutality, are you?"
> "We both know there are other ways of destroying a man, Tom." Dumbledore said calmly [...]. "Merely taking your life would not satisfy me, I admit—"
> "There is nothing worse than death, Dumbledore!" snarled Voldemort.
> "You are quite wrong," said Dumbledore [...]. "Indeed your failure to understand that there are things much worse than death has always been your greatest weakness."[13]

Rowling consistently underlines the immorality of Voldemort's magic, which extends his life and power at the expense of innumerable others, and which instrumentalizes people free of love and kindness.

Yet even if one accepts the shallowest of readings of *Harry Potter* as a text that celebrates the power of magic, it is unclear why these concerns would be directed at a *fictional* text. There is no real Harry Potter engaged in witchcraft, no children casting spells or engaging necromancers. One could, perhaps, just as easily call for the banning of *Hamlet* on the grounds of his consulting with spirits. Or, to take it to its logical conclusion, call for the ban of any text representing murder, given the obvious "thou shalt not kill" prohibition in Exodus 20:13 (KJV). That there is no such a prohibition on representation at all suggests that here is a cultural quilting point, a source of ideological tension that is constantly being pulled apart and sutured together by partial explanations and practices. In order to register the emergence of these tensions towards the fantastic then, one must read genealogically, situating the discourse of the fantastic as occult as part of a greater historical discourse about witchcraft in the United States.

Puritanism and witchcraft

Accusations of "witchcraft" or "the occult" directed at *Harry Potter* have their roots in an old religious tradition—the curiously American blend of "colonial theological text, civic ritual and contemporary pulp horror formula."[14] The origins of the reading of fantastic texts as occult and satanic emerge most clearly from early Puritan practices and the works of theologians Increase and Cotton Mather and Jonathan Edwards, transmitted through nineteenth- and twentieth-century evangelical writings (most prominently in the form of dispensation- alist evangelicalism from John Nelson Darby, Cyrus Scofield, and their modern-day heirs). Historian Paul Boyer, for instance, suggests that Rapture theology originates with Increase Mather and that, "in a sense, Darby did nothing new."[15] Cotton Mather, famous chronicler of the Salem witch trials, wrote about the "late Stupendious [*sic*] growth of Witches among us"[16] and "the whole plot of the Devil, against *New-England*."[17] He states, "Tis agreed, That the Devil has made a dreadful Knot of *Witches* in the Country."[18] Reverend John Hale of Beverly, Massachusetts, wrote that "[Magic] serves the interest of those that have a vain curiosity to pry into things God has forbid- den, and concealed from discovery by lawful means."[19]

Though the *Harry Potter* novels themselves are fantasy novels, evan- gelical criticisms sit squarely within a distinctly American tradition of Gothicized theology, a "mode of memory" as David Punter put it.[20] Politically, the invocation of demonic imagery has been used as a boundary marker, a means of forming Christian communities against "the nightmare of limitless possibilities"[21] embodied by the aberrant text. Vilifying *Harry Potter* has less to do with the specific properties of the text than by the perennial need to repeat such scapegoating rituals in American Christendom. In short, readers may consider texts such as *Harry Potter* as being discursively constructed *as* witches, and thus in need of purging from the greater body of believers.

In his *The Enemy Within*, American historian John Demos traces practices of witch-hunting through the two thousand years since the birth of Christ. Curiously, though such practices are chiefly condemned through reference to the Hebrew Bible (the Christian "Old Testament"), witch-hunting appears largely unknown on a large scale in Jewish communities. This oddity may be due to the fact that, as Demos points out, the greatest goal of witch-hunting is a social scapegoating, something of which Jews have historically been more victims than perpetrators. Witch-hunting belongs to a "capacious terrain that also includes racism, sexism, and anti-Semitism, as well as pogroms, lynchings, genocide and ethnic cleansing."[22] Yet witch- hunting differs from most of the manifestations of these removals of a "despised 'other' [in finding] the other within its own ranks."[23] Witch-hunting is thus first and foremost directed at the community *itself*, which in Christianity means scrutinizing a community of members who outwardly appear to be Christian believers.

Demos describes an elaborate taxonomy of witchcraft in Puritan New England, a "broad spectrum of belief and practice"[24] containing "high magic" such as alchemy, natural astrology, and numerology and "folk" magic, which included divining, image magic ("poppets"), charms, fortune-telling and healing. While high magic was well regarded as a form of learning among New England's elite, it was folk magic which attracted the attention, for it was this learning that contained an element of *maleficium*—malevolence or misfortune. Demos documents numerous cases brought against women over issues of dead cows, children, and other misfortunes. Witch-hunting in the Puritan communities of colonial New England took the form of a scrutiny of mostly middle-aged, married women with no or few children, primarily those renowned for their sharp tongues.[25]

In the case of *Harry Potter*, opposition to the series comes most strongly in the Bible Belt where Christian, indeed conservative Protestant, belief and practice are near compulsory. Though it is couched in the rhetoric of the embattled religious Right, ironically it occurs in areas where Christianity is least at risk. Perhaps it is this irrationality that explains why the fear of witchcraft migrated from the early Puritans in New England to primarily the South and Midwest of the country, as well as other hotbeds of evangelical activity such as Colorado. Yet it did so without the full context of the early Puritan practice—the criticisms of *Harry Potter* lack the specifically gendered nature of New England witch-hunting, and the element of *maleficium*. It is unlikely that Joseph Chambers or the Pentecostals in *Hell House* blame *Harry Potter* for the loss of livestock or other misfortunes. Instead, the discourse of the occult poses a *metaphysical* rather than material threat, a shift that has much to do with the cultural changes of the post-Enlightenment United States and its effects on the field of the religious.

Detraditionalization

Demos argues that belief in witchcraft was near universal on both sides of the Atlantic at the time of the early American colonies.[26] Why then has belief survived for so long in the United Sates when it is all but unknown in the United Kingdom and its other Anglophonic former colonies Canada and Australia? Part of the answer lies in what sociologists call detraditionalization. Sociologist Paul Heelas defines the term as a shift of authority; from "without" to "within." It entails the decline of belief in pre-given or natural orders of things. Individual subjects are themselves called upon to exercise authority in the face of the disorder and contingency which is thereby generated.[27]

In the case of Christians, the shift towards detraditionalization has been the disembedding of large-scale religious institutions such as the Catholic Church and the Church of England. While still powerful, neither retains its almost exclusive purchase on hegemonic power in religious, let alone social terms. In the United States, many of the early Christian settlers fled from religious persecution by these institutions, thus creating the conditions for the marked increase of proliferation of Protestant denominations of the United States. If the Church of England has *waned* significantly as a powerful presence in the UK, its absence from the American religious imaginary arguably hastened the detraditionalization process infinitely.

As sociologists Ulrich Beck and Elisabeth Beck-Gernsheim point out, this "does not mean that tradition no longer plays any role [...]. But traditions must be chosen and often invented, and they have force only through the decisions and experiences of individuals."[28] This explanation reflects the dominant American conception of a sovereign individual, who reflexively and consciously makes his or her decisions. The modern individual, then, is in stark contrast to the pre-modern member of estates or classes, who "used to be born into traditional societies, as they were into social classes or religions. Today even God himself must be chosen."[29]

And so, in concert with institutions such as the welfare state and the capitalist creation of individual "consumers," religious detraditionalization produces an atomization, a society comprised of individuals first and foremost. Brian Massumi makes this point clear when he says, contra-Foucault, "it's no longer disciplinary institutional power that defines everything, it's capitalism's power to produce variety—because markets get saturated. Produce variety and you produce a niche market."[30] Demos points out that the individualization and detraditionalization of Protestant belief may have opened the door for a more sustained belief in the occult with fewer defenses than the traditional accoutrements of Catholicism. In a key passage, he argues that:

> to the extent that Protestants, more than Catholics, stressed the absolute sovereignty of God and the utter inability of man—to that extent magic became an even greater, more blasphemous challenge.

In fact, Protestantism may have unwittingly *invited* such challenge. For Protestants were, relative to Catholics, effectively disarmed with traditional "intercessionary" means denied them. No more saying of rosaries, no use of holy water or holy relics, no recourse to elaborate and enveloping church ritual: no potentially comforting doctrine of salvation by works. Instead, inherent sin and irrefutable weakness in the face of an all-powerful, largely inscrutable Deity.[31]

It is for this reason that Catholic accoutrements still even today appear in horror films and television series as a means of warding off witchcraft of all kinds. And it is here perhaps that readers can account for the dissemination of the Puritan belief in witches throughout much of American Protestantism—to Southern Baptists, evangelicals, fundamentalists. What these denominations share most of all is the detraditionalized shift, the Protestant centering of the individual's relationship with God and concurrent responsibility of the individual for their own salvation. As Edward J. Ingebretsen puts it nicely, "a [Puritan] culture authorized by Revelation in effect organized itself according to a semiotics of terror and uncertainty."[32] Though they are detraditionalized and thus organized in a rather more dispersed fashion than the Catholic Church and the Church of England, there is nevertheless a fairly direct through line from the Puritans to modern evangelical and fundamental Protestants. Ingebretsen also points out that the Puritans engendered the Gothic nightmares of H. P. Lovecraft, Stephen King and other horror writers and film-makers. To use a patrilineal metaphor, modern evangelicals may be considered the Puritans' *legitimate* heirs, while the religiously inflected American Gothic tradition may be considered decidedly more illegitimate and unofficial.

For modern Protestants, the issue slides between two fears. First, that *Harry Potter* is satanic itself, and that the series is a tool of Satan to recruit more followers. For the first, what critics might call the strong position, Chambers and his ilk are fairly clear that *Harry Potter* is "a creation of hell."[33] *Harry Potter* is unambiguously occult and satanic. This is undoubtedly the minority position, but it is the more virulent. For the second more popular position, what critics can call the weak position, it is less that *Harry Potter* is occult per se but that it opens the way for the occult—letting Satan into the reader's heart. As portrayed in the *Hell House* monologue, *Harry Potter* becomes the first step of a slippery slide towards being controlled by the Devil. The problem, therefore, is that *Harry Potter's* representations of magic produce an *openness* towards the occult, which can then take on more serious, soul-destroying effects. Even moderate apologias of the series such as Burkhart's are sympathetic to this position, with their concern to ward off the occult from children's interpretations of the series. Evangelicals—and especially children—are thus positioned as peculiarly vulnerable to the effects of the occult-by-proxy text. Like the Dursleys of Privet Drive, evangelicals fear the unexpected irruption of the supernatural (that is, the demonic) in their midst.[34]

This fear of the susceptibility of the Christian to the occult is found heavily in Puritan writings. Mather suggests that "the Devils may sometimes have permission to represent an Innocent Person as Tormenting such as under Diabolical Molestations. But such things are Rare and Extraordinary."[35] Though Mather would like to rule out of the possibility of an innocent tormented by the Devil, he nevertheless fears that such a distinction is not possible. Demos makes clear that this fear springs from the very ethos of conversion that motivates the Protestant revolution. He says:

> as conversion—*metanoia*—was the religious motivation in the first place, and metamorphosis of various kinds became the great fear, a shadowy threat articulated in sermon and text as a fear of declension, slippage, or falling away.[36]

Thus the "conversism" of evangelical Protestants unwittingly produces the fear of its opposite, of being converted or seduced away from one's faith (a similar fear lurks behind accusations of homosexuals "recruiting" good heterosexuals). This fear of falling away from God remains strong in the present day, and is colloquially referred to among Southern Baptists and Pentecostals as "backsliding." If one can be born again, then surely one can just as easily be lost again.

Creating heaven through hell

If the reasons for criticizing *Harry Potter* seem tenuous and more related to the anxieties of American variants of Protestantism, what cultural purpose does the discourse of the occult serve? In his *Maps of Heaven, Maps of Hell*, American literary critic Ingebretsen argues that, from the Puritans onward, a discourse of the hellish has powerfully bound together American Protestant communities. Terror, Ingebretsen suggests, points the faithful towards heaven through a fully fleshed narrative of the demonic, which is conjured only to be rejected. He points out that, "though they spoke long and eloquently about God's love, it was God's inescapable terror that compelled their allegiance."[37] The fear of hell proved—and continues to prove—a powerful motivator for America's Protestants, who unlike the pre-modern Christians "born into traditional communities [or] religions,"[38] bear the sole responsibility for their fate. The individualizing nature of religious practice has had profound influences on American psyches, culture, religion, and politics.

Indeed, in the protestations (sincere or otherwise) of the faith of presidents downwards, personal religious conviction can be seen to motivate public policy at every level of American government. This trend is indeed most noticeable in evangelical religious communities, which have in the last decade especially exerted a profound influence on American politics. Recall Bebbington's point that activism is a core value of evangelicalism—the active political remaking of the world. The American Library Association has reported that *Harry Potter* has remained among the nation's most removed books from public and school libraries over the last decade.[39] Purging *Harry Potter* from school curricula may serve as a talismanic form of evangelical activism, warding off the broader danger of the occult with the specific purging of one particular text.

The evangelical criticisms of *Harry Potter* participate in an American Protestant practice of scapegoating that dates back to the witch-hunting of the Puritan era. Yet compared to other hysteric episodes in American history (Salem, McCarthyism), the anti-*Harry Potter* phenomenon is relatively mild. Boyer suggests that "simply because prophecy belief does not *absolutely* determine most people's worldview, critics cannot safely dismiss it altogether."[40] The discourse of the occult expressed through antagonism towards *Harry Potter* and other fantastic texts serves to do a number of things, culturally. It expresses the anxieties about the conversism of Protestantism, binding together evangelical and fundamentalist communities through antagonism towards hated Other, which poses a threat inside the community. Further, it fulfills the evangelical need for activism and takes a politically easy target.

Yet perhaps evangelicals grasp at a partial truth, since the texts *do* take a definite pleasure in imagining the ability of humans to perform supernatural acts—a pleasure which is undoubtedly played up in the film adaptations (especially the first two films, which insert magical scenes mostly for affective rather than plot reasons). One of the undoubted pleasures of the series, whether on page or on screen, is the make-believe of an enchanted world, where inanimate objects teem with life, and almost nothing is impossible. Russian structuralist Tvetan Todorov would class the text as marvelous, for it is never *meant* to be an ontologically grounded Realist depiction of life as it is.[41] Nevertheless, in its textual suspension of the rules of real-life, *Harry Potter* lives unwittingly "on the border that joins and separates belief and unbelief."[42] This is the power of fiction, the pleasurable suspension of disbelief that every literary text produces. Though evangelical Protestants see this as a cause for concern, even denunciation, it is clear that purging *Harry Potter* and texts like it will not suffice to resolve the tension within Protestant thought and practice itself, for the fears conjured by the evangelical conversism are simply specters themselves. Though the reaction to *Harry Potter* is relatively benign, as American history demonstrates, these fears if stoked enough can be far more dangerous than the "occult."

Notes

1. *Hell House* (2003) Directed by George Ratliff. Performed by Aria Adloo, Ashley Adloo, Amy Allred, Gabriel Allred, Cherie Asbjornson. DVD. Plexifilm.

2. D. M. Soulliere, "Much Ado about Harry: The Creation of a Moral Panic," *Journal of Religion and Popular Culture* 22(1) (2010). Available at: http://www.usask.ca/relst/jrpc/pdfs/art22%281%29-PotterPanic.pdf (accessed September 17, 2010).

3. J. Chambers, *The Harry Potter Series: A Vision of the Antichrist* (2009). Available at: http://www.pawcreek.org/end-times/harry-potter-antichrist (accessed September 17, 2010).

4. C. Neal, *What's a Christian to Do with Harry Potter?* (New York: Waterbrook, 2001).

5. J. Killinger, *God, The Devil and Harry Potter: A Christian Minister's Defense of the Beloved Novels* (New York: Thomas Dunne, 2002).

6. G. Burkart, *A Parent's Guide to Harry Potter* (Downers Grove, IL: InterVarsity, 2005).

7. *Ibid.*: 17.

8. *Ibid.*: 44.

9. E. J. Ingebretsen, *Maps of Heaven, Maps of Hell* (Armonk, NY: M. E. Sharpe, 1996): xxiii.

10. Soulliere: para. 9.

11. D. W. Bebbington, *Evangelicalism in Modern Britain: A History from the 1730s to the 1980s* (London and New York: Routledge, 2002): 3.

12. Chambers, *op cit.*

13. OP[A]: 814.

14. Ingebretsen: xi.

15. P. Boyer, *When Time Shall Be No More: Prophecy Belief in Modern American Culture* (Cambridge, MA: Harvard University Press, 1992): 88.

16. C. Mather, *Wonders of the Invisible World: Being an Account of the Trials of Several Witches Lately Executed in New England* (Whitefish, MT: Kessinger, 2010): 81.

17. *Ibid.*: 6.

18. *Ibid.*: 16.

19. As cited in J. Demos, *The Enemy Within: 2000 Years of Witch-hunting in the Western World* (New York: Viking, 2008): 101.

20. D. Punter, *The Literature of Terror: A History of Gothic Fictions from 1765 to the Present Day* (New York: Longman, 1996): 409.

21. Ingebretsen: xxiii.

22. Demos: 3.

23. *Ibid.*

24. *Ibid.*: 95.

25. *Ibid.*: 117–18.

26. *Ibid.*: 98.

27. P. Heelas, "Introduction: Detraditionalization and its Rivals," in P. Heelas, S. Lash and P. Morris (eds.), *Detraditionalization: Critical Reflections on Authority and Identity* (Cambridge, MA: Blackwell, 1996): 1–20, at 2.

28. U. Beck and E. Beck-Gernsheim, *Individualization: Institutionalized Individualism and its Social and Political Consequences* (Thousand Oaks, CA: Sage, 2001): 26.

29. *Ibid.*: 23.

30. M. Zournazi and B. Massumi, "Navigating Movements: A Conversation with Brian Massumi," in M. Zournazi (ed.), *Hope* (Annandale, NSW: Pluto Press Australia, 2002): 210–44, at 224.

31. Demos: 100.

32. Ingebretsen: xix.

33. Chambers: para. 2.

34. In a certain sense, this fear of the unexpected incursion of alterity may also be considered an attempt to ward off the sacred (something Ingebretsen's analysis would endorse, I think). The necessity of being open to alterity and making an unconditional, undifferentiated embrace of the Other in order to usher in the sacred has been a hot topic among deconstructionists in the last decade or two, with Jacques Derrida introducing the idea in *The Gift of Death* (trans. David Willis; Chicago: University of Chicago Press, 1994), John D. Caputo extending it in his work, *The Weakness of God: A Theology of the Event* (Bloomington, IN: Indiana University Press, 2006) and Richard Kearney mounting a critique in *The God Who May Be: A Hermeneutics of Religion* (Bloomington, IN: Indiana University Press, 2001).

35. Mather: 18.

36. Demos: xiii.

37. Ingebretsen: 5.

38. Beck and Beck-Gernsheim: 23.

39. The American Library Association lists Rowling as the fourth most "challenged" author in American Libraries between 1990 and 2004, a challenge being a formal, written complaint requesting the material be removed from the library. While most challenges tend to address sexual content or "offensive" language, clearly Rowling has attracted these

challenges because of the fantastic elements in her works. See the ALA website for a full list of challenged authors: http://www.ala.org/ala/oif/bannedbooksweek/challengedbanned/challengedbanned.htm#mfcb

40. Boyer: xii.
41. T. Todorov, *The Fantastic: A Structural Approach to a Literary Genre*, trans. Richard Howard (Cleveland, OH: Case Western Reserve University, 1973).
42. M. C. Taylor, *Erring: A Postmodern a/Theology* (Chicago: University of Chicago Press, 1984): 5.

8

Wizard's Justice and Elf Liberation: Politics and Political Activism in *Harry Potter*

Marcus Schulzke

Part of what makes the *Harry Potter* series so appealing to a large, international audience is the books' emphasis on discovery. As readers progress through the series, they find answers to the many mysteries that drive the plot, they learn more about characters and their motivations and, most importantly of all, they discover a new world. Readers are newcomers to the wizarding world, and they are guided through it by a main character who is likewise struggling to understand its culture and institutions. Harry and the readers begin the series naively, with little sense of the depth of the world they are about to encounter. Over the course of the series, that world comes into focus first as a world of black and white dichotomies between good and evil, and then as an increasingly complex world of hidden agendas, corruption, and moral ambiguity. Many of the wizarding world's nuances appear when the books address political topics such as justice, the nature of authority, and political activism.

The wizarding world is replete with myriad overlapping conflicts and interests. These political themes are an important part of what makes the books so entertaining, as many of the conflicts they describe are cultural and institutional battles that parallel readers' own.[1] The precise meaning of these parts of the narrative is the subject of intense debate, with commentators finding liberal and conservative themes in the books' portrayal of government. Given the books' popularity, their status as social artifacts, and the influence they have had on several generations of readers, it is important that these themes be explored to understand what kind of political lessons have been transmitted to the books' millions of readers. The books are also useful from a pedagogical perspective and have been used as the basis for political science classes,[2] among others. As a series with such a large following, the *Harry Potter* books have become a reference point that transcends cultural, class, and ethnic barriers, and can be drawn on to explore topics that might otherwise be opaque.

Thus, it is valuable to explore several of the prominent political themes in the series and to chart their development. The promotion of a skeptical attitude about politics, the encouragement of resistance, and the dilemma of how to mobilize support for a controversial cause are among the many political themes, but these deserve consideration because they join together to advocate a form of democratic political engagement. Although the books are often radical and subversive in that they show the faults of leaders and their policies, they do not consistently support any particular ideology. Instead of promoting an ideology, they promote an analytical attitude that is also critical and action-oriented. The books encourage an engaged, yet still judicious, orientation—one that is never satisfied by appeals to authority or power and that is always ready to take action against injustice.

Searching for an ideology

Whether the *Harry Potter* books are conservative or progressive depends on a critic's own political values and which parts of the story are focused on. The books show countervailing political themes, so uncovering an ideological message is a matter of choosing which parts of the story to consider most salient. Some critics have accused the books of elitism, especially those who come from countries such as Sweden with highly egalitarian values.[3] The books affirm competition and do little to challenge the wizarding world's clear discrepancies in wealth, which makes them seem somewhat conservative. Many characters tacitly accept their anonymous power over events in the Muggle world without feeling any duty to inform the Muggles about events as significant as civil war. There are many injustices, even in Hogwarts, a place that is supposed to be enlightened and tolerant,[4] and it is possible to read the intense loyalty students have to their houses as encouraging nationalistic attitudes of exclusion.[5] However, there is ample evidence to show that the books support egalitarian values. The books promote openness and tolerance, overtly criticizing adults' attempts to hide information from the young students. They also show Harry and his friends questioning discrimination and challenging traditional institutions,[6] which is hardly something readers would expect of a piece of conservative fiction.

Readers can find events or institutions to support both the conservative and the progressive interpretations. For example, some critics argue that the books include many capitalist themes.[7] Hogwarts often seems as though it is training students to be extremely competitive and acquisitive, as they are encouraged to win games of Quidditch, earn points for the House Cup contest, score well on tests, and beat other students in the numerous other tournaments and duels, and, of course, to win the myriad social conflicts that arise among teenagers.

However, the celebration of competition is counterbalanced by the books' glorification of generosity and the negative representations of elites. Harry, Ron, and Hermione are extremely generous. Harry gives money to the Weasley twins, shares his possessions, and risks his high status to help his friends. Hermione regularly uses her superior intellect to assist friends with their academic work and their more serious challenges. Ron, having little to offer materially, is always willing to risk himself to help his friends. Their willingness to help Harry is made clear when they help him find the Sorcerer's Stone, and they show the same commitment throughout the books when they choose to accompany him on dangerous quests. The same generosity can be found in most of the books' heroes: the Weasley family, Lupin, Sirius Black, Dumbledore, and many others. Furthermore, many of the story's wealthy characters are cast in a negative light. The Malfoys are elitist and malevolent; the Dursleys are gluttonous and wasteful. It is easy to see these two families as representing the worst of capitalist societies.

Given the texts' openness to different interpretations, uncovering political themes in the *Harry Potter* series is not as simple as spotting signs of ideological bias. Readers must see that, in such a dynamic world, a world built on mystery and discovery, such one-dimensional answers invariably miss important counterevidence. For that reason, this essay goes beyond the search for partisan messages in the text to comment on several of the series' central political themes and to show that the nuanced treatment of these themes encourages readers to take a nuanced view of real world political issues.

Taking a critical perspective

The characters' view of politics and politicians changes enormously throughout the series. During the first two books they are uncritical. They give readers little reason to question the morality of government policies and only some doubt of the ministers' competence. Harry and his friends learn about their world without coming into conflict with its institutions. However, readers do receive some sense of what is to come later. Quirrell and Snape are not government officials, but they are authority figures whose behavior encourages the adoption of a skeptical attitude. The former turns out to be a tool for Voldemort's return to power; the latter wrongly bullies Harry for the actions of his father. Both of these characters become warnings about the potential for duplicity and abuse of authority. They provide the characters' early lessons in why it is important to pay careful attention to the actions and motives of others. Gilderoy Lockhart, the epitome of narcissism, is particularly dangerous, as he turns out to be both incompetent and willing to harm others for nothing more than the advancement of his image. After their encounters with these teachers, the three main characters learn that they must always be attentive to others' hidden motives. This lesson turns out to be quite important when the friends interact with the government in the following books.

Authority figures become increasingly suspect in *The Prisoner of Azkaban*. When readers expect Harry to be severely punished for using magic outside school, he is given very lenient treatment. This action makes Minister of Magic Cornelius Fudge appear benevolent, especially given his personal dedication to Harry's safety. However, over the course of the book, readers learn that this benevolence is only a cover for ineptitude and injustice. This book marks a turning point in the series' arc, as the idealistic view of the forces that control the wizarding world is upset. Harry learns that the prisoners at Azkaban are subjected to extremely cruel punishment that goes beyond any kind of torture that exists in the Muggle world. If Muggles knew about this facility torturing its prisoners, it would be considered a violation of British law and of international agreements on human rights. The existence of this prison shows that the wizarding world is not constrained by the same liberal values as the country's Muggle population. Its Dementor guards even become Harry's new enemy, briefly rising to supersede Voldemort in their capacity to inspire fear in him. They are agents of the state and yet so malicious that they are among the series' greatest villains. In the following books, they return to play a menacing role and, in the end, they join forces with Voldemort, who is considered their natural ally.[8] Their allegiance to Voldemort raises serious doubts about the politicians who employed the Dementors.

The condemnation of Sirius Black is more evidence of institutional failure. Those entrusted with judging guilt and innocence are incapable of rethinking their verdict or even giving Black a fair trial before he is sentenced to Azkaban. The decision shows that

Fudge and his administrators are more interested in preserving their reputation and silencing dissent than in actually pursuing justice. This view of the wizards' system of justice makes Azkaban and the Dementors even more terrible. Not only does the government abuse its prisoners, it even fails to provide the accused with fair trials. In the end, justice is only served when Harry and his friends free Sirius and help him start a new life as an outlaw. This act of subverting the power of the highest officials in the Ministry of Magic is a radical statement of the duty of ordinary people to take a stand against abuses of power.

The themes of inept government and abuse of authority are taken up more forcefully in *The Order of the Phoenix*, as the Ministry takes control of Hogwarts to eliminate dissent, suppress the rumors of Voldemort's return, and undermine the school's defenses. If this plan had succeeded, it would have left the school nearly defenseless during the Death Eater attack the following year. Dolores Umbridge, the Ministry's representative who takes control of Hogwarts during Harry's fifth year, is an especially complex villain. She is not simply an embodiment of evil as Voldemort is. She is a more nuanced character whose evil is hidden by a happy exterior and good intentions. She is abusive, but unlike Voldemort, she still seems to think that she is doing the right thing and protecting the students. This approach leaves Harry and his friends with the difficult problem of how to fight someone who cannot be attacked directly. They undertake a covert strategy of subtly undermining her authority and using their secret association to strengthen the school's defenses.

In the sixth and seventh novels, the government's true character finally becomes clear. By this time, Harry and his friends are deeply skeptical of authority figures who have not proven that they deserve their status, and they are committed to taking action and resisting illegitimate authority. They are mature enough to understand how to combat government ineptitude without challenging it, as directly as they did in *The Prisoner of Azkaban*. One of the clearest examples of their attitude comes in the seventh book when Harry, Ron, and Hermione not only refuse Minister Rufus Scrimgeour's offer to assist the government but also attempt to hide their intentions and the purpose of the gifts that Dumbledore left them. Harry is defiant when Scrimgeour asks for help; he criticizes the minister for imprisoning innocent people and for using Harry to legitimize the government's misguided fight against Voldemort. Their dialogue perfectly captures the series' critique of those who abuse their authority and Harry's demand that authority figures prove their worth. When Scrimgeour says that Harry should learn some respect, Harry responds by telling him "It's time you earned it."[9]

Throughout the series, Dumbledore plays an important role in shaping the leading characters' attitudes about those in power. He consistently encourages the students to develop their critical faculties and to challenge authority figures. He guides them through some of their challenges, and often plays the role of a *deus ex machina*, but he is not overbearing. He gives the students so many opportunities to solve problems on their own that he almost seems neglectful, but he always seems to be there to ensure that the students never face challenges that they will not be able to overcome. Dumbledore's noble character may have something to do with his withdrawal from a political life that could have corrupted him.[10] Yet even Dumbledore is shown to be less than perfect when Rita Skeeter begins analyzing his past. For a time, Harry doubts his friend and questions Dumbledore's character, but the exploration of Dumbledore's past in *The Deathly Hallows* helps to moderate the critique of authority. Harry is able to see the difference between Dumbledore's imperfections and the dangerous abuses of power displayed by so many other characters. Harry learns that he should not be excessively judgmental of others and that he must be willing to accept some authority figures despite their flaws, provided they have earned respect and overcome their past errors.

The many critiques of authority lead Benjamin Barton to accuse the books of encouraging dissent against the government.[11] Others argue that critique of government is not as thorough as Barton seems to think because there are some reliable elements of it. Arthur Weasley and the members of the Wizengamot court that finds Harry not guilty in *The Order of the Phoenix* are more admirable figures.[12] The abuses of power by members of the government and some Hogwarts professors outnumber the positive examples, and this knowledge has a profound effect on the characters. Harry and his friends become deeply suspicious of authority figures. In itself, this may not be a positive message, as this kind of skepticism can be taken to excess. Luckily, the characters' critical awareness of their world does not lead them to cynicism. Instead, it gives them even stronger motivation to take action against injustice. By the end of the series they consistently demand that authority figures, especially those in government, prove their worth. When they cannot rely on their leaders for help, they are ready to take the initiative and act on their own.

Resisting injustice

The critical narrative in each of the books is complemented by a parallel narrative of taking responsibility for improving the wizarding world. Given the circumstances, taking political action often means resistance. The characters are left with few alternatives when officials refuse to investigate Voldemort's return and attempt to use force to suppress different perspectives. From the beginning of the series to the end, those who take it upon themselves to resist injustice, whether it comes from Voldemort, from the government, or from the Death Eaters, are portrayed as heroes. This is true even when the actions they take are somewhat misguided, as Harry's were at the end of the first and fifth books, when his actions actually bring his opponents closer to victory by showing Quirrell how to find the Sorcerer's Stone and by aiding the Death Eaters' attempt to retrieve the prophecy. While not always helpful, the activist students not only have the right intentions, but they also always act with sensitivity for others. In the end, this choice turns out to be what leads them to victory over Voldemort.

The theme of resistance is, like the critiques of injustice and illegitimate authority, one that runs throughout the books and increases as the story develops. The themes are often linked, as the resistance is often driven by injustices. When Harry is persecuted by the Dementors in *The Prisoner of Azkaban*, he does not quietly accept their abuse even though they are powerful representatives of the state. He pushes himself to learn the very advanced Patronus charm and defeat them. Lupin encourages Harry and sees that the fear of the Dementors is also a powerful motivating force that can help Harry learn advanced spells that will allow him to become more independent. The book concludes with a message of self-reliance, as Harry discovers that he, and not his father, was the one who cast the Patronus charm that saved him from the army of Dementors that attacked him.[13] In *The Order of the Phoenix*, Harry takes a much larger step, albeit reluctantly, by organizing Dumbledore's Army to resist Umbridge. This decision is another of the turning points in the series, and it is fitting that it comes in the book that probably does the most to disrupt the characters' trust of authority. The club is a resistance organization dedicated to teaching fighting skills that the government does not want the students to learn. Again, this is an incredibly radical theme given the age of many readers and the author's approving tone. The students propagate a forbidden ideology and learn spells that give them the power to fight against the Death Eaters in *The Half-blood Prince*. During that battle, the students take on more skilled opponents and beat them with nothing more than their own skill and a little bit of luck.

The Deathly Hallows provides still more positive examples of activism, as the Hogwarts students lead the fight against Voldemort and the

Death Eaters. Harry, Ron, and Hermione continue to be the central figures in this fight, but other students also rise to new levels of heroism. Neville, formerly a loyal though somewhat incompetent character, is redeemed when he becomes the leader of Hogwarts' opposition movement. The choice of leaders is important. Neville is, despite his faults, a symbol of courage who rises to greatness because he takes the initiative to act. In the first book, he had the strength of conscience to stand up to his friends. The fact that he takes Harry's place as leader of Dumbledore's Army shows the power of Neville's moral courage; it is also evidence that even someone as clumsy and unlucky as Neville can become a leader by setting an example of courage that others can follow. During the final battle with Voldemort, Neville again proves himself by fighting even when defeat seems certain. The Sorting Hat gives him Godric Gryffindor's sword, a confirmation of Neville's courage, and he uses the sword to kill Nagini, Voldemort's last known Horcrux. This triumph by a student who spent much of the series being a figure of ridicule is a way of showing that even those who lack the natural abilities of people such as Harry and Hermione can accomplish great things.

The paradoxes of resistance

Being critical of authorities and taking action against injustice are among the clearest and most consistent political messages of the series. Taken by themselves, these are valuable messages. Nevertheless, the books' glorification of critical thinking would be incomplete if they did not also complicate these messages to show that some problems do not have easy answers, even for those with the intelligence and commitment to search for them. Rowling understands that activism must have a conscience, as she makes it clear that, when it comes to issues more complex than fighting against evil, it is essential to carefully consider a cause and the effects it could have on others.

One of the series' unresolved dilemmas is whether Hermione's attempt to liberate the house-elves is benevolent or misguided. As a student with Muggle parents, Hermione is continually harassed by racists such as Draco Malfoy. Her experience of intolerance gives her a deep understanding of how it feels to be an outsider, and it motivates her to work on behalf of other marginalized groups. She attempts to free the elves who work in the Hogwarts kitchen and to enlist the help of other students in her campaign of elf liberation. To build support for this project, she creates the Society for the Promotion of Elfish Welfare (S.P.E.W.), a group with an unattractive name that hides the noble intentions of the cause. Hermione receives surprisingly little support, even from her most tolerant friends. Ron continually teases her, Harry seems indifferent, and even Dumbledore, whom one would expect to be receptive of the project given his support of the students' activism, seems to think that Hermione's efforts are misguided. Almost everyone Hermione attempts to recruit for her cause is content to allow their world's racist institutional structure to persist.[14]

The greatest problem with this project, however, is that few of the elves actually want to be free. They are so offended by Hermione's efforts to liberate them that they refuse to clean the Gryffindor common room, an unusual expression of self-determination by a group of elves determined to remain slaves. This little rebellion provides an excellent statement of a recurrent problem of political activism. Progressive activists sometimes find that the people they hope to liberate are happy and have no desire for social change. One of the most recent expressions of this experience comes in the Marxist theory of class-consciousness.[15] After the failure of communist revolutions throughout Europe in the early twentieth century, some socialists decided that the workers were incapable of seeing that their objective class interest was revolution. They explained this observation with the idea of false consciousness: workers who do not want to fight for a more egalitarian society are being misled by the ruling class's ideology, and they end up siding with their oppressors. Although Hermione is dealing with slaves rather than wage laborers, she discovers the same problem. The elves claim to love their servitude, and they resist her attempts to help them. Their behavior raises the question of whether the elves' happiness is based on the ideology they have been taught to accept, or whether it is a genuine expression of happiness that does not show false-consciousness.

Jean-Jacques Rousseau argues that people living in his ideal participatory democracy may have to be "forced to be free"[16]—a claim that perfectly expresses Hermione's own thinking. Her hope seems to be that, once free, the elves would be happier and realize that they were previously misguided. Dobby provides some evidence that she might be right. After Dobby is freed, he experiences a transformation that allows him to live a more fulfilling life of voluntary work for those he cares about. However, not all freed elves are as open-minded as Dobby. Winky hates her freedom and is eternally depressed at the thought of life without servitude. Readers are thus presented with the dilemma of whether to side with Hermione and support elf liberation, even though the elves claim that they do not want freedom, or to allow the elves to live as they wish, even if it means accepting an immoral institution.

The dilemma of resisting injustice against the wishes of those being harmed is never resolved, so one cannot rely on the books for an answer. It is left as a thought experiment that raises questions about which values activists ought to prioritize. As Brycchan Carey points out, taking part in an organization such as S.P.E.W. is the closest thing most of the book's readers will have to a battle against evil.[17] Any political challenges readers encounter will likely be more nuanced than a war against an evil villain; they will require a greater capacity to see issues from multiple perspectives and to struggle in finding solutions. It is therefore important that readers who are inspired by the activist message of the series think carefully about Hermione's problems with the elves and to find their own answers to this persistent challenge of political activism.

Learning from *Harry Potter*

The *Harry Potter* books deal with serious political issues in an engaging way. They manage to entertain readers while leading them to consider familiar ideas from a new perspective. Each of the political themes covered here—the critiques of authority, encouragement to activism, and warnings about the paradoxes of resistance—encourages readers to think about their own values. The themes show how important it is to maintain a critical perspective on government and to question those in positions of authority when they are acting inappropriately. To support this attitude, the books provide many positive examples of people organizing themselves to resist injustice, but they also caution activists to be attentive to the desires of others. When taken together, these are excellent lessons, as they provide a model for engaged, democratic citizenship. Whatever their ideology, readers can relate the books' themes to their own experience of politics. Liberal and conservative readers alike may each find institutions that they consider unjust or individuals who wield undeserved authority, and they can use the idea of spirited, but contentious activism to inform their own efforts to engage in contentious politics.

Notes

1. K. E. Westman, "Specters of Thatcherism: Contemporary British Culture in J. K. Rowling's Harry Potter Series," in L. A. Whited (ed.), *The Ivory Tower and Harry Potter: Perspectives on a Literary Phenomenon* (Columbia, MO: University of Missouri Press, 2002): 305–28.
2. S. Deets, "Wizarding in the Classroom: Teaching Harry Potter and Politics," *PS: Political Science and Politics* 42(4) (2009): 741–4.

3. A. Towns and B. Rumelili, "Foreign yet Familiar: International Politics and the Reception of Potter in Turkey and Sweden," in D. H. Nexon and I. B. Neumann (eds.), *Harry Potter and International Relations* (New York: Rowman and Littlefield, 2006): 61–79.

4. W. P. MacNeil, *Lex Populi: The Jurisprudence of Popular Culture* (Stanford, CA: Stanford University Press, 2007).

5. A. P. Mills, "Patriotism, House Loyalty, and the Obligations of Belonging," in W. Irwin and G. Bassham (eds.), *The Ultimate Harry Potter and Philosophy: Hogwarts for Muggles* (Hoboken, NJ: John Wiley & Sons, 2010): 97–112.

6. M. A. Gemmill and D. H. Nexon, "Children's Crusade: The Religious Politics of Harry Potter," in D. H. Nexon and I. B. Neumann (eds.), *Harry Potter and International Relations* (New York: Rowman and Littlefield, 2006): 79–100, at 93.

7. J. Sterling-Folker and B. Folker, "Conflict and the Nation-State: Magical Mirrors of Muggles and Refracted Images," in D. H. Nexon and I. B. Neumann (eds.), *Harry Potter and International Relations* (New York: Rowman and Littlefield, 2006): 103–26, at 106.

8. I. B. Neumann (2006) "Naturalizing Geography: Harry Potter and the Realms of Muggles, Magic Folks, and Giants," in D. H. Nexon and I. B. Neumann (eds.), *Harry Potter and International Relations* (New York: Rowman and Littlefield, 2006): 157–76, at 163.

9. DH[A]: 130.

10. D. L. Williams and A. J. Kellner, "Dumbledore, Plato, and the Lust for Power," in W. Irwin and G. Bassham (eds.), *The Ultimate Harry Potter and Philosophy: Hogwarts for Muggles* (Hoboken, NJ: John Wiley & Sons, 2010): 128–40.

11. B. H. Barton, "Harry Potter and the Half-Crazed Bureaucracy," *Michigan Law Review* 104(6) (2006): 1523–38.

12. B. Admiraal and R. L. Reitsma, "Dumbledore's Politics," in W. Irwin and G. Bassham (eds.), *The Ultimate Harry Potter and Philosophy: Hogwarts for Muggles* (Hoboken, NJ: John Wiley & Sons, 2010): 113–27.

13. PA[A]: 411.

14. J. C. Horne, "Harry Potter and the Other: Answering the Race Question in J.K. Rowling's *Harry Potter*," *The Lion and the Unicorn* 34(1) (2010): 76–104, at 83–4.

15. G. Lukács, *History and Class Consciousness: Studies in Marxist Dialectics* (Cambridge, MA: Massachusetts Institute of Technology Press, 1972).

16. J.-J. Rousseau, "The Social Contract," in *The Social Contract and The Discourses* (New York: Everyman's Library, 1993): 108–305, at 194.

17. B. Carey, "Hermione and the House-Elves: The Literary and Historical Contexts of J.K. Rowling's Antislavery Campaign," in G. L. Anatol (ed.), *Reading Harry Potter: Critical Essays* (Westport, CT: Greenwood Publishing Group, 2003): 103–15, at 106.

9

What it Means to Be a Half-Blood: Integrity versus Fragmentation in Biracial Identity

Tess Stockslager

Late twentieth-century England, where the *Harry Potter* series is set, was a multicultural place. This plurality is represented to a minor extent in the student body of Hogwarts, with students such as Cho Chang and the Patil twins representing Britain's large population of Asian immigrants, for example.[1] Nevertheless, these characters and other students of color are so secondary to the main action that racial relations among the students cannot be examined with any adequate depth. The students from the French school Beauxbatons and the North European school Durmstrang who appear in *The Goblet of Fire* are gross stereotypes. The teachers of Hogwarts, as far as the reader knows, are homogenously white. Some critics have attributed the little diversity that does exist in the series to politically correct tokenism on Rowling's part.[2]

However, this allegation is not to say that race is a neglected topic within the series. Just as magic itself is a vehicle for exploring the issue of giftedness,[3] issues such as racism, interracial marriage, and biraciality find their analogues within the practice of monitoring the amount of magical "blood" in one's pedigree. Though open-minded wizards denounce the practice, insisting that no true "pure-blood" wizarding family could possibly remain in England—Ron Weasley, for example, makes this argument in *The Chamber of Secrets*[4]—families such as the Malfoys and the Blacks continue to use their genealogies to enforce a sharp distinction between themselves and those with Muggles in their ancestry.

In such a racially stratified world, it is easy for most people to find their place. Being a pure-blood comes with privilege (largely intangible though it may be), but it also comes with expectations.

A Hogwarts student of purely magical blood, for example, is expected to have an aptitude for magic, which is why Neville Longbottom is such a spectacular failure. A Muggle-born student such as Hermione Granger, conversely, may be the victim of racism and may lack the cultural knowledge base required to operate comfortably in the wizarding world, but she is also not held to such lofty expectations. Other characters, such as Professor Slughorn, repeatedly express wonder at her great achievement in magic, and they usually attribute their sense of wonder to her parentage.[5] A high-performing pure-blood student would not be such a spectacular prodigy.

However, for half-blood witches and wizards, navigating society involves traversing the precarious chasm in the middle of the binary. Whether they try to maintain a balanced position in the center, or whether they renounce either their magical or Muggle origins and cling to the other, they will always be dogged by the knowledge that they belong fully to neither one.

As Barfield points out, an exact counterpart to Rowling's version of magic does not exist outside the world of the novels; thus readers can make sense of it only by analogy.[6] Rowling constructs magical endowment as both a race issue and a giftedness issue. It is racial in the sense that it is typically passed down through the family bloodline, but the fact that a Muggle-born young person can receive wizarding abilities complicates this picture. In this essay, I emphasize the racial aspect to draw an analogy between half-blood identity and biracial identity. Several of the experiences of the three half-blood characters in the series bear striking resemblances to common experiences of biracial and bicultural people, magical and Muggle alike. I begin with Seamus Finnegan, whose half-blood status helps early in the series to introduce the ultimately crucial issue of race, and whose Irishness creates an interesting real-world parallel with half-bloodedness. I then look at two more prominent half-blood characters: Severus Snape, whose acceptance of his half-blood identity allows him to achieve an integrated personality, and Tom Riddle, who attempts to perform a pure-blood identity. First, however, the essay's central term needs to be defined.

The term "half-blood"

Because of the dual configuration of magic as both an inherited characteristic and a gift or talent, there are at least two ways to define the term *half-blood* in the magical sense. One possible meaning is employed when characters such as Tom Riddle[7] and Bellatrix Lestrange[8] refer to Harry Potter as a half-blood—understandably so, since he comes from a Muggle family on his mother's side and a wizarding family on his father's side. Though Harry is indeed a half-blood by lineage (Harry's mother Lily, though a witch, had no magical "blood" strictly speaking), the fact that both of his parents had magical abilities makes the designation less fitting.

A stricter definition of the term *half-blood* would limit it to those wizards and witches who have one magical parent and one Muggle parent. This is the better definition for the purposes of this essay, not only because it restricts the subjects of inquiry to those who are most clearly suspended between two cultures, but also because it limits these subjects to a manageable number. There are only three such half-bloods identified in the series: Seamus Finnegan, Harry's inquisitive and often hapless Gryffindor roommate; angry and enigmatic potions master Severus Snape; and Tom Riddle, better known as Voldemort, the Dark wizard who sets the plot of the series in motion. Each of these characters has a magical mother and a Muggle father, and each of them illustrates advantages, difficulties, and tragedies associated with half-bloodedness and with its real-life counterpart, biraciality.

Seamus Finnegan: half-blood Irishman

Seamus Finnegan's half-blood status is not at all crucial to the plot; basically, it serves to introduce the concept and to prefigure elements that will appear in more sinister or painful forms in the other two half-blood stories. Though magical pedigree is briefly discussed when Harry encounters Draco Malfoy in Diagon Alley,[9] Seamus is the first character within the series to mention the concept of half-bloodedness. Shortly after being sorted into Gryffindor, the talkative, sandy-haired boy tells his housemates that his "dad's a Muggle" and his mother is a witch.[10] His frankness about his origins puts him in stark contrast to Tom Riddle, who goes to violent lengths to deny his half-blood status, and Severus Snape, who is silent about his half-blood status, as he is about most details of his life.

Seamus adds to this revelation an apparently humorous piece of family history, stating that it was a "[b]it of a nasty shock"[11] for Mr. Finnegan when he found out that his new bride was a witch. So this was not a mutually agreed-upon interracial marriage (if one may use this term), and thus it foreshadows the account of the seduction and elopement between Merope Gaunt and Tom Riddle, Sr. However, judging from Seamus's jovial attitude toward the circumstances of his birth, the Finnegan marriage, after the "nasty shock," seems to have been happy, or at least uneventful. Seamus's housemates chuckle at the brief story and then move on to another topic. The issue of race will not lift its head above the surface of the narrative again until the second book, when the Heir of Slytherin will target Muggle-born students.

Seamus's magical biraciality is most interesting when considered along with another prominent aspect of his character, his Irishness. In the *Harry Potter* series, Seamus Finnegan appears repeatedly as an archetypal Irish character. His speech carries markers popularly identified as Irish, even though they might technically be features of certain dialects in England as well (e.g., "Me mam,"[12]). He is easily angered and predictably fiery when angry (see in particular his row with Harry over Seamus's mother's assessment of Harry's sanity[13]). He enjoys telling tall tales.[14] He is apparently not a very competent wizard,[15] a trait that the films turn into a running joke and that plays on the persistent stereotype that the Irish are slightly less intelligent than the English[16]; the first film also creates an amusing scene out of what was only a passing reference in the book to Seamus's attempt to turn a cauldron of water into rum, bringing the stereotype of the drunken Irishman into play. He and his mother display fierce national pride at the Quidditch World Cup, even though the Ministry of Magic disapproves,[17] thus validating the proverbial concept that the Irish are rebels. He even has a cousin named Fergus,[18] a quintessentially Irish name—much like the name *Seamus* itself, which is the Irish equivalent of *James.*

While detractors of Rowling's work might attribute Seamus's obvious and stereotypical Irishness to tokenism, once again, or a lack of originality in characterization, it actually has a meaningful thematic purpose closely related to his half-bloodedness. For centuries—in culture, in politics, and most overtly in literature and the popular imagination—the Irish have occupied an uneasy position on the boundaries of English society. They live in the British Isles, but on a separate island. They are Christian, but not Protestant (at least not stereotypically). They speak English, but with a distinctive accent and alongside a language of their own. They are white, but not Anglo-Saxon. These are generalizations, of course, but in literature generalizations become powerful myths. Edward Said exposed this myth-making tendency (of Western writing in particular) in his landmark 1979 work *Orientalism,*[19] the book that brought the concept of the Other into critical parlance. Said's goal in *Orientalism* is "to ask whether there is any way of avoiding the hostility expressed by the division, say, of men into 'us' [...] and 'they'"[20]; "they" are, of course, the Other. The Other is a socially constructed concept of a person or group encompassing the traits from which the society in power wishes to distance itself.

Barfield notes that the *Harry Potter* books employ the rhetoric of Otherness through the language of blood.[21] If Muggles and Muggle-borns (who may as well be Muggles from a pure-blood's viewpoint) are the Other, then half-bloods are somewhere in between the Other and the people who set the terms. Historically, the Irish occupy a similar position in the British consciousness. In British colonial writing, natives of Africa, Asia, and the Pacific islands are clearly the Other, but the status of the Irish is not so clear. In Victorian rhetoric in particular, the Englishman is the normative complete man. The implication, not always tacit, is that a male of another race is perhaps not a man at all. The further implication is that an Irishman must be only half a man. In the same way, anyone who shares, for instance, the Black family's views on magical racial politics would consider Seamus Finnegan to be only half a wizard.

Unfortunately, because Seamus is a minor character, there is little room for Rowling's narrator to explore what his Irishness and half-bloodedness might mean for his relationship with his fellow students (most of whom are English), his performance in school, his relationship with his parents, and even his sense of his own masculinity with regard to the concept of "halfness." Seamus serves primarily to introduce ideas that reappear in sublimated form as the series progresses.

Severus Snape: Half-Blood Prince

Our next half-blood, far from occupying the teeming ranks of minor characters like Seamus, plays a pivotal role in the series. Severus Snape is one of only two characters, other than Harry, who have the distinction of being mentioned in one of the novel titles. (The other is Sirius Black.) Snape appears to be a relatively minor figure in *Harry Potter and the Half-Blood Prince*, a novel dominated by flashbacks of Tom Riddle and Harry's obsession with Draco Malfoy's suspicious behavior—until the last few chapters, of course. However, Orson Scott Card points out that the events of the novel are bookended with Snape's actions and that he is present throughout the story in the notes in Harry's potions textbook. "Volume six," Card says, "is Snape's book."[22] It is significant that the name by which Snape is immortalized in eponym is a name that draws attention to his blood status. Severus Snape's half-bloodedness is more than just a clever plot device; it is a factor that significantly shapes his identity.

Like Seamus Finnegan, Severus Snape is the son of a witch (Eileen Prince) and a Muggle (Tobias Snape). Rowling stated in an interview that he was "a child conceived outside of love."[23] Brief glimpses of his childhood pre-Hogwarts suggest that his parents were constantly at odds and that his father may have been violent.[24] Though the reader is never given an explicit reason for this conflict—poverty and personalities were no doubt contributors—it probably resulted at least in part from the clash of cultures. If this was the case, the young Severus had two options (besides trying to make peace, an option he evidently did not take) for survival in his tumultuous home: escape or learn to play both sides. Hogwarts was a place of escape for him, as was the playground where he watched and later met Lily[25] and even his bedroom.[26] However, escape was surely not always possible, and thus Severus had to learn to avoid displeasing both of his parents, the witch and the Muggle. Like many children of two cultures, he probably became quite adept at domestic double-agency.

Snape carries this skill to Hogwarts, with a major difference: in a place where there are no Muggles, he now finds himself suspended between the Dark wizards and those who stand against them. At school, he carries on contradictory alliances with the kind, popular, and decidedly anti-Voldemort Lily Evans and with his fellow Slytherins and future Death Eaters.[27] However, his relationships with both parties are uneasy. Snape is well aware of the fact that fitting in is difficult for him, a state of affairs that he may associate with his bicultural identity. It is during his time at school that he first (as far as readers know) uses the name "Half-Blood Prince," recording it in his sixth-year potions textbook. No evidence exists that he ever discloses this name to anyone else (if he had, Harry would not have had such a hard time identifying the mysterious Prince[28]), but the fact that he uses it at all, especially during his teenage years when self-description is such an important part of identity formation, demonstrates that his status as a half-blood, and thus an outsider, is a key component in the way Severus Snape thinks about himself, and remains so throughout his adulthood.[29] He may not publicize his half-bloodedness, but this fact does not mean he is ashamed of it; he does not publicize any personal information. He may not consider being a half-blood something to celebrate, but he clearly accepts it as fact, which puts him in direct contrast to Tom Riddle.

After graduating from Hogwarts, Snape once again finds himself in a position of alienation. Following a brief period of loyalty to Voldemort, he enters into a contract of service to Albus Dumbledore that will last the rest of his life. His skill of switching between two cultures becomes crucial to Dumbledore's ultimate plan, especially after Voldemort returns to bodily form and reassembles his Death Eaters. Hogwarts faculty and students as well as members of the Order of the Phoenix place a tenuous trust in him only because Dumbledore trusts him.[30] Snape is not fully trusted by the other side, either; Bellatrix Lestrange, arguably Voldemort's closest supporter, calls his loyalty into question.[31] Bellatrix, of course, turns out to be right. Just as the young Severus, skilled though he may have been at keeping himself out of both parents' displeasure, never considered joining Muggle society, the adult Snape, once he has made up his mind to join Dumbledore, does not switch his loyalties. However, this does not lessen the isolation of his position—the isolation to which, as a half-blood, he has become accustomed.

Snape is not only, in a magical manner of speaking, biracial, but bilingual as well. As a child, he must have learned to use both wizarding and Muggle terminology—a skill that cannot be taken for granted in a pureblood witch or wizard.[32] As an adult, his adeptness at learning two languages allows him to converse with both Death Eaters and members of the Order of the Phoenix, usually without raising suspicion. As is true of many bilingual people, he practices code switching, a term generally used to describe the act of shifting between a dialect and a majority language depending on one's inter-locutors and the purpose of the communication.[33] Code switching is a complex process that requires sensitivity to one's environment and the ability to think quickly. Snape, who is highly intelligent and hyper-vigilant (a trait not surprising in a person who experienced abuse at school and probably at home as well), is good at it, though not flawless. At one point during Occlumency lessons, Harry catches Snape referring to Voldemort as the Dark Lord. Harry, whose dislike of Snape makes him particularly astute in this case, points out that only Death Eaters use this term. Snape is spared from having to answer this question when the lesson is interrupted,[34] and Harry never brings up the matter again, although he uses it to stock his personal arsenal of reasons not to trust Snape. Aside from this one false step, Snape is a successful code switcher who uses his bilingual ability to great advantage.

While Snape's half-blood status may condemn him to lifelong alienation, it also enables him to play a crucial role in the downfall of Voldemort. Perhaps more importantly, his *acceptance* of his half-blood status marks a major distinction between himself and Voldemort, a distinction that makes all the difference in the two wizards' character development.

Tom Riddle: half-blood racist

Tom Riddle's mother Merope Gaunt, much like Thomas Hardy's Tess Durbyfield, is the unappreciated daughter of an impoverished rural family, who, partly as an escape from her dreary home life, bears the child of a wealthy and heartless local heir. Merope is not just any downtrodden country girl, however; she is the descendant of two of the wizarding world's oldest and most famous families: the Slytherins and the Peverells.[35]

The exquisite irony of the younger Tom Riddle's parentage is that he is descended on one side from Muggles and on the other side from the most virulent Muggle-hater in history. Salazar Slytherin is legendary as the Hogwarts founder who, after his demand that the school accept only pure-blood students was denied, built the Chamber of Secrets and placed within it the basilisk with the purpose of destroying Muggle-born students.[36] Tom Riddle, as the Heir of Slytherin, will open this chamber during his time at Hogwarts and later cause it to be opened again. The main criteria for acceptance into the Hogwarts house named after Slytherin are ambition and cunning,[37] but the house also carries on its founder's exclusionary legacy in that it traditionally draws from pure-blood families such as the Blacks, the Malfoys, and the Lestranges. Exceptions do occur, however; while there are no known Muggle-borns in Slytherin house, readers are told of two half-bloods who get in (Riddle and Snape).

Another great irony is that when he first finds out that he is a wizard, young Tom assumes that he must be a half-blood and does not seem to be bothered by it. Already associating power with immortality, he concludes that since his mother was too weak to keep herself alive, she must not have had magical abilities.[38] For a brief time, he seems to accept his half-bloodedness as immutable fact, much as the other two half-bloods in the series do. However, when Tom Riddle gets to Hogwarts, two significant landmarks in his identity formation occur. First, though the novels are silent about his induction into the racially hierarchical wizarding world, one can surmise that he learns quickly enough from his Slytherin housemates the stigma attached to being anything but a pure-blood. This knowledge probably leads in part to the second major event: his search for information about the Hogwarts career of his father, who he initially assumes must have been a wizard. When this search proves to be fruitless, he turns his attention toward his mother's family, embarking on some field research during the summer before his sixth year at Hogwarts, when he is sixteen years old.[39]

The sixteenth year of a person's life, occurring as it does in the middle of the teenage years, is a significant period in identity development. At age sixteen Severus Snape takes an important step toward acceptance of an unchangeable aspect of his identity by writing the name "Half-Blood Prince" in his sixth-year potions textbook. At age sixteen, Tom Riddle, now styling himself as Voldemort, takes a drastic step in the opposite direction by killing his Muggle father and grandparents (significantly, Harry Potter is sixteen when he finds out about both of these actions). Dumbledore attributes the triple murder equally to two motivations, "obliterating the last of the unworthy Riddle line and revenging himself upon the father who never wanted him,"[40] but, characteristically of Dumbledore's generous nature, he probably overemphasizes the second, more human motivation and underemphasizes the first. Voldemort demonstrates a lifelong pattern of indifference toward relationships with other people; he comes close to showing affection only to his snake, Nagini. Judging by his general behavior, the sixteen-year-old patricide likely acted less out of hurt toward an absent father than out of his compulsion to eliminate an unwanted element from his magical pedigree and thus achieve purity of blood.

Voldemort violently literalizes the concept of race as performance. This concept provides one possible resolution of the difficulty of defining race, which has been variously described as a biologically determined trait or as a social construct, among other definitions. Simply stated, race as performance means that a person is what that person chooses to act like. This concept lies behind the actions of many light-skinned people of mixed racial ancestry in pre–civil rights America who attempted to "pass" as white. In a gross distortion of this generally harmless behavior, Voldemort tries to pass as a pure-blood wizard not only by talking like one (e.g., using the term "Mudblood"[41]) and setting in place a political agenda that would satisfy the most exclusivist pure-blood (e.g., using the Ministry of Magic to hunt down Muggle-borns[42]), but also by forcibly altering his family tree.

On the surface, Voldemort's attempt at passing is successful. His pure-blood followers never question his ancestry (cf. Harry's daring disclosure to the Death Eaters of Voldemort's half-blood status[43]), and Dumbledore repeatedly emphasizes the guesswork involved in tracing information about Voldemort's parents[44]; clearly, Voldemort is not careless with his biographical details. Interestingly, Tom Riddle-as-memory does tell Harry that he is a half-blood.[45] It is possible that he believes that Harry, who is practically a half-blood himself, will not consider this important enough information to spread around. Additionally, he offers this revelation right after a racist tirade against his "foul, common Muggle" father.[46] Clearly, this single self-disclosure of Riddle's blood status is not an indication that Voldemort accepts his racial identity.

Psychologically, Voldemort's quest for genetic homogeny is less successful. Dumbledore often talks about subtleties that the literal-minded Voldemort cannot understand—love, for example.[47] Characteristically, Voldemort fails to grasp the elementary truth that, by killing the remaining Muggles in his family tree, he cannot change the fact that they were his family and an inescapable part of his identity. He is uncomfortable with the disunity—the halfness—of his ancestry. This discomfort is normal, but instead of learning to live with the inevitable contradiction in his identity, he tries to get rid of it. Significantly, this fundamental psychological problem hinders Voldemort from achieving true personhood.

Conclusion: integrity versus fragmentation

Similar to many other themes in the *Harry Potter* novels, half-bloodedness is introduced in a seemingly insignificant form by a minor character (Seamus Finnegan in this case) only to return as a major plot and thematic device. In Severus Snape and Tom Riddle, Rowling presents two different ways of dealing with being a half-blood. Riddle hates diversity of any kind, perhaps believing it to be a chink in his invincibility, and thus he forcibly creates a monolithic family heritage for himself. However, ironically, his thirst to be immortal, which is also part of his obsession with invincibility, leads him to split his soul into seven pieces. Through the Horcruxes, the wizard who loathes the idea of being half a man becomes a seventh of a man—actually less, since, as the final book reveals, the remaining piece of Voldemort's soul resides in Harry. To put it in psychological terms, because Tom Riddle is unable to accept his unchangeable identity as a half-blood, he is also unable to achieve an integrated personality.

Severus Snape, on the other hand, accepts his identity. Harry is wrong when he says that Snape is "just like Voldemort. Pure-blood mother, Muggle father ... ashamed of his parentage, trying to make himself feared using the Dark Arts, gave himself an impressive new name."[48] What Harry overlooks is that Snape's "impressive new name," unlike Voldemort's, bears explicit testimony to his blood status. Though he never advertises his parentage, Snape clearly self-identifies as a half-blood. Because of his ability to accept the identity given him at birth, he is free to be a whole person. Snape may be a skilled liar and Occlumens, but he is a man of integrity—quite literally, he is integrated. When he stops serving Voldemort, he stops (unlike Peter Pettigrew) for good, because he knows himself. This difference is why the newly enlightened Harry can tell Voldemort with confidence, "Snape was Dumbledore's, Dumbledore's from the moment you started hunting down my mother."[49] While Voldemort strives for genetic unity but becomes fragmented in the process, Snape accepts his genetic duality and achieves integration. Put another way, Voldemort fails in attaining purity of blood, but Snape succeeds, in large part, in attaining purity of character.

This difference in results is a crucial concept, not only for half-blood wizards and for biracial Muggles, but also for everyone; a large part of psychological health is knowing the difference between what humans can and cannot change about themselves. This is, of course, not always such a simple distinction. Fatalism versus free will is a major theme in the *Harry Potter* series, beginning with Harry's worries over the reason for the Sorting Hat's decision not to put him in Slytherin, and the resulting conversation with Dumbledore.[50] The introduction of the prophecy complicates this theme, leading to a couple of similar conversations.[51] Voldemort's reaction to the prophecy is another example of his inability to consider more than one possible interpretation or course of action.

What Voldemort seems unable to understand is that trying to change one's ancestry is at best frustrating and at worst destructive. Trying to change one's character, on the other hand—whether that means quitting the Death Eaters or learning how to love—may be a long and painful process, but it is possible. More than any brilliant potion-making tip, this is the most important lesson of the Half-Blood Prince.

Notes

1. See K. E. Westman, "Specters of Thatcherism: Contemporary British Culture in J. K. Rowling's *Harry Potter* Series," in L. A. Whited (ed.), *The Ivory Tower and Harry Potter: Perspectives on a Literary Phenomenon* (Columbia, MO: University of Missouri Press, 2002): 305–28, at 307.

2. E. E. Heilman and A. E. Gregory, "Images of the Privileged Insider and Outcast Outsider," in E. E. Heilman (ed.), *Harry Potter's World: Multidisciplinary Critical Perspectives* (New York: RoutledgeFalmer, 2003): 241–59, at 255.

3. S. Barfield, "Of Young Magicians and Growing Up: J. K. Rowling, Her

Critics and the 'Cultural Infantilism' Debate" in C. W. Hallett (ed.), *Scholarly Studies in Harry Potter: Applying Academic Methods to a Popular Text* (Lewiston, NY: Edwin Mellen, 2005): 175–97, at 186.

4. CS[A]: 116.
5. See W. Wandless, "Hogwarts vs. 'The "Values" Wasteland': *Harry Potter* and the Formation of Character," in C. W. Hallett (ed.), *Scholarly Studies in Harry Potter: Applying Academic Methods to a Popular Text* (Lewiston, NY: Edwin Mellen, 2005): 217–40, at 229.
6. Barfield: 186.
7. CS[A]: 317.
8. OP[A]: 784.
9. SS[A]: 78; cf. Westman: 313.
10. SS[A]: 125.
11. *Ibid.*
12. OP[A]: 217.
13. *Ibid.*: 216–19.
14. SS[A]: 144.
15. *Ibid.*: 171 and elsewhere.
16. See Fran Pheasant-Kelly's essay titled "Bewitching, Abject, Uncanny: Other Spaces in the *Harry Potter* Films," Chapter 4 in this book, for further discussion of this idea.
17. GF[A]: 82.
18. HP[A]: 355.
19. E. Said, *Orientalism* (New York: Vintage-Random House, 1979).
20. *Ibid.*: 45.
21. Barfield: 186.
22. O. S. Card, "Who Is Snape?" in A. Berner, O. S. Card and J. Millman (eds.), *The Great Snape Debate* (N.p.: Borders, 2007): 80–109, at 96.
23. Quoted in P. Appelbaum, "The Great Snape Debate," in E. E. Heilman (ed.), *Critical Perspectives on Harry Potter*, 2nd edn (New York: Routledge-Taylor & Francis, 2009): 83–101, at 89.
24. OP[A]: 591; DH[A]: 667.
25. DH[A]: 663–5.
26. OP[A]: 591.
27. DH[A]: 673.
28. Cf. HP[A]: 638.
29. *Ibid.*: 604.
30. GF[A]: 605; HP[A]: 332, 615–16.
31. HP[A]: 21–35.
32. See CS[A]: 47 for one of Mr. Weasley's malapropisms for a Muggle invention.
33. See J. O. Milner and L. F. Milner, *Bridging English*, 3rd edn (Upper Saddle River, NJ: Merrill-Prentice Hall, 2003): 330–2.
34. OP[A]: 593.
35. HP[A]: 207–8.
36. CS[A]: 150–1.

37. SS[A]: 118.
38. HP[A]: 275.
39. *Ibid.*: 362–3.
40. *Ibid.*: 367.
41. DH[A]: 12.
42. *Ibid.*: 208–9.
43. OP[A]: 784.
44. HP[A]: 197, 214, 362.
45. CS[A]: 317.
46. *Ibid.*: 314.
47. HP[A]: 444; see also 559.
48. *Ibid.*: 637.
49. DH[A]: 740.
50. CS[A]: 333.
51. OP[A]: 842–4; HP[A]: 509–12.

10

Magic, Medicine, and *Harry Potter*

Clyde Partin

The rich tradition of medicine is deeply embedded in the seven *Harry Potter* novels, yet the steady undercurrent of medical issues and themes in the story has received scant attention from critics. Traditional medical topics such as anatomy, embryology, physiology, and especially pharmacology permeate the books. There is even a reference to the vigorous demands and prerequisites needed for the wizarding equivalent of medical school. Medical care delivered in the magical world at St. Mungo's Hospital and at the school infirmary is modeled on standard empathetic, humanistic, and professional values. The various medical afflictions from which the characters suffer are considered metaphors for illnesses that affected Rowling's family members or helped her advance the points of view she wanted to express. Thus, it is important to delineate and to explore the threads of medicine and medical care woven into the novels, both in a socio-medical context and a psychological/psychiatric aspect since they are the most thematically developed. In this vein, one must examine the characters and their afflictions and explore the basic sciences as they are taught by the professors at Hogwarts.

Medicine's role with the characters

Literary critics emphasize Rowling's extensive background reading of childhood classics to provide inspiration for her writing. Others note how much of the story she has mined from her own life. After an abusive failed marriage, Rowling finds herself a single mother occupying government-subsidized housing in Edinburgh, Scotland. Rowling's real-life emotional struggles are dealt another blow when her mother is diagnosed with multiple sclerosis and, after grappling with the disease for a decade, succumbs at age forty-five. Some critics postulate that Hogwarts' Professor Lupin's chronic incurable illness is a metaphor for not only multiple sclerosis but also "people's reaction to illness and disability."[1] Lupin was bitten by a werewolf during a research expedition, was subject to periodic transformations, and thus was ostracized despite his avuncular nature. In the third novel, *Harry Potter and the Prisoner of Azkaban*, Lupin is the person who warns Harry, "get too near a Dementor and every good feeling, every happy memory will be sucked out of you."[2] Like a Prozac pill, the Patronus charm is offered as an antidote to the Dementors. The ability to produce a Patronus is no mean feat and attests to Potter's burgeoning talents. Professor Lupin, who teaches Harry how to do this, tells Harry that "the Patronus is a kind of positive force, a projection of the very things that the Dementor feeds upon—hope, happiness, the desire to survive—but it cannot feel despair as real humans can, so the Dementors can't hurt it."[3]

Other characters exhibit afflictions that have medical counterparts. Professor Quirrell, the "D-Defence Against the D-D-Dark Arts"[4] instructor not only has a speech impediment but seems to suffer an anxiety disorder, perhaps post-traumatic stress syndrome. A ghastly encounter with vampires in the Dark Forest during a year of field research left him trembling, nervous, never the same since and "scared of the students, scared of his own subject."[5] More subtle is the play on words when Hogwarts student Pansy Parkinson comes to our attention as "she raised a shaking arm"[6]: a shaking arm (or palsy) is a symptom of Parkinsonism. At some point, Rowling must have reviewed the disease of lockjaw, for she refers to *risus sardonicus*, the deathly grimace frozen on the faces of those so infected. Professor McGonagall, rather irritated with a colleague whom she does not respect, offers a retort "with an attempt at a reciprocal smile that made her look as though she had lockjaw."[7]

Alcoholism also makes an appearance in the stories. Hagrid, the tender-hearted gamekeeper at Hogwarts, has an undue fondness for distilled spirits, a penchant for large, dangerous animals and a tendency to experience motion sickness (for example, during the cart ride at Gringott's). Predictably, Hagrid has a cure for the last problem—a "pick-me-up" at the Leaky Cauldron, the favored watering hole.[8] A genetic misfit, Hagrid is a half-breed giant whose size seems to exceed even abnormal levels of growth hormone as a rational explanation. Hagrid is not the only character to struggle with alcohol. Winky the house-elf is "getting through six bottles a day now."[9]

The constant cursing of Peeves, a poltergeist, suggests Tourette's syndrome. The house-elf Dobby is fond of self-flagellation. His most egregious injury is ironing his hands in self-retribution for making Platform 9¾ impermeable to Harry as he attempted to cross the magical barrier. Dobby's penchant for self-injury is reminiscent of Lesch-Nyhan syndrome, although Roger Highfield has pointed out that the genetic disorder Williams Syndrome may be a possible explanation.[10] Victims of Williams Syndrome

> have subnormal intelligence and are acutely sensitive to sound. They are loving, caring, and sensitive to the feelings of others. Despite having low IQs, many are good storytellers and have a talent for music, notably perfect pitch. Most striking of all is their appearance. A relatively large number are short. They have childlike faces, with small upturned noses, oval ears, and broad mouths with full lips and a small chin. They look and behave like the traditional description of elves.[11]

Harry's cousin, the aptly named Dudley Dursley, over-indulged and overweight, is destined for sleep apnea. "The silence in the dark house was broken only by the distant, grunting snores of his enormous cousin, Dudley,"[12] and "he heard his cousin Dudley give a tremendous grunting snore from the next room," writes Rowling.[13] Dudley could be a poster child for the movie *Super Size Me*, a modern-day literary stand-in for Fat Boy Joe in Charles Dickens's novel *The Pickwick Papers*. One reader suggests Dudley "clearly descends from Dahl's Augustus Gloop, whose gluttony Rowling can make even more contemptible by implicitly calling on current concern about obesity and inactivity among couch-potato kids."[14] Unable to resist the urge for the illegal misapplication of magic, Hagrid zaps Dudley with a tail; predictably, it is porcine. Dudley must go to London seeking the services of a plastic surgeon for a supernumerary caudalectomy.

Mendelian genetics and magic

On a higher social plane, class discrimination is manifested by whether or not a person is a pure-blood wizard, or a hybrid product (Mudblood) of a pure-blood and a Muggle (someone who has no wizard powers/blood). Rowling appears to get the genetics of this reasonably correct. An article in *Nature* explores these genetics, which the authors feel is inherited in standard Mendelian fashion. They suggest that the wizard/witch allele (W) is recessive to the Muggle allele (M). Thus, pure-blood wizards are WW. Incomplete penetrance, they speculate, may be represented by Neville Longbottom, who is WW but is a lackluster wizard with limited skills.[15] Others question this conclusion, suggesting that the "assumption that wizarding has a genetic basis [is] deterministic and unsupported by available evidence," pointing out that

> in incomplete penetrance, individuals either display the trait or not: they do not display an intermediate degree of the trait. Impoverished wizarding skills might be indicative of variable expressivity of an allele. However, both variable expressivity and incomplete penetrance are associated with dominant alleles. If the wizarding skills were dominant, rather than recessive as suggested, wizarding children such as Hermione could not be born to non-wizarding parents.[16]

Explaining the genetic concepts further, Emory University geneticist Rachelle M. Spell argues that "traits can exhibit both incomplete penetrance (there or not there) and variable expressivity (to different degrees). Longbottom could be an example of this." Spell goes on to partially quench the genetic theorizing, stating

> the idea that class is inherited in our society is represented in these stories by the notion that magic is inherited. Whether scientists describe wizarding as dominant or recessive is trivial compared to the idea that it is heritable. I found a supposed quote from Rowling that suggests her agreement: "Magic is a dominant and resilient gene."[17]

Indeed, Rowling does make that statement on her website, but logic suggests that subjecting wizarding genetics to too much scientific scrutiny, while fun, falls prey to over-analysis. Moreover, the issue of genetics sets the foundation for the more sinister theme of ethnic cleansing that periodically singes the atmosphere of the higher institutional levels of wizarding authorities.

Medical training in the stories

In the British educational system, as at Hogwarts, a wide range of ages exists in one school, allowing the young students to benefit from the older students. This approach is reminiscent of the teaching scheme the renowned medical educator Sir William Osler envisioned for his model of medical education in the 1890s at Johns Hopkins Medical School. Senior residents would supervise junior residents and interns, who would in turn pass along knowledge and experience to medical students. As in medicine, "hands-on experience and real-life activity are vital to learning."[18] Hogwarts teachers such as Professors Lupin and McGonagall employ this system of education with varying degrees of success. J. Conn observes that these "experienced clinical teachers have a richer and more tightly connected knowledge of their subject matter than do novice teachers, allowing them to integrate or link information with knowledge from other disciplines and to place a clinical situation in its appropriate context."[19] In contrast, the close-ended questioning style, favored by Professor Snape, for example, employed in a humiliating, antagonistic, threatening manner is not conducive to a nurturing learning experience. Successful clinical teachers whether in medicine or magic are adaptive and imaginative, and, while the former do not have to contend with "unscheduled explosions, wayward broomsticks or invading trolls, they are challenged by complex, diverse and rapidly changing learning environments" such as might be found on the wards of a teaching hospital.[20] An essay on "Harry Potter and the Acquisition of Knowledge" makes it clear that learning is a vital theme in the life of Hogwarts students, and "the philosophy of the school is unmistakably centered on discovery, teaching, and the slow steady cumulative acquisition of knowledge."[21]

There is a demanding pre-med option offered to aspiring Healers. One student, at a career advice day, after reviewing the leaflet on requirements for Healers, despairs of the demands—"You need at least an E in NEWT level in Potions, Herbology, Transfiguration, Charms and Defence Against the Dark Arts. I mean … blimey… don't want much, do they?"[22] These rigorous academic credentials are analogous to the demanding requirements of our medical school admission boards. Hermione shrewdly retorts, "Well, it's a very responsible job, isn't it?"[23]

Magical clinical care

An astonishing number of minor and sometimes major injuries are incurred by the Hogwarts students and faculty. Numerous sojourns—between ten and fifteen per novel—to the "Hospital Wing" or infirmary are recorded. It is implied that many of the visits lead to admission and overnight observation; although in most cases, it is left murky as to how much time a student spends in the clinic or the specific treatment. Concussions, dermatologic disasters, animal bites, laboratory accidents, and magical misadventures are the most common reasons for seeking care. The Quidditch contests provide for plenty of injuries; in fact, the first injury recorded in the novels occurs when Neville loses control of his broomstick in his inaugural flying lesson, suffering a broken wrist. The longest visit, a fortnight, is endured by Hermione Granger, who develops fur and feline features after a transfiguration plan goes awry. Reversing this error seems to be a real test of the skills of the clinic's healthcare provider, Madam Pomfrey. Fortunately, as Harry observes, Madam Pomfrey "never asks too many questions."[24]

In fact, the yoke of utilization review is nowhere to be found in the novels. Discharge seems to be motivated by youthful exuberance tempered by the sage wisdom of Madam Pomfrey, her name no doubt an allusion to the source of opium, whose medical credentials are vague but seem to be along the lines of a nurse practitioner. She displays the classic attributes of an accomplished old-school head nurse—stern but kind, tough yet gentle. She runs the ward with an iron hand, is loved by the students, and is respected by the school authorities. Her splendid care is rendered in a concerned, competent, and compassionate manner. Her judicious dispensation of chocolate, TLC and the tincture of time seem to be the most cost effective and efficacious of treatments. Her therapeutic armamentarium is not infrequently augmented by magical medicine and potions. Madam Pomfrey is the epitome of dedication and devotion to duty. Irritated by an unwarranted and cowardly attack on a faculty member, she exclaims, "If I wasn't worried what would happen to you students without me, I'd resign in protest."[25] The victim of this attack, Professor McGonagall, sustains injuries severe enough to warrant transfer to the tertiary care hospital in London, St. Mungo's Hospital for Magical Maladies and Injuries. This is one of only two times that Madam Pomfrey transfers a patient, the other incident being schoolmate Katie Bell, the target of an Imperious Curse, who is sent to St. Mungo's the day after being victimized.[26] Whatever admirable qualities Madam Pomfrey may possess, she is not immune to the pitfalls of polypharmacy. Hermione Granger is admitted to the hospital wing suffering from chest wall trauma—"quite enough damage to be going on with"[27]—in Pomfrey's estimation. Pomfrey prescribes ten potions, but fortunately, there are no potion-potion interactions or deleterious consequences.

In the second novel, somewhere at the intersection of practicing medicine without a license, inept administration of a potion and misapplication of magic is the closest thing there is to a malpractice case. Harry fractures his arm during a Quidditch match when the Bludger rams it. In dramatic fashion, Potter ignores his useless arm, grabs the Snitch, thus winning the game for his side, and passes out from the pain as he crash-lands his broom in the mud. Unfortunately, the inept Professor Lockhart comes to his aid and, instead of mending his arm with a charm, makes all the bones in Harry's arm disappear. Harry repairs to the Hospital Wing, where Madam Pomfrey prescribes "Skele-Gro," which overnight painfully, but successfully, regenerates the standard thirty-three bones of the upper extremity.

Occasionally, in Potter's world, more serious treatments are needed than can be handled by Pomfrey's clinic. In these circumstances, witches and wizards are referred to St. Mungo's Hospital for Magical Maladies and Injuries. The description of the hospital setting is uncannily accurate. The very name of the hospital invokes traditional Catholic benevolence. The hospital entrance, just off a non-descript London street, is disguised as an entrance to a department store scatologically called Purge and Dowse Ltd. In the crowded hospital reception area, "rows of witches and wizards sat upon rickety wooden chairs, looking perfectly normal and perusing out-of-date copies of *Witch Weekly*, others sporting gruesome disfigurements such as elephant trunks."[28] Portraits of famous Healers line the hospital corridors. On one ward, a sign informs us: "*Healer-in-Charge: Hippocrates Smethwyck. Trainee Healer: Augustus Pye.*"[29] The fundraising fountain traditionally found at the entry of a hospital even makes an appearance at St. Mungo's, where Harry later dumps the entire contents of his moneybag in support.[30]

Providing stark contrast with the Healers at St. Mungo's, doctors, described as "Muggle nutters,"[31] are not held in high esteem in the wizard world. They prefer their own version of healthcare providers, known as Healers, whose emblem is a wand and bone embroidered on their lime-green robes.[32] They consider what human physicians practice as complementary medicine and the Healer trainee Augustus Pye is quite interested in that. He discovers a Muggle remedy and advises that "stitches work very well on Muggle wounds."[33] Unfortunately, stitches turn out not to be efficacious in the wizard world.

The long-term care facility at St. Mungo's is depicted as a "special ward for people whose brains have been addled by magic."[34] This ward "bore unmistakable signs of being a permanent home to its residents. They had many more personal effects around their beds," the healer notes. "For permanent spell damage you know. Of course, with intensive remedial potions and charms and a bit of luck, we can produce some improvement."[35] This facility is likely where Harry's classmate Neville Longbottom's parents reside. They "were tortured into insanity by You-Know-Who's followers,"[36] a condition we would probably call post-traumatic stress syndrome, perhaps evolving into an age-related dementia. In *The Half-Blood Prince*, the Junior Minister Herbert Chorley, who has had his brains addled by a "poorly performed Imperious Curse"[37] is also the beneficiary of a team of healers from St. Mungo's Hospital.

Medical care in the wizarding world is not confined to the clinics and hospitals. One of the more interesting traumatic magical injuries sustained is splinching. The capacity to apparate, or suddenly disappear and reappear elsewhere, is Ministry-of-Magic regulated and a difficult task. When attempted by wizards not fully trained in the technique, the result can be disastrous. Incomplete apparition, or splinching, leads to certain parts of the anatomy being left behind, a most inconvenient development. Fortunately, Ministry of Magic authorities maintain a constant vigilance for such mishaps and quickly dispatch members of the Accidental Magic Reversal Squad to do what all the king's men apparently could not do—put the Humpty-Dumpty wizard back together. A version of hypnosis also exists. Should a Muggle become a victim of magic, the Accidental Magic Reversal Department will send a representative out to repair the damage and perform a memory modification on the victim so that person has no recollection of the incident.

Magical medicine

The magical potions described by Rowling are imaginative, sometimes humorous and many have a vestigial basis in pharmacological reality. In the first novel, the apothecary shop in Diagon Alley is depicted in detail, "which was fascinating enough to make up for its horrible smell, a mixture of bad eggs and rotted cabbages. Barrels of slimy stuff stood on the floor, jars of herbs, dried roots and bright powders lined the walls, bundles of feathers, strings of fangs and snarled claws hung from the ceiling."[38] At Hogwarts, the students take herbology, taught by the aptly named Professor Sprout, exhorting them "to take care of all the strange plants and fungi and find out what they were used for."[39] Professor Snape, a most unlyrical character, eloquently tells his students in the potion-making class, "I don't expect you will really understand the beauty of the softly simmering cauldron with its shimmering fumes, the delicate power of liquids that creep through human veins, bewitching the mind, ensnaring the senses … I can teach you how to bottle fame, brew glory, even stopper death."[40] The text for the class is *One Thousand Magical Herbs and Fungi* by Phyllida Spore! Like any useful pharmacology class, they explore antidotes, with a practical twist—Professor Snape might be poisoning one of them before Christmas to test their antidote.

Rowling is said to have consulted Nicholas Culpeper's classic text, *Culpeper's Complete Herbal*, first published in 1814, as she concocted her potions.[41] First mentioned is the powerful sleeping potion, the *Draught of Living Death*, comprised of asphodel[42] and wormwood. Perhaps the two are synergistic, since Culpeper devotes four pages to the virtues of wormwood and two paragraphs on asphodel but does not mention any soporific qualities, although wormwood is an ingredient in absinthe. Culpeper must be a believer in the Doctrine of Signatures, for he writes of the asphodel root, "I know no physical use of the roots; probably there is, for I do not believe God created any thing of no use."[43] The *Draught of Peace*, "a potion to calm anxiety and soothe agitation,"[44] seems to be a less-potent version of the *Draught of Living Death*. When tested on formulating this potion, Harry demonstrates his limited aptitude for pharmacology and potion-making by forgetting to add the syrup of hellebore. Ordinarily, "the roots of the hellebore are very effectual against all melancholy diseases, especially such as are of long standing, as quartan agues and madness," Culpeper claims.[45] Harry is at least diligent when one evening finds him studying scurvy-grass, lovage, and sneezewort. These "plantes are most efficacious in the inflaming of the braine, and are therefore much used in *Confusing and Befuddlement Draughts*, where the wizard is desirous of producing hot-headedness and recklessness."[46] Scurvy-grass and lovage are catalogued in Culpeper but "inflaming of the braine" does not seem to be an attribute known to Culpeper.

The first potions lesson involves a simple nostrum to cure boils, highly pragmatic for the acne-prone adolescent population of Hogwarts. Unfortunately for Neville, his attempt at combining dried nettles, slugs, crushed snake fangs, and porcupine quills misfires. The mixture splashes on Neville, causing angry red lesions to erupt and start to fester as he heads to the Hospital Wing, hoping Madam Pomfrey has an antidote. According to Culpeper, the "juice of the (nettle) leaves, or the decoction of them, or of the root, is singularly good to wash either old rotten, or stinking sores or fistulous, and gangrenes, and such as fretting, eating or corroding scabs, manginess and itch."[47] Speaking of antidotes, Rowling seems to have been inspired by Pythagorean's Theorem in describing Golpalott's Third Law: "the-antidote-for-a-blended poison-will-be-equal-to-more-than-the-sum-of-the-antidotes-for-each-of-the-separate-components."[48] *Pepper-Up Potion* and *Wit-Sharpening Potion* make their debut in the fourth novel, but it is *Veritaserum* that seems to have a real life counter-part—pentothal. It is described as a "Truth Potion so powerful that three drops would have you spilling your innermost secrets."[49] Just as with any Food and Drug Administration-controlled substance, "use of this Potion is controlled by very strict Ministry Guidelines."[50]

Professor Sprout also teaches the students about herbs useful in many magical situations. A biological theorem states that ontogeny recapitulates phylogeny, but Gillyweed does this in reverse. In the second task of the Triwizard Tournament, confronted with the need to swim underwater for an hour, Potter finds the solution in a dose of Gillyweed. After ingesting some, Harry develops gills, allowing him to spend a comfortable hour making a dramatic rescue deep in the lake. As the "gillyweed wears off, he emerges from the water like a baby coming forth from the womb, his lungs bursting as he finally reaches the surface and gasps for air,"[51] in a potent symbolic moment of rebirth that presages Voldemort's reappearance in an infantile state towards the end of the novel.

Rowling even toys with medically inspired gag gifts and candies. A window advertisement asks, "Why Are You Worrying about You-Know-Who? You SHOULD Be Worrying about U-NO-POO—the Constipation Sensation That's Gripping the Nation!"[52] Similarly, Fred and George Weasley continually try to invent and market various novelties to their fellow students. Sweets are deviously disguised items such as Puking Pastilles, Fainting Fancies, Fever Fudge, and Nosebleed Nougats. As a matter of ingenious marketing, the candies are sold with the antidote. A well-timed ingestion might get one out of a boring class early. The horrified teacher sends the unfortunate victim to the Hospital Wing. As soon as the teacher is out of sight, the antidote is self-administered and the ruse is successful. The boys are challenged on this by Hermione Granger, who questions the brothers' right to try their new ideas on younger students, emphatically stating, "you can't test your rubbish on students! [...] It could be dangerous!"[53] Age aside, lack of informed consent is a serious breach of professional protocol. The concept of informed consent has been around since December 1900 when the Prussian Parliament felt obliged to enact legislation protecting patients involved in clinical research.[54]

Patent medicine makes a cameo appearance in the series as well. *Baruffio's Brain Elixir* is passed around by some students, no doubt targeted to the attention deficit disorder crowd. It seems a "flourishing black-market trade in aids to concentration, mental agility and wakefulness had sprung up among the fifth- and seventh-years," as they approach their important OWL exams.[55] Just as in the real world, pharmacology as depicted in these novels prays on the unwary, promises more than it can deliver, is geared to the standard ills of school-age children and adolescents, is fraught with side effects and toxicities—but on occasion can serve a useful purpose.

Various regulatory and licensing agencies such as the Ministry of Magic, akin to America's Food and Drug Administration, oversee the application and misapplication of magic. Even the language of the Harry Potter pandemic has public health allusions—"Crazes, fashions and Pottermania are the measles and whooping cough of the mind, spreading horizontally, from child to child."[56] With over 400 million copies sold, it is easy to appreciate the epidemiologic dimensions. Others see anecdotal testimonial healing powers in the novels. After receiving an email from a former student, recovering from a serious illness and associated depression, requesting advice on some books she might read to help lift her depression, a college literature professor suggested the *Harry Potter* books. The student regained her health and returned to school.[57]

The *New England Journal of Medicine*[58] devoted one page to the death of Susan Sontag who penned the well-known book *Illness as Metaphor*. Sontag's opening line is quoted, "Illness is the night-side of life, a more onerous citizenship."[59] Readers may not find that kind of writing in Harry Potter, but certainly, illness as metaphor can be found. For those readers and physicians who embrace the notion that art and literature reflect life, there are medical and social lessons on disease, the practice of medicine and the human condition to glean from the *Harry Potter* novels. There is much to appreciate in the author's skillful blending of magic and medicine. "There is probably no more fascinating story than that of the rise of scientific medicine. Its beginnings were in mystery and superstition; its progress encumbered with ignorance and quackery. Above these it has risen to become the most beneficent science of the modern world" notes Yale University physician Howard Haggard.[60] In his third of three laws of prediction, science fiction writer Arthur C. Clarke states, "Any sufficiently advanced technology is indistinguishable from magic."[61]

The practice of medicine is considered the artistic application of scientifically based knowledge. Nonetheless, many days I am spell-bound by the results I obtain by a pharmaceutical potion I have chosen to give a patient. My cardiology and surgical colleagues, with tantalizing success, seem to be practicing some healthy brand of magic with their laparoscopes, angioplasties, and brew-eluding stents. Yet Harry and his Hogwarts schoolmates, like medical students and interns, discover that mastering their chosen craft does not come easy. Bringing special talents to the table helps, but it does not replace hard work and diligence. Medicine, like magic, does not possess all the answers. Death does take the upper hand in many cases, despite our best efforts. Magic is not immune to the finality of death. We are cruelly aware of that from the beginning when Harry's parents are killed. Hogwarts Headmaster Dumbledore again reminds us of this when Hogwarts student Cedric Diggory dies in a vicious contest gone awry, saying heavily "No spell can reawaken the dead."[62] Child educators and parents should give credit to author J. K. Rowling for reawakening children's interest in literature. Similarly, the medical community can revel in the creative and benevolent light she has cast upon the practice of medicine.

Notes

1. P. Nel, *Harry Potter Novels: A Reader's Guide* (New York: Continuum, 2001): 15.
2. PA[B]: 140.
3. *Ibid.*: 176.
4. PS[B]: 55.
5. *Ibid.*
6. DH[A]: 610.
7. OP[B]: 368.
8. PS[B]: 59.
9. GF[A]: 536.
10. R. Highfield, *The Science of Harry Potter: How Magic Really Works* (New York and London: Penguin Books, 2002).
11. *Ibid.*: 192–3.
12. PA[B]: 10.
13. GF[B]: 22.
14. E. Teare, "Harry Potter and the Technology of Magic," in L. A. Whited (ed.), *The Ivory Tower and Harry Potter* (Columbia, MO: University of Missouri Press, 2002): 329–42, at 338.
15. J. M. Craig, R. Dow, and M. A. Aitken, "Harry Potter and the Recessive Allele," *Nature* 436 (August 11, 2005): 776.
16. A. N. Dodd, C. T. Hotta, and M. J. Gardner, "Harry Potter and the Prisoner of Presumption," *Nature* 437 (September 15, 2005): 318.
17. R. M. Spell, PhD, personal communication, February 26, 2009; September 21, 2010; September 30, 2010.
18. G. M. Booth and M. Z. Booth, "What American Schools Can Learn from Hogwarts School of Witchcraft and Wizardry," *Phi Delta Kappa* (December 2003): 310–15, at 313.
19. J. Conn, "What Can Clinical Teachers Learn from *Harry Potter and the Philosopher's Stone?*" *Medical Education* 36 (2002): 1176–81, at 1177; Woolfolk, 1998 as quoted by Conn: 1177.

20. *Ibid.*: 1179.
21. L. Hopkins, "*Harry Potter* and the Acquisition of Knowledge," in G. L. Anatol (ed.), *Reading Harry Potter: Critical Essays* (Westport, CT: Praeger, 2003): 25–34, at 28.
22. OP[B]: 578.
23. *Ibid.*: 579.
24. CS[B]: 168.
25. OP[B]: 644.
26. HP[B]: 242.
27. OP[B]: 746–7.
28. *Ibid.*: 427–8.
29. *Ibid.*: 430.
30. *Ibid.*: 142.
31. *Ibid.*: 428.
32. *Ibid.*
33. *Ibid.*: 448.
34. *Ibid.*: 321.
35. *Ibid.*: 452.
36. *Ibid.*: 454.
37. HP[B]: 23.
38. PS[B]: 62.
39. *Ibid.*: 99.
40. *Ibid.*: 102.
41. N. Culpeper, *Culpeper's Complete Herbal and English Physician* [1814] (Glenwood, IL: Meyerbooks, 1990).
42. Asphodel, the only flower that blooms in hell, is much beloved by poets. It covers the Elysian meads. From Sir Thomas Browne 1658—*The dead are made to eat Asphodels about the Elysian meadows*. From Pope St Cecilia's Day 1713—*Happy souls who dwell in yellow meads of asphodel* (*Oxford English Dictionary*, 28th US printing, 1989: 124). William Carlos Williams wrote a long poem *Asphodel, That Greeny Flower*, confessing his marital indiscretions and seeking "abiding love in the gathering shadows of death."
43. Culpeper: 218–19.
44. OP[B]: 210.
45. Culpeper: 93.
46. OP[B]: 340.
47. Culpeper: 127.
48. HP[B]: 351.
49. GF[B]: 517.
50. *Ibid.*: 448.
51. M. K. Grimes, "Harry Potter: Fairy Tale Prince, Real Boy, and Archetypal Hero," in L. A. Whited (ed.), *The Ivory Tower and Harry Potter* (Columbia, MO: University of Missouri Press, 2002): 89–122, at 104.
52. HP[B]: 113.
53. OP[B]: 229.

54. T. G. Benedek, "From Bizarre Experiments to Informed Consent," Abstract #45, *38th Annual Meeting of the American Osler Society*, May 4–7, 2008.
55. OP[B]: 624.
56. Highfield: 275.
57. S. Black, "Harry Potter: A Magical Prescription for Just about Anyone," *Journal of Adolescent and Adult Literacy* 46(7) (April 2003): 540–4.
58. R. Charon, "Bearing Witness: Sontag and the Body," *New England Journal of Medicine* 352(8) (2005): 756.
59. S. Sontag, *Illness as Metaphor* (New York: Farrar, Straus and Giroux, 1978): 3.
60. H. W. Haggard, *Mystery, Magic and Medicine: The Rise of Medicine from Superstition to Science* (Garden City, NY: Doubleday, Doran and Company, 1933): 5.
61. A. C. Clarke, "Hazards of Prophecy: The Failure of Imagination," Chapter 2 in *Profiles of the Future: A Inquiry into the Limits of the Possible* (New York: Holt, Rinehart and Winston, 1984): 27–39, at 36.
62. GF[B]: 531.

11

Harry Potter and the Myriad Mothers: The Maternal Figure as Lioness, Witch, and Wardrobe

Roslyn Weaver and Kimberley McMahon-Coleman

Families are important in the *Harry Potter* series. Harry's loss of his parents is a key focal point of the narrative, and the series is book-ended by scenes that focus on family. Book One[1] begins with Harry's placement as a baby into the Dursley family environment—the opening sentence of the series setting up the issue of families, normality, and belonging—while Book Seven[2] concludes with a scene about the adult Harry's own family with his wife and children.

A particular recurring theme is Harry's mother's love that protects and sustains him as he endures many trials and adventures. In this respect, mothering becomes a key concern throughout the series. In Harry's own life, the early loss of his heroic biological mother, Lily Potter, leads to a myriad of substitute mothers in both magical and Muggle worlds, ranging from the cruelly absurd (Aunt Petunia) to the loving provider (Mrs. Weasley) and the authoritative teacher (Professor McGonagall). Indeed, Harry's ongoing sense of his loss of immediate family is balanced by his gain of an alternative family in the staff and students of Hogwarts, as well as the Weasley family, who ultimately come to view him as one of their own. Throughout the series, Harry also learns of other maternal figures who are weak (Merope Riddle), neglectful (Eileen Prince), and eccentric (Mrs. Longbottom). Mothers, therefore, have an important role in the books. Beyond the covers of *Harry Potter*, J. K. Rowling's own media identity as a single mother and Cinderella figure played a large role in shaping the books in the public imagination. Depictions of motherhood in *Harry Potter* and a greater understanding of the roles and status of the women who perform motherhood duties are key investigative paths for analyzing the series.

Across the spectrum of positive and negative portrayals, three main types of mothering emerge in *Harry Potter*, although characters may occupy more than one category across the books: those mothers who protect and defend children, even to the point of death (the Lioness); those who reject and neglect children, failing entirely as mothers (the Witch); and those who care and provide for children, offering material—and moral—care (the Wardrobe). These category names are adapted from C. S. Lewis in recognition of both Lewis's and Rowling's status as classic British children's fantasy writers and also their similarities of writing about children who grow into maturity in magical worlds in the absence of their parents. Although other readings claim that there are serious flaws in the books in terms of gender and feminism, Rowling's multi-faceted depictions of mothers give the subject more depth than such analyses might suggest. Critical readers must recognize the complex issues at work in motherhood as represented in *Harry Potter*.

Gender and parenting in the *Harry Potter* series

Many critics have dismissed the gender roles in *Harry Potter* as outdated and narrow depictions that favor male over female characters,[3] while others assess the series more positively.[4] Given that gender has received much scholarly attention, the concern here lies with the specifics of the mothering role rather than a broad analysis of male and female depictions in *Harry Potter*.

The removal of the protagonist's parents is common in literature generally,[5] and the mother in particular is a frequent casualty in children's literature and fairy tales.[6] In Rowling's series, Harry lost his parents when he was a baby, and his interest in his biological family provides much of the emotional resonance of his adventures. John Kornfeld and Laurie Prothro note that Harry's search for his family is an important concern in the narrative.[7] Some critics have taken a psychoanalytic approach to the series,[8] while other work has applied a Kristevan reading to the novels.[9] Fathers have received some passing attention in *Harry Potter* scholarship, with critics remarking on Harry's many substitute father figures.[10]

However, given the narrative focus on Harry's mother's love, it seems reasonable to pay particular attention to the mothers in the novels. This analysis is informed by Nancy Felipe Russo's 1976 work critiquing the "motherhood mandate," where a "good mother" remains at home or feels guilty for working.[11] One view of motherhood sees it as a woman's "single destiny and justification in life."[12] Traditional motherhood stereotypes include caring for the family and the home environment, operating as a moral guide, and nurturing children as a preferably full-time occupation.[13] As Lawrence Ganong and Marilyn Coleman note, "This myth of motherhood contends, among other things, that mothers are either all good or all bad. They are either perfectly loving, kind, patient, and giving, or they are rejecting, cold, and controlling."[14] Within popular perceptions of family structures, married mothers have typically fared better in positive stereotypes than stepmothers, divorced mothers, and unmarried mothers.[15] Rowling herself has critiqued the marginalization of single mothers in politics.[16]

Harry experiences a range of familial environments, beginning with the Dursleys, moving to Hogwarts as an alternative home, and then finding substitute parents in the Weasleys, an act that ultimately augurs the start of his own family with Ginny Weasley. Throughout the series, his mother's love becomes the standard against which maternal roles are measured. Although Harry is an orphan, his interactions with other characters provide the reader with a myriad of mothering figures. These characters perform roles popularly associated with mothering: comfort, advice, discipline, moral guidance, and care. This discussion of mother figures largely follows Harry's progression across homes from the Dursleys to Hogwarts to the Weasleys and concludes with a look at the ideal mother in the series, together with the related discourse of mothering outside the covers of the books.

The Lioness

The mother as Lioness is a protector and defender of children, even to the point of death. The primary representative of this type is Lily Potter, whose invisible presence throughout the series offers an epitome of motherhood. Although Rowling reveals very little of Lily Potter, it is clear that Harry's mother was a gifted witch, and that she was willing to sacrifice herself to save her infant son. This act causes Voldemort's curse to backfire, making Harry the only person known to have survived the Unforgivable killing curse, and marking him with the scar that is visible proof of the bond created between Harry and Voldemort. Lily's sacrifice offers Harry ongoing protection as a "shield" around him,[17] as even Voldemort must admit that a mother's love contains powerful magic: "His mother left upon him the traces of her sacrifice ... this is old magic."[18] As M. Katherine Grimes notes:

Lily is her son's savior. [...] [She] returns to Harry when he is threatened by dementors; he hears her voice from the past. [...] And when

Voldemort tries to kill him again at the end of *Harry Potter and the Goblet of Fire*, the spirit of his mother comes from her killer's wand. It is she who gives him the instructions that save his life.[19]

Lily's Lioness traits of courage, sacrifice and love are themes repeated across other maternal figures later in the series, such as Barty Crouch's mother, who gives up her life to save her son. Indeed, the inclusion of another Lioness mother, Tonks, results in a new Harry figure in the concluding pages of the final book: Teddy Lupin. In a narrative move that is strongly reminiscent of Harry's own childhood, Teddy is orphaned when his mother, Tonks, dies beside her husband during the final battle against Voldemort in *The Deathly Hallows*. This event appears to be Rowling's move to produce a circular plot, whereby the conclusion of the novel sees a new orphan boy, Teddy, striking out on adventures at Hogwarts. Teddy's upbringing in his maternal grand-parents' home, however, is implied to be vastly different to Harry's childhood. Frances Devlin-Glass writes, "The ultimate motherly act is to die for one's child,"[20] a point that Kornfeld and Prothro also suggest of Lily as well as Mrs. Crouch.[21]

Yet rather than simply self-sacrifice, the moral influence of the mother becomes a key theme across the *Harry Potter* novels. The more nuanced and arguably more idealized versions of mothers through-out the series are not stereotyped into one role. Thus, as the story progresses, it becomes clear that Lily demonstrated not only courage but also the traditional motherhood trait of moral guidance that aligns with the Wardrobe-mother figure: she was pure, loving, and protective, and she brought out the best in those around her. Throughout the course of the series readers learn that Lily was close to her sister Petunia, at least until she left for Hogwarts, and that she had a good influence on the young Severus Snape[22] and on the somewhat narcissistic adolescent version of James Potter.[23] Her influence on Harry is also notable: "his deepest nature is much more like his mother's,"[24] and Harry often draws on this knowledge of his mother's goodness and sacrifice as he makes his own decisions in life. In self-sacrifice, and in moral influence, Lily remains the standard of motherhood against which all other maternal figures in the series are measured.

The Witch

Although Lily is the key mother in the series, it is her sister Petunia Dursley who offers the first major example of motherhood to the reader. Throughout the novels Petunia is contrasted unfavorably with

Lily. The opening lines of the first novel position the Dursley nuclear family as one that values normality and conformity:

> Mr and Mrs Dursley, of number four, Privet Drive, were proud to say that they were perfectly normal, thank you very much. They were the last people you'd expect to be involved in anything strange or mysterious, because they just didn't hold with such nonsense.[25]

The reader quickly becomes aware that the Dursleys are far from the ideal family with their narrow-minded rejection of difference and imagination. Petunia is rarely differentiated from her partner and child, and rarely mentions her departed sister throughout the series, instead denouncing her as a "freak," "strange," and "*abnormal.*"[26] Even though Petunia prizes "normality" above all else, her refusal to offer Harry anything more than very rudimentary food, shelter, schooling, and clothing is closely aligned with traditional "wicked witch" or evil stepmother stereotypes in fairy tales, as others have noted.[27] It is ironic, therefore, that her fury at Harry and his "kind" is all because of the "abnormality" of her sister, a witch whose selection to attend Hogwarts led to their ultimate estrangement. Rowling's descriptions of Petunia—"thin and blonde and had nearly twice the usual amount of neck"[28]—reinforce Petunia's deficient character in the same manner that traditional fairy tales often demarcated good and evil by physical appearance.

Petunia proves unable to mother either son or nephew appropriately, failing as a mother by infantilizing and spoiling her biological son Dudley while neglecting her nephew Harry. Indeed, a number of critics have suggested that her neglect of Harry constitutes child abuse.[29] Petunia therefore embodies the second motherhood type, the Witch, which is used here in its traditional sense as an evil female figure, rather than Rowling's strictly gendered usage (witches and wizards compared to Muggles). In Rowling's work, the mother as Witch neglects and rejects children, whether physically or morally, ignoring or even attacking their welfare in ways that widely diverge from the motherhood mandate of moral guidance and nurturing. Petunia does enforce discipline, but only subjectively (to Harry), and never fairly.

Harry's time in the Dursley household introduces the idea of the mother as Witch, and when he moves away to attend Hogwarts, it becomes clear that Petunia is not alone in bad mothering. In this category, Petunia is joined by Narcissa Malfoy, Eileen Prince, and Merope Riddle, all of whom prove unable to nurture and guide and protect their children. The measure of mothering (and parenting) success that Rowling uses throughout the series is the children, and Dudley is a mirror of his parents: insufferably cruel and small-minded. Dudley is a failure, and therefore his parents are as well. Like Dudley, the sons of Narcissa, Eileen, and Merope inherit the sins of their mothers. Draco, Snape, and Voldemort (Tom Riddle) are boys who lack a moral compass, a position that is traditionally occupied by the mother. Dudley and Draco both suffer an excess of maternal affection that is not tempered by moral discipline, while Snape and Voldemort suffer neglect and rejection from their mothers. Their family background is again less than ideal, and in many ways influences their choices. It is implied that the "cross and sullen" Eileen Prince[30] grows up to be a neglectful mother for Snape,[31] while the dysfunctional Merope is responsible for the ultimate villain of the series, Voldemort. This is particularly evident in that Voldemort's disadvantaged birth with an unstable, sole parent is largely blamed for his later choices. Merope lacked Lily's courage, and instead "chose death in spite of a son who needed her."[32] Elizabeth Heilman and Trevor Donaldson have also noted this theme, writing that Merope's "poor mothering" is a likely cause of Voldemort's evil:

> The central theme of the novels, the battle between good Harry and bad Tom seems to have roots in their mothers—the good, self-sacrificing, pretty, charming mother Lily and the bad, self-destructive, failed, "plain, pale" mother, Merope.[33]

Rowling appears to be making a case for nurture over nature in such family environments, with a particular exception of Harry, whose ability to make positive choices and develop into a hero clearly happens despite his extremely negative family environment as a child.

As much as these mothers fail their children, some do move beyond the Witch category because they fulfill the motherhood mandate of lavishing sacrificial love on their child. Dudley and Draco are maligned throughout the series as petty thugs who victimize other children, yet Rowling does develop this characterization at later stages to depict the boys with more sympathy. Whatever their other faults, Petunia and Narcissa do display great love for their sons, and perhaps it is this relatively stable nuclear family upbringing with doting mothers willing to sacrifice themselves for their sons that redeems them in some way. Other sons find redemption because of their own love for others, despite their mother's shortcomings. For example,

Snape's love for Lily is the sole reason for his redemptive acts in the series, highlighting again her elevated position as moral guide.

The Wardrobe

As Harry attends Hogwarts, he comes into contact with a broader range of people and thus a variety of mother figures, and it is here that readers see a third distinct mother figure: the Wardrobe. The Wardrobe figure provides material care and comfort for Harry and other children. Indeed, the Hogwarts setting becomes a kind of substitute family, complete with Dumbledore and Professor McGonagall cast in the role of parents. As with the other students, Harry is sorted into one of four houses that represent the home environment, where a student's "house will be something like your family within Hogwarts."[34] Deborah De Rosa points out that material caring and provision are evident in Hogwarts in that "the departure from the childhood 'home' effects a period of physical nurture rather than a time of fasting and deprivation."[35] Ruthann Mayes-Elma suggests that the only alternatives to mothering for female characters in the series are stepmothers and teachers.[36] Yet the series allows the maternal role to be filled by any female character, including the teacher Professor McGonagall, Head of Gryffindor House, whose position as disciplinarian and advisor is no less genuine than that offered by those women with biological ties to the children.

The main example of the Wardrobe figure at Hogwarts is thus Professor McGonagall. From the outset, Harry's Head of House (a position referred to in some real-life boarding schools as a "House Mother") is introduced as a "sensible person"[37] whose beliefs are in stark contrast to the Dursleys. Interestingly, her argument with Dumbledore regarding leaving Harry in the Dursleys' care centers on Petunia's mothering capabilities, or lack thereof:

> Dumbledore—you can't. I've been watching them all day. You couldn't find two people who are less like us. And they've got this son— I saw him kicking his mother all the way up the street, screaming for sweets.[38]

Professor McGonagall is depicted as strict, stoic, sensible, and protective. Heilman notes that she is "something of a mother figure, concerned that students get enough sleep and stay well."[39] Professor McGonagall also occasionally shows affection for students in her care, especially Harry.

Alongside Professor McGonagall in the capacity as Wardrobe stands Mrs. Longbottom, whose no-nonsense disciplinarian strategies are often viewed as anachronistic and, in some cases, ill-judged. Mrs. Longbottom is established first and foremost as a Witch, and is initially portrayed as harsh and authoritarian, openly criticizing her grandson Neville for bringing "shame" on his family[40] and constantly reminding him of his father's standing as a wizard, which the hapless Neville struggles to honor. She is generally configured only in terms of her harshness and her unusual dress sense, which often features a tall hat topped with a stuffed vulture, a long green dress, a fox-fur scarf, and large red handbag. As the series progresses, however, readers learn that Mrs. Longbottom has not only provided material care for Neville but also facilitated his ongoing relationship with his ailing parents, who no longer recognize him.

It is through the safe space and family-like structure of Gryffindor that Harry comes into contact with the Weasleys. Harry's *de facto* family is the Weasleys, who provide Harry with the stable setting that foreshadows the beginning of his own family with Ginny. Mrs. Weasley is the most obvious example of the Wardrobe, providing material and moral care to Harry as well as her own children, despite the Weasleys' poverty. She considers Harry to be "as good as" her own son[41] and sends him gifts for Christmas as she does her own children.[42] Devlin-Glass calls Mrs. Weasley "a suburban earth mother with a fine line in motherly magic [...] She invariably understands Harry's emotional needs and is happy to be the surrogate Mother that Mrs Dursley is too fearful to become."[43] Kornfeld and Prothro highlight Mrs. Weasley's "nurturing" qualities of "cooking, cleaning, and caring for the children,"[44] exemplifying the traditional household in which mothers care for children at home while fathers work.[45] In this way, Mrs. Weasley fulfills the motherhood mandate of full-time mothering.

Although Mrs. Weasley becomes a substitute mother for Harry, Suzanne Lake argues that Harry enjoys the "good parent figures" of the Weasleys at a distance, "always one step removed from full access to and relatedness with them. Because of this, Harry exists in a state of continual longing and deprivation."[46] Similarly, Terri Doughty suggests that Mrs. Weasley's motherly role is as "a distant supplier of good food and knitted jumpers rather than a key figure in Harry's life."[47] However, although Harry is inevitably an "adopted" son of the Weasleys rather than a born one, the Weasleys' wholehearted embrace of Harry closes some of this distance and places him firmly within their family unit, a position that is made official when Harry marries Ginny at the series' conclusion. Rowling's depiction of Mrs. Weasley has drawn criticism from commentators who dismiss her as a failure as a mother, with several critics aligning Mrs. Weasley with Petunia as ineffective, over-involved mothers who cannot effectively manage their children.[48] This reading seems to miss the significant influence Mrs. Weasley has in Harry's life in providing support and stability. Furthermore, if the children are used as the measure of mothering, as Rowling implies, it is clear that the goodness and courage of all her children prove Mrs. Weasley successful in her efforts.

While Professor McGonagall, Mrs. Longbottom, and Mrs. Weasley appear to function as Wardrobe-mothers, providing material care for children, each moves beyond this category to be Lioness as well. Readers learn Professor McGonagall was a member of the original Order of the Phoenix with the Potters, and throughout the series she is prepared to defend the children and the castle. Mrs. Longbottom also proves herself to be something of a Lioness, often defending Harry's actions and ultimately fighting against Voldemort and the fallen Ministry of Magic, after first hospitalizing one of Voldemort's Death Eaters. Heilman and Donaldson point out that:

> Mrs. Weasley, initially a narrowly written, exclusively domestically minded, worrying mother, seems transformed in the final battle of *Deathly Hallows*. She sheds the apron and oven mitts for a fierce and aggressive tone as she engages Bellatrix Lestrange in a duel [...]. Rowling's most matriarchal character finally leaves "The Burrow" and involves herself first-hand in violent conflict with the Death Eaters.[49]

Although Heilman and Donaldson reject this role shift as simply reinforcing Mrs. Weasley's function as protective mother,[50] it does seem that there is a latitude of movement afforded to the mothering role at least that suggests Rowling's gender roles are not as narrow and stereotypical as others might argue.

Future mothers

Two witches are explicitly positioned as the mothers of the future who embody the best of the Lioness and the Wardrobe: Hermione and Ginny. As the series closes, readers briefly read about the children of Harry and Ginny, and Ron and Hermione, as they begin their journey to Hogwarts. Hermione comes under attack from several critics who dismiss her as unconvincing or passive,[51] yet Mayes-Elma suggests otherwise: "Hermione enacts her agency through mothering many times throughout the text. When Harry or Ron is sick or injured, Hermione is the caregiver, helper, and worrier."[52] Heilman and Donaldson write that Hermione adopts "an overwhelmingly matriarchal role" in the quest section of the final book, providing food and assistance for Harry and Ron.[53] Ginny is a second example of future mothers, and is also, and perhaps significantly, redheaded like Lily. Both Hermione and Ginny display courage and loyalty through-out the series. The importance of stable families and devoted mothers is a theme that is never lost within the narrative, and Rowling's conclusion highlights the loving support and moral guidance that Hermione and Ginny offer as mothers.

Rather than being confined to stereotypes, doomed to perform one role only, Rowling's characters therefore represent a broad range of choices women may make in the maternal role. This option indi-cates that there is some depth to gender roles in the series, at least for females. These characters who occupy and move across a spectrum of maternal types suggests a flexibility of identity available to the myriad mothers in the *Harry Potter* books.

Mothering beyond the *Harry Potter* series

Beyond these three types of fictional mothers, and Hermione and Ginny as future mothers, however, it is worth concluding with a note about another discourse about mothering that cannot be separated from the *Harry Potter* series: that of Rowling as mother. If Lily is the invisible presence whose motherly love marks every part of the series, the presence of Rowling and her mother have also left ghostly traces of a motherhood discourse around the series itself. From the early media attention on the success of the novels, coverage focused on and in some ways created Rowling's iconic status as an impoverished single mother, invoking a discourse of triumph through adversity and poverty, in which a single mother overcomes her difficulties to build a better life for her child. Rowling has dismissed media reports of more dramatic details, such as living in an unheated flat in Edinburgh,[54] yet in her own words she frames her experience in decidedly fairytale terms:

> [In 1997] I was a single parent with a four-year-old daughter, teaching part-time but living mainly on benefits, in a rented flat. Eleven months later, I was a published author who had secured a lucrative publishing deal in the US, and bought my first ever property: a three-bedroom house with a garden.[55]

Rowling's status as single mother was not the only discourse of mothering around the books. Media reports have also highlighted the influence her mother's death had on the series, a fact Rowling herself notes in an interview when speaking of her mother's death six months after first writing of the orphaned Harry:

> And [my mother's death] made an enormous difference because I was living it, I was living what I had just—what I had just written. The Mirror of Erised is absolutely entirely drawn from my own experience of losing a parent. "Five more minutes, just, please, God, give me five more minutes."[56]

Rowling's own shifting maternal identity in the media, from Cinderella figure to single mother advocate, perhaps reflects the possibilities afforded to the range of mothers in her *Harry Potter* novels.

Notes

1. PS[B].
2. DH[B].
3. M. Cherland, "Harry's Girls: Harry Potter and the Discourse of Gender," *Journal of Adolescent and Adult Literacy* 52(4) (2008/9): 273–82; F. Devlin-Glass, "Contesting Binarisms in *Harry Potter*: Creative Rejigging, or Gender Tokenism?" *English in Australia* 144 (2005): 50–63; E. E. Heilman, "Blue Wizards and Pink Witches: Representations of Gender Identity and Power," in E. E. Heilman (ed.), *Critical Perspectives on Harry Potter* (New York: Routledge, 2003): 221–39; E. E. Heilman and T. Donaldson, "From Sexist to (sort-of) Feminist: Representations of Gender in the Harry Potter Series," in E. E. Heilman (ed.), *Critical Perspectives on Harry Potter*, 2nd edn (New York: Routledge, 2009): 139–61; T. Pugh and D. L. Wallace, "Heteronormative Heroism and Queering the School Story in J. K. Rowling's *Harry Potter* Series," *Children's Literature Association Quarterly* 31(3) (2006): 260–81; J. Zipes, *Sticks and Stones: The Troublesome Success of Children's Literature from Slovenly Peter to Harry Potter* (New York: Routledge, 2001).
4. C. A. Cothran, "Lessons in Transfiguration: Allegories of Male Identity in Rowling's *Harry Potter* Series," in C. W. Hallett (ed.), *Scholarly Studies in Harry Potter: Applying Academic Methods to a Popular Text* (Lewiston, NY: Edwin Mellen Press, 2005): 123–34; E. T. Dresang, "Hermione Granger and the Heritage of Gender," in L. A. Whited (ed.), *The Ivory Tower and Harry Potter: Perspectives on a Literary Phenomenon* (Columbia, MO: University of Missouri Press, 2002): 211–42; M. Fry, "Heroes and Heroines: Myth and Gender Roles in the Harry Potter Books," *New Review of Children's Literature and Librarianship* 7(1) (2001): 157–67.
5. R. E. Rothenberg, "The Orphan Archetype," *Psychological Perspectives* 14(2) (1983): 181–94.
6. M. F. Apseloff, "Abandonment: The New Realism of the Eighties," in

S. Egoff, G. Stubbs, R. Ashley and W. Sutton (eds.), *Only Connect: Readings on Children's Literature*, 3rd edn (Toronto: Oxford University Press, 1996): 359–64; S. Henneberg, "Moms Do Badly, But Grandmas Do Worse: The Nexus of Sexism and Ageism in Children's Classics," *Journal of Aging Studies* 24 (2010): 125–34; M. Warner, "The Absent Mother: Women against Women in Old Wives' Tales," in S. Egoff, G. Stubbs, R. Ashley, and W. Sutton (eds.), *Only Connect: Readings on Children's Literature*, 3rd edn (Toronto: Oxford University Press, 1996): 278–87.

7. J. Kornfeld and L. Prothro, "Comedy, Conflict, and Community: Home and Family in *Harry Potter*," in E. E. Heilman (ed.), *Critical Perspectives on Harry Potter* (New York: Routledge, 2003): 187–202.

8. S. Lake, "Object Relations in *Harry Potter*," *Journal of the American Academy of Psychoanalysis and Dynamic Psychiatry* 31(3) (2003): 509–20; K. Noel-Smith, "Harry Potter's Oedipal Issues," *Psychoanalytic Studies* 3(2) (2001): 199–207.

9. A. Mills, "Harry Potter and the Terrors of the Toilet," *Children's Literature in Education* 37(1) (2006): 1–13.

10. Devlin-Glass, *op. cit.*; T. Doughty, "Locating Harry Potter in the 'Boys' Book' Market," in L. A. Whited (ed.), *The Ivory Tower and Harry Potter: Perspectives on a Literary Phenomenon* (Columbia, MO: University of Missouri Press, 2002): 243–57; M. K. Grimes, "Harry Potter: Fairy Tale Prince, Real Boy, and Archetypal Hero," in L. A. Whited (ed.), *The Ivory Tower and Harry Potter: Perspectives on a Literary Phenomenon* (Columbia, MO: University of Missouri Press, 2002): 89–122; M. Nikolajeva, "Harry Potter and the Secrets of Children's Literature," in E. E. Heilman (ed.), *Critical Perspectives on Harry Potter*, 2nd edn (New York: Routledge, 2009): 225–42.

11. N. F. Russo, "The Motherhood Mandate," *Journal of Social Issues* 32(3) (1976): 143–53, at 150.

12. A. Rich, *Of Woman Born: Motherhood as Experience and Institution*, 10th Anniversary edn (New York: W. W. Norton & Company, 1986): 34.

13. L. H. Ganong and M. Coleman, "The Content of Mother Stereotypes," *Sex Roles* 32(7/8) (1995): 495–512; K. A. Gorman and B. A. Fritzsche, "The Good-Mother Stereotype: Stay at Home (or Wish that You Did!)," *Journal of Applied Social Psychology* 32 (2002): 2190–201.

14. Ganong and Coleman: 496.

15. H. E. Bullock, K. F. Wyche, and W. R. Williams, "Media Images of the Poor," *Journal of Social Issues* 57(2) (2001): 229–46; E. M. DiLapi, "Lesbian Mothers and the Motherhood Hierarchy," *Journal of Homosexuality* 18(1) (1989): 101–21; Ganong and Coleman, *op. cit.*

16. J. K. Rowling, "The Single Mother's Manifesto," *The Times*, April 14, 2010, available at: http://www.timesonline.co.uk/tol/comment/columnists/guest_contributors/article7096786.ece (accessed August 25, 2010).

17. OP[B]: 737.

18. GF[B]: 566.

19. Grimes: 115.
20. Devlin-Glass: 61.
21. Kornfeld and Prothro: 191.
22. DH[B]: 538, 540–5, 593.
23. OP[B]: 570, 576, 591.
24. DH[B]: 549.
25. PS[B]: 7.
26. *Ibid.*: 44.
27. Grimes: 115; R. Mayes-Elma, *Females and Harry Potter: Not All that Empowering* (Lanham, MD: Rowman & Littlefield, 2006): 100.
28. PS[B]: 7.
29. J. Lacoss, "Of Magicals and Muggles: Reversals and Revulsions at Hogwarts," in L. A. Whited (ed.), *The Ivory Tower and Harry Potter: Perspectives on a Literary Phenomenon* (Columbia, MO: University of Missouri Press, 2002): 67–88, at 80; F. Mendlesohn, "Crowning the King: Harry Potter and the Construction of Authority," in L. A. Whited (ed.), *The Ivory Tower and Harry Potter: Perspectives on a Literary Phenomenon* (Columbia: MO: University of Missouri Press, 2002): 159-81, at 162; R. Natov, "Harry Potter and the Extraordinariness of the Ordinary," in L. A. Whited (ed.), *The Ivory Tower and Harry Potter: Perspectives on a Literary Phenomenon* (Columbia, MO: University of Missouri Press, 2002): 125–39, at 126; M. Pharr, "In Medias Res: Harry Potter as Hero-in-Progress," in L. A. Whited (ed.), *The Ivory Tower and Harry Potter: Perspectives on a Literary Phenomenon* (Columbia, MO: University of Missouri Press, 2002): 53–66, at 57.
30. HP[B]: 502.
31. DH[B]: 538.
32. HP[B]: 246.
33. Heilman and Donaldson: 153.
34. PS[B]: 85.
35. D. De Rosa, "Wizardly Challenges to and Affirmations of the Initiation Paradigm in *Harry Potter*," in E. E. Heilman (ed.), *Critical Perspectives on Harry Potter* (New York: Routledge, 2003): 163–84, at 168.
36. Mayes-Elma, *op. cit.*
37. PS[B]: 14.
38. *Ibid.*: 15.
39. Heilman: 225.
40. PA[B]: 201.
41. OP[B]: 85.
42. CS[B]: 159.
43. Devlin-Glass: 61.
44. Kornfeld and Prothro: 189.
45. Heilman and Donaldson: 153; Kornfeld and Prothro: 189.
46. Lake: 511.
47. Doughty: 252.
48. Heilman and Donaldson, *op. cit.*; Mayes-Elma, *op. cit.*
49. Heilman and Donaldson: 143.

50. *Ibid.*: 144.
51. Cherland, *op. cit.*; Devlin-Glass, *op. cit.*
52. Mayes-Elma: 97.
53. Heilman and Donaldson: 147.
54. J. K. Rowling, "Harry Potter and Me" (2001), available at: http://www.accio-quote.org/articles/2001/1201-bbc-hpandme.htm (accessed August 25, 2010).
55. Rowling (2010), *op. cit.*
56. Rowling (2001), *op. cit.*

12

"I Knew a Girl Once, whose Hair...": Dumbledore and the Closet

Jim Daems

When J. K. Rowling announced at a reading at Carnegie Hall in October 2007 that Albus Dumbledore is gay—an outing that "must count as the most unlikely in literary history"[1]—positive and negative responses were immediate.[2] Popular responses generally divided into two clearly defined stances: those seeing Rowling's announcement favorably praised her for creating a positive portrayal of a gay character; unfavorable responses mainly came from the Christian right, who had already, in large part, condemned the *Harry Potter* books and films for their positive representation of wizardry and magic. For the Christian right, Dumbledore's sexuality now became another reason to keep impressionable children away from the contaminating effects of these works. Academics soon entered the debate, and, while generally supportive of Rowling's announcement, began to examine critically the underlying premises of the controversy created by the now gay Dumbledore. While readers can be sympathetic to the arguments for acceptance that the debate has prompted, significant problems exist in embracing Rowling's outing of Dumbledore: first, as literary scholars, readers must be aware of the old critical notion of the intentional fallacy; second, positive responses rely on a far too broad definition of "queer," forcing them into tenuous allegorical readings of the *Harry Potter* series; and, finally, positive and negative reactions often both rely on a historically problematic association of wizards, werewolves, and homosexuals. In effect, without textual support for Rowling's claim, positive readings are trapped within negative stereotypes in attempting to see Dumbledore's sexuality as a step towards greater cultural acceptance. Readers need to be wary of potentially reinforcing these stereotypes.

It is worth recounting the events leading to Rowling's announcement. Apparently, the outing was prompted while Rowling reviewed the film script for *Harry Potter and the Half-Blood Prince*. Rowling states, "I was in a script read-through for the sixth film, and they had Dumbledore saying 'I knew a girl once, whose hair...' I had to write a little note in the margin and slide it along to the scriptwriter: 'Dumbledore's gay!'"[3] Rowling also "ensured director David Yates was made aware of the truth about her character."[4] Yates' mistake, however, is understandable. What is significant here is the fact that the marginal comment only results in an erasure in the script—a troubling silence. No correction occurs beyond removing the phrase. As Yates noted shortly after Rowling's announcement, there were not to be "any changes to the way Dumbledore is portrayed in" *Harry Potter and the Half-Blood Prince*.[5] The potentially heterosexual reminiscence is replaced by an authorial assertion of homosexuality in contexts exterior to the works themselves, evident in the public reassertion at Carnegie Hall. If there is a closet in the *Harry Potter* books and films, then, it is not the one occupied by Harry under the stairs, but that of Dumbledore who is nowhere allowed to express his feelings for Grindelwald. Dumbledore is gay only because his creator, as the series ends, tells readers he is. However, literary criticism teaches readers that an author's statements of intention or meaning must be assessed against the work itself—or ignored completely. This requirement allows a fascinating opportunity for students, many of whom grew up reading the books and watching the films, to engage critically with Rowling's announcement. In the case of the *Harry Potter* books and films, critics can find no support for this claim. More troubling is the fact that the debate this claim sparks comes to rely on stereotypes, and it is here that critics must be most wary.

Popular responses to Rowling's announcement

Positive popular responses to Rowling's announcement are intriguing. For example, gay rights advocate Peter Tatchell saw the outing as a step forward, but added,

> I am disappointed that she [Rowling] did not make Dumbledore's sexuality explicit in the Harry Potter book [*sic*]. Making it obvious would have sent a much more powerful message of understanding and acceptance.[6]

However, Mary Bousted, general secretary of the Association of Teachers and Lecturers, disagrees with Tatchell: "I am glad that she didn't write his sexuality into the stories. Dumbledore's sexuality has absolutely nothing to do with the fact that he is a headmaster of Hogwarts."[7] Similarly, Melissa Anelli, webmaster of the Leaky Cauldron, reported that a strong majority of those that contacted her were "delighted" with Rowling's announcement. Anelli believes that Dumbledore's outing is enough in itself, and praises Rowling for presenting "it as matter of fact. She is not saying it's a reason to level judgement against him. It's just something else about the character, like the fact that he is a teacher."[8] These responses point to certain limitations relating to the outing of Dumbledore. Rowling tells readers that Dumbledore is gay, but critics really cannot find any explicit evidence of this in either the books or the films. "Making it obvious would have sent a much more powerful message"[9] belies the fact that the books and films really send no message at all. The authorial comment now only points to a closeted Dumbledore—that is "the reality of gay people" even in the Potterverse.[10] As Tison Pugh and David L. Wallace note, "Ultimately, it was J. K. Rowling who put Dumbledore in the closet, and she now receives credit for taking him out of it."[11] Anelli's and Bousted's comments only support this closeting.

This is evident also in the representation of "fact" in Anelli's and Bousted's responses. While supportive of Rowling's announcement, both believe the posthumous "fact" of Dumbledore's sexuality should not be, as it indeed is not, explicitly stated in the books. Both women also, curiously, relate Dumbledore's sexuality to his profession as a teacher. The point seems to be that one's private life should be kept private. Now, on one level, it does not matter—in the sense that a teacher can be gay or straight and still be a good or bad teacher. Yet, what can be implied in statements such as these is that any representation of Dumbledore as gay would be somewhat disconcerting—for example, there is nothing sexually explicit in Ron's coming of age. Yet, one can ask if it is necessary to the books, or is it just a "matter of fact" that could go unsaid? Clearly, Dumbledore's feelings for Grindelwald could be expressed in much the same way (with some allowance for maturity), without being disconcerting for readers. Indeed, he need only say somewhere in the books that he unambiguously loves Grindelwald. Still, for Rowling to make the announcement suggests that she feels it does matter now that the series of books has ended. While the announcement reinforces Rowling's claim that her novels are a "prolonged argument for tolerance,"[12] the posthumous outing becomes a sort of misappropriated *Out Week* or Absolutely Queer broadside tactic.

However, critics should recall Adrienne Rich's discussion of being a lesbian and a teacher, as so many of the responses to Rowling's announcement touch on Dumbledore's purported sexuality and his profession:

> I have felt my identity as a feminist threatening to some, welcome to others; but my identity as a lesbian is something that many people would prefer not to know about. And this experience has reminded me of what I should never have let myself forget: that invisibility is not just a matter of being told to keep your private life private; it's the attempt to fragment you, to prevent you from integrating love and work and feelings and ideas, with the empowerment that that can bring.[13]

Anelli and Bousted impose this invisibility on Dumbledore; however, to a degree, that is a consequence of Rowling's decision not to mention his sexuality in the books. Including it in the series would certainly have empowered both the representation of her character and the identities of her queer readers. Rich's comment and Anelli's and Bousted's statements also relate this Harry Potter controversy to an old debate within the gay community that goes back to at least the first Mattachine convention in 1953:

> The assimilationists insisted that gay people are just the same as heterosexuals except for what they do in bed. The appropriate strategy for attaining equality, then, was to stress the common humanity of homosexuals and heterosexuals and keep sexuality as such private. It was an approach founded on an implicit contract with the larger society wherein gay identity, culture, and values would be disavowed (or at least concealed) in return for the *promise* of equal treatment [...]. Tolerance would be earned by making difference unspeakable.[14]

This sort of compromise was most notable in the U.S. military's policy of "don't ask, don't tell," and it can only lead to further representations of "gay" characters such as Dumbledore in children's literature.

Instead, Dumbledore's invisibility and fragmentation empower negative responses to the outing. Rebecca Combs of the Christian Coalition of America states, "It's not a good example for our children, who really like the books and the movies. I think it encourages homosexuality [...]. I would never allow my own children or grandchildren to read the books or watch the movies, and other parents should do so too."[15] As part of a wide-ranging, and nonsensical, homophobic rant, Laurie Higgins ties Harry Potter in with,

> The movement [...] to include positive portrayals of homosexuals and the transgendered in all textbooks from kindergarten on up. I have no objections to textbooks including the important invention and discovery

of a homosexual or transgender person so long as their homosexuality or transgenderism is not mentioned.[16]

A troubling similarity exists between these condemnations of a gay Dumbledore and the comments of praise; in both cases, what these commentators are reacting to is not in the books or films. If anything, the *Potter* books and films represent the "reality" of gay people for the Christian right—closeted—while pointing to the hypocrisy of still seeing something that, in Higgins' case, "is not mentioned" as a problem of conspiratorial proportions. Readers are back to either the sin not to be named or the love that dare not speak its name. Both favorable and unfavorable responses converge, ultimately, in the closet.

How "queer" is Dumbledore?

Perhaps this is not entirely surprising. Following from Eve Kosofsky Sedgwick's assertion that the closet is still a defining feature of gay identity,[17] Andrew Buzny attempts to transcend this by arguing that, "Within a queer paradigm Dumbledore appears to exist beyond not only an in/out gay identity, but also the gay/straight binary perpetuated by the heterosexual matrix to substantiate its claims to intelligibility through an 'us' versus 'them' dichotomy."[18] This observation, to me, is giving Rowling too much credit with the hindsight provided by her announcement, and it would also be beyond her target audience's understanding of identity. The problem is, again, present in that, without textual evidence to support substantially queer readings, critics have relied on a very broad definition of "queer" in order to find some sort of evidence in light of Rowling's announcement. In relation to the current debate, this broad definition develops from Michael Bronski's pre-outing argument in "Queering Harry Potter." Bronski writes,

> The Harry Potter books are, in a word, queer. As used today, "queer" means "homosexual," but it has larger connotations too. The word also suggests a more generally deviant, nonconformist, renegade identity. In its oldest, original sense, queer means "deviating from the expected or normal; strange" or "odd or unconventional in behaviour."[19]

From Bronski's definition in order to support his argument that the *Harry Potter* books are "queer," it is conceivable to make almost anything "queer"—Christ is queer, for example, in the sense of "deviating from the expected or normal." Sedgwick makes this point more forcefully:

> a lot of the way I have used it [queer] so far in this dossier is to denote, almost simply, same-sex sexual object choice, lesbian or gay, whether or not it is organized around multiple criss-crossings of definitional lines. And given the historical and contemporary force of the prohibitions against *every* same-sex sexual expression, for anyone to disavow those meanings, or to displace them from the term's definitional center, would be to dematerialize any possibility of queerness itself.[20]

Buzny is aware of the problems created by Bronski's definition, and he works to remove the negative notions of abnormality from the definition by resorting to the notion of performativity: "It is imperative to recognize that gender and sexuality are performative; that is, they are not biologically inherent to a subject but are performed through an adherence to or negation of certain social norms."[21] Certainly, gender and sexuality are performative, and "eccentricities" and variations from the norms of behavior, dress, or speech may be termed queer—perhaps even abnormal by some—in this broad sense. However, critics need to confirm these performances by finding concrete evidence of homosexuality in the texts, not just "stereotypical clues"[22] that only call out for further explicit confirmation—and this includes confirmation beyond Rowling's announcement, even if her statement may be motivated by an awareness of queer readings by slash fans.[23] Otherwise, critics construct a queer Dumbledore that forever remains separate from Rowling's assertion that he is gay. As Pugh and Wallace note while defining their terms, it is conceivable that "one can be queer without being homosexual; likewise, one can be homosexual without being queer."[24] In a purely performative way, this is true. However, the two terms, following from Bronski's broad definition, do not seem to come together in Dumbledore as gay, and this does "dematerialize any possibility of queerness itself."[25]

In a sense, if "stereotypical clues" do provide critics with enough evidence to support Rowling's claim, these essentially work to make difference unspeakable. Difference remains in the closet—everyone knows that there are homosexuals, but to find that purported one in *Harry Potter* requires much more than the effortless reading Bronski claimed in 2003. As Pugh and Wallace state, "queer readings [...] must remain figurative and depend on queer readers bringing their own metatextual knowledge to the text to make the parallels."[26] Indeed, Bronski's 2007 article pulls away from even attempting to maintain his earlier parallels: "In *Harry Potter and the Deathly Hallows* the Potterverse becomes increasingly normalized [...]. At the end of the book, in a short epilogue, readers see that after the death of Voldemorte [sic] the world has returned to normal."[27] As the books became increasingly, assertively heteronormative, primarily because of the sexual coming-of-age of its young, straight characters, queerness was quashed. Then, Rowling made her announcement, which tends to confirm Dumbledore's sexuality as a deviant/abnormal eruption within the heteronormative Potterverse. Queer becomes the disem-powered term in the homo/hetero binary. There is no other place for the queer in *Harry Potter* because, as Sedgwick argues,

> "Queer" seems to hinge much more radically and explicitly on a person's undertaking particular, performative acts of experimental self-perception and filiation. A hypothesis worth making explicit: that there are important senses in which "queer" can signify only *when attached to the first person*. One possible corollary: that what it takes—all it takes—to make the description "queer" a true one is the impulsion *to* use it in the first person.[28]

Queer cannot signify within the Potterverse without being attached to Dumbledore in the first person. This connection is evident in the erasure of any sign of sexuality that occurred following Rowling's marginal comment on the screenplay of *Harry Potter and the Half-Blood Prince*. Pugh and Wallace effectively capture the dilemma that results: "Given the books' avowed interest in resisting cultural norma-tivity, the ways in which heteronormativity nonetheless contain queer readings points to its crushing ideological weight."[29] Pugh and Wallace's readings (2006 and 2008), as well as the contrast between Bronski's 2003 and 2007 articles, demonstrate how effective this containment is.

Historical parallels and negative stereotypes

Critics can further elucidate the difficulties posed by heteronormativity in *Harry Potter* by examining stereotypes in relation to historical links between magic, werewolves, and homosexuals (a term that is anachronistic in earlier time periods). Alan Bray's work highlights the negative associations which condemned the "sodomite" in early modern England. The "sodomite" was "part of a mythology, embrac-ing werewolves and basilisks, sorcerers, and devilry [...] and it was within its mould that the images of the sodomite were cast."[30] Within this context, no self-conscious identity could be developed—the "sodomite" was something entirely alien. Indeed, the first-person impulsion of self-conscious identity only developed, according to Bray, late in the seventeenth century with the Molly houses of London. The negative associations of the werewolf, witch, and "sodomite" still retain some of their force in readings of *Harry Potter* that engage with Rowling's outing of Dumbledore. This problem arises from the fact that in both the books and movies "wizards are only queer magically; they are never queer sexually."[31] As Pugh and Wallace state, in the diverse fantasy world that Rowling creates in the series, she "nonetheless never ventures into the realm of non-normative sexualities."[32]

How far, then, can critics press any allegorical reading of anything *Potter* as gay? For example, if critics do read werewolves as gay by linking the marginalization of werewolves in *Harry Potter* with the historical marginalization of gays and lesbians, they run into some troubling issues which hearken back to the historical connections that Bray calls our attention to. Pugh and Wallace highlight the underlying problem of this association:

> If werewolves thus serve as a queer figure within the world of the *Harry Potter* books, it becomes distressingly apparent that they must then also serve as figures of pederasty and child sexual abuse. Certainly, the texts invite a link between lycanthropic and homosexual hysteria surrounding the employment of werewolves and queers in schools.[33]

This is still a strong homophobic stereotype associating homosexuality with pederasty, which plays a key part in the movement to remove gay teachers from classrooms. This attitude may, in part, explain Anelli's and Bousted's "matter of fact" responses. As Pugh and Wallace argue, our queer readings are problematically contained by the heteronormative in the *Potter* series.[34] If critics associate werewolves and gay men, they reinforce the pederastic stereotype through Fenir Greyback's behavior. Equally troubling is the fact that, if critics look at a more favorable representation of a werewolf in the Potterverse, Lupin, they still cannot break away from these stereotypes:

> Because this sympathetic figure [Lupin] suffers a life of seclusion due to circumstances beyond his control, one might expect Lupin to condemn lupophobia as irrational and baseless discrimination; on the contrary, the reader sees that the prejudices against werewolves are neither hysterical nor unfounded. [...] From the initial congruency between werewolves and queers, the parallels slip increasingly into the realm of pederasty rather than of homosexuality [...]. Given the diseased nature of lycanthropes in the texts, the metaphor between werewolves and gay men marks all queers as quite literally sick.[35]

As Lupin is a sympathetic figure, the lack of condemnation here calls into question the overall "argument for tolerance" in the *Harry Potter* series, which is made more problematic now by the need to go back through the books as a result of Rowling's announcement. Clearly, readings that attempt to find parallels between characters in the *Harry Potter* series and homosexuals end up reinforcing some very negative and harmful stereotypes, feeding into calls from the Christian right that these works be kept away from children.

In fact, this example is further problematized by another statement made by a far from likeable character when Dudley taunts Harry with homophobic comments about his relationship with Cedric Diggory in *The Order of the Phoenix*. However, "Since Dudley, one of the most unappealing characters in the books, voices this homophobic jibe, it is clear that the books do not explicitly endorse homophobia."[36] This is not to conclude that Rowling is implicitly homophobic in this instance. It may be that Rowling is not openly condemning either lycophobia or homophobia because she wants her readers to exercise their own judgment—although, other than in the case of Lupin, it is difficult to sympathize with werewolves. However, what is also interesting here is how this homophobic passage relates to the issue of "stereotypical clues." Same-sex male desire is here associated with effeminization—Dudley's "high-pitched, whimpering voice" and Harry's tears. This does not make Harry queer, nor do Dumbledore's tears elsewhere in the works make him queer in a specifically homosexual sense. These two examples quoted above support Pugh and Wallace's argument regarding the crushing weight of the heteronormative in the *Harry Potter* series, which can be developed further by noting how this relates to what Hélène Cixous calls "patriarchal binary thought."[37] From her feminist perspective, Cixous demonstrates how the underlying binary of Western thought is the male/female pair and the positive and negative values ascribed to these. Furthermore,

> Cixous then goes on to locate *death* at work in this kind of thought. For one of the terms to acquire meaning [...] it must destroy the other. The "couple" cannot be left intact: it becomes a general battlefield where the struggle for signifying supremacy is forever re-enacted. In the end, victory is equated with activity and defeat with passivity; under patriarchy, the male is always the victor.[38]

This is, importantly, how homophobia works in conjunction with misogyny in Western culture—effeminize the gay male in order to condemn him by using the negative, disempowered feminine side of the patriarchal binary, precisely how Dudley attempts to enact "verbal dominance"[39] over Harry.

Binaries, homosexuality, and the death of Dumbledore

This approach allows a discussion of gender binaries and the value judgments that these create. Mary Eagleton's *Working with Feminist Criticism*, for example, includes some useful exercises to prompt students to think about gender and what readers accept as "normal." These can easily be expanded upon by adding in a consideration of homosexuality. Hence, the problem is much larger than just "heteronormative heroism" that Pugh and Wallace identify at work in the *Harry Potter* series; rather, it is a problem of language itself. As written by Rowling, Dumbledore cannot, contra Buzny, "resist the demands of heteronormativity."[40] It is not only with the death of Voldemort that the Potterverse returns to "normal"; if readers do see Dumbledore as gay, then his death also ensures this. Kenneth Kidd raises the key question: "Shouldn't the fact (if we can call it a fact) that he [Dumbledore] is now gay *and dead* give us pause?"[41] The character is dead, the books are done (though there is always a possibility of more), and the film series is now complete and unable to venture too far from the books. Indeed, following Rowling's announcement, Yates and producer David Barron stated that there would be no changes to Michael Gambon's portrayal of Dumbledore.[42] In effect, Rowling's posthumous announcement simultaneously outs Dumbledore while closing off the possibilities of reading him as gay. Perhaps, as Catherine Tosenberger states,

> Rowling appears to be unaware of the longstanding trope in literature and film—including early entries in the young adult genre to which her later books belong—that gay characters must be not just lonely and celibate but dead.[43]

In the erasure of "I knew a girl once whose hair..." readers are to assume that the absence of heterosexual reminiscence equates with its binary opposite—if there is no evidence of heterosexuality (the default position of "signifying supremacy"), then he must be homosexual (even though there is no evidence to support the latter). Hence, despite Rowling's announcement, there is a troubling silence in the books and films, but that silence is commensurate with the disempowered side of the binary that the homosexual conventionally exists in and has struggled to emerge from through positive affirmations of identity. To recall Sedgwick, "there are important senses in which 'queer' can signify only *when attached to the first person.*" In this case, readers are left clutching at straws to affirm Dumbledore's sexuality because, if he is gay, he has been portrayed as, and may forever remain, closeted and complicit in that silence.

Notes

I would like to thank Andrew Buzny for providing me with a copy of his paper presented at Accio in 2008.

1. C. Hastings, "Harry Potter and the Secret of Albus," *Telegraph*, October 21, 2007, available at: http://www.telegraph.co.uk/culture/books/booknews/3668677/Harry-Potter-and-the-Secret-of-Albus.html (accessed July 15, 2010): para. 2.
2. See Chapter 13, Pamela Ingleton's essay, "Neither Can Live while the Other Survives": *Harry Potter* and the Extratextual (After)life of J. K. Rowling" for further discussion of this topic.
3. Hastings: para. 12.
4. BBC News, "JK Rowling Outs Dumbledore as Gay," October 20, 2007, available at: http://www.bbc.co.uk/1/hi/entertainment/7053982.stm (accessed August 3, 2010): para. 11.
5. T. Masters, "Potter Stars React to Gay Twist," BBC News, November 12, 2007, available at: http://news.bbc.co.uk/2/hi/entertainment/7085863.stm (accessed July 16, 2010): para. 8.
6. BBC News: paras. 11–12.
7. As cited in Hastings: para. 16.
8. As cited in Hastings: para. 14.
9. BBC News: para. 12.
10. *Ibid.*: para. 11.
11. T. Pugh and D. L. Wallace, "A Postscript to 'Heteronormative Heroism and Queering the School Story in J. K. Rowling's *Harry Potter* Series'," *Children's Literature Association Quarterly* 33(2) (2008): 188–92, at 191.
12. BBC News: para. 14.
13. A. Rich, "Invisibility in Academe," in T. Roberts *et al.* (eds.), *The Broadview Anthology of Expository Prose* (Peterborough, ON: Broadview Press, 2002): 291.
14. B. D. Adam, *The Rise of a Gay and Lesbian Movement*, rev. edn (New York: Twayne, 1995): 69.
15. As cited in E. Garcia, "Conservatives Urge Ban on 'Harry Potter' over Witchcraft, Homosexuality," *Christian Post*, October 30, 2007, available at: http://www.christianpost.com/article/20071030/conservatives-urge-ban-on-harry-potter-over-witchcraft-homosexuality (accessed July 15, 2010): para. 3-4.
16. L. Higgins, "Q & A: *Harry Potter* Author J. K. Rowling's 'Gay' Dumbledore Announcement Manipulates Children," *Americans for*

Truth about Homosexuality, October 22, 2007, available at: http://www. americansfortruth.com/news/q-a-harry-potter-authors-gay-dumbledore-announcement-manipulates-children.html (accessed July 15, 2010): para. 6.

17. E. K. Sedgwick, *Tendencies* (Oxford and New York: Taylor & Francis, 1994).

18. A. J. Buzny, "Did You Really Think Dumbledore Was Straight? Queering the Hogwarts Headmaster," Accio—UK Harry Potter Conference, 2008: 5.

19. M. Bronski, "Queering Harry Potter," September 2003, available at: http://www.zmag.org/zmag/viewArticle/13675 (accessed July 15, 2010): para. 5.

20. Sedgwick: 8.

21. Buzny: 1.

22. *Ibid.*

23. C. Tosenberger, "'Oh my God, the Fanfiction!' Dumbledore's Outing and the Online Harry Potter Fandom," *Children's Literature Association Quarterly* 33(2) (2008): 200–6, at 201.

24. T. Pugh and D. L. Wallace, "Heteronormative Heroism and Queering the School Story in J. K. Rowling's *Harry Potter* Series," *Children's Literature Association Quarterly* 31(3) (2006): 260–81, at 277.

25. Sedgwick: 8.

26. Pugh and Wallace (2006): 266.

27. M. Bronski, "Harry Potter and the Death of Queerness?" September 2007, available at: http://www.zmag.org/zmag/viewArticle/15626 (accessed July 15, 2010): para. 4.

28. Sedgwick: 9.

29. Pugh and Wallace (2006): 268.

30. A. Bray, *Homosexuality in Renaissance England*, 2nd edn (New York: Columbia University Press, 1995): 21.

31. Pugh and Wallace (2006): 266–7.

32. *Ibid.*: 264.

33. *Ibid.*: 267.

34. Pugh and Wallace (2006).

35. *Ibid.*: 267–8.

36. *Ibid.*: 277.

37. M. Eagleton, *Working with Feminist Criticism* (Oxford: Blackwell, 1996): 147.

38. Toril Moi quoted in M. Eagleton, *Working with Feminist Criticism* (Oxford: Blackwell, 1996): 147.

39. Pugh and Wallace (2006): 267.

40. Buzny: 6.

41. K. Kidd, "Introduction Outing Dumbledore," *Children's Literature Association Quarterly* 33(2) (2008): 186–7, at 186.

42. Masters: para. 8–11.

43. Tosenberger: 203.

13

"Neither Can Live while the Other Survives": *Harry Potter* and the Extratextual (After)life of J. K. Rowling

Pamela Ingleton

On June 23, 2011, a week after initiating a countdown somewhat cryptically heralding the advent of a new web-based Harry Potter project, J. K. Rowling released an online video officially announcing "Pottermore": an interactive online interface facilitating an "online reading experience unlike any other," the content of which, Rowling claimed, would come to be provided by both Rowling herself and fan participants. In the video, Rowling suggests that fans and readers will build Pottermore, though she quickly adds that her presence will be obvious as she shares information about Harry Potter's world that she has been hoarding since she started the series. While this latest *Potter* project seems to have been designed at least in part to traverse the presumably discrete realms of author and reader, as I will argue in the following pages, Pottermore, rather, is simply the latest example of Rowling's insistent need to constantly assert and reassert (authorial) control over her text(s) and carefully monitor and indeed police her brand and literary universe. In the following chapter, I situate the release of Pottermore, Rowling's *Harry Potter* addenda or supplementary publications and especially her controversial "outing" of the Professor Dumbledore character back in 2007, alongside various authorship theories, in an attempt to offer some tentative conclusions about the ways and means of Rowling's authorship and the anxieties informing the management of authority in our contemporary publishing landscape.

Amidst the hype surrounding the *Harry Potter* series, the personal story of author J. K. Rowling has become as well known and as oft-quoted as Harry's own; one would be hard pressed to find any Harry Potter fans completely unaware of their fetish's auteur. Since rising to prominence with the unprecedented success of *Potter*, Rowling has been the subject of several biographies (e.g. *J. K. Rowling: The Wizard behind Harry Potter, J. K. Rowling: A Biography*), documentaries (e.g. *J. K. Rowling: A Year in the Life, J. K. Rowling: The Interview*) and television specials (e.g. "J. K. Rowling: One-on-One" on NBC's *Today*, "Oprah and J. K. Rowling in Scotland" on *The Oprah Winfrey Show*). Several of Rowling's television appearances occurred (well) after the release of the seventh and final instalment of the *Harry Potter* series, *Harry Potter and the Deathly Hallows*; much of the content of these post-*Hallows* interviews reveals an impulse on Rowling's part to ensure that her work, and her control and authority over it, remains intact now that the *Harry Potter* saga has (presumably) drawn to a close. Challenged by pre-publication speculation like that of *Maclean's* columnist Brian Bethune who examined the possibility of "killing the main character to control his afterlife,"[1] Rowling was forced to consider the future of Harry—and her *own*—beyond, or *post*-publication, when there would be nothing more to reveal and no more books in which to reveal it. Or so readers thought. On the contrary, in the time since *Hallows'* publication, Rowling has been anything but quiet. In fact, she has had much to say.

Like her fictional uber-villain Lord Voldemort, Rowling's biggest fear appears to be death—in this case, the death of the author. One might say that, in the face of Barthesian assaults on conventional notions of authorship (further outlined in the subsequent section of this chapter), Rowling refuses to die. While critics such as Suman Gupta have claimed that Rowling "ceases to be the author of the phenomenon and simply becomes part of the phenomenon as author,"[2] Rowling has instead actively and continuously worked to reaffirm her control over the *Harry Potter* series, an inclination reflected in her publication history and publicity appearances. For example, she published the final book with an epilogue, positioning her characters "Nineteen Years Later" and solidifying, to a certain extent, their post-textual existence. Moreover, she produced realizations of three of the fictional books mentioned within the *Harry Potter* series, further extending—and *demarcating*—the description of her fictitious world: *Fantastic Beasts and Where to Find Them*,[3] *Quidditch through the Ages*,[4] and *The Tales of Beedle the Bard*, the original copy of which sold to Amazon.com for four million dollars in December 2007, and was later mass-produced in time for Christmas 2008.[5] Finally, Rowling welcomed a media circuit following the publication of *Hallows* that had her filling in the holes and answering unanswered questions about the final volume and the series as a whole. Enter Rowling the "secret keeper," a role now extended beyond the final textual revelation; apparently there is *still* more to know, and once again readers must to turn to her—author and creator—to find it out. What follows is an attempt to begin to trace this "extratextual" existence, Rowling's "extratextual conversations" in the form of interviews, documentaries, supplemental publications, etc., and to interrogate the ways in which they function to affirm her position as creator or traditional, original genius in a postmodern framework that implicitly denounces such a possibility.

J. K. Rowling and the death of the author

First broached most notably by Roland Barthes in his now canonical essay, "The Death of the Author,"[6] the notion of author as original genius has been interrogated and largely replaced, at least within academia, by critical deconstructions, re-evaluations and demystifications of the role of the contemporary author within concepts like Michel Foucault's "author function": that which "does not refer purely and simply to a real individual,"[7] but rather invokes "the subject as a variable and complex function of discourse."[8] Or as Barthes more apocalyptically puts it: "writing is the destruction of every voice."[9] With such potent, prolific statements working to remove the author from the text—or suggest, perhaps, that the two were never as inextricably linked as traditional notions of authorship might assume—to where has the author been displaced? And how do contemporary authors, in light of such theories, configure or *reconfigure* themselves?

J. K. Rowling is, in Barthes's term, Potter's "final signified,"[10] or at least she is very concerned with establishing herself as such. In her remarks to director James Runcie in an interview for his documentary, *A Year in the Life of J. K. Rowling*, she insists that everything to do with Potter needs to be her version, as the official version, since it all comes from her imagination.[11] With this statement Rowling extends the boundaries of the "official version" of the *Potter* story to include that which she has "not written" within the books themselves: the comments she makes *now*, *post*-publication, outside of the text, or her extratext or extratextual conversations. Perhaps the most interesting and critically rich post- or extratextual comment was the shocking and controversial "outing" of Hogwarts headmaster Albus Dumbledore at Carnegie Hall in October 2007.[12] To quote Rowling's statement directly, "Dumbledore is gay [...] I would have told you earlier if I knew it would make you so happy."[13] "I would have told you earlier'? Earlier *when*? Perhaps in the texts themselves? The ambiguity of what exactly in this statement might constitute "earlier" is intriguing and institutes a timeframe that extends the author's participation with the text beyond the moment (or moments) of writing. While this ambiguous timeframe alongside the amorphous, perpetually changing details of the Harry Potter world seem to propose a certain openness to the texts, Rowling's need to assert these details herself and assert the prominence, as she emphasizes, of *her* version of *her* world,[14] paradoxically negates the process and effectively *closes* the text.

As Barthes writes, "To give a text an Author is to impose a limit on that text [...] to close the writing."[15] If the creator of Dumbledore claims that Dumbledore is gay, Dumbledore is then refused to be anything but—or is he, if such a claim were made outside of the text? Are authorial "extratextual conversations" part of universal understandings of the texts themselves, or are they to be disregarded? *Can* they be disregarded? And what constitutes a "universal" understanding of a text in the first place?

According to Catherine Tosenberger, Rowling's specific phrasing suggests that she would not actually consider her comments on Dumbledore's sexuality to fall within the realm of an "extratext," and that they belong, rather, to the text proper: "Rowling appears to believe that her announcement of Dumbledore's gayness is not, in fact, extratextual. During a press conference after her Carnegie Hall appearance, she indicated that she felt the nature of Dumbledore's feelings for Grindelwald was evident within the text."[16] In "Is Dumbledore Gay? Who's to Say?," Tamar Szabó Gendler offers a slightly different take on the matter, proposing that the extratext is not only recognizable but endorsable from the perspective of the reader, and though extratextual, the information obtained therein is no less legitimate for it: "for most Potter fans, Rowling is the patented owner and creator of the Potter universe. She's the master storyteller who has the right—indeed, the unique prerogative—to authoritatively fill out, embellish, and continue her story."[17] Gendler's essay also asks how readers are to interpret what she refers to as "extra-canonical"[18] commentary, reading the difficulty with the extratext in relation to the philosophical problem of "*truth in fiction*."[19] If Rowling's Carnegie Hall comments are indeed extratextual (in that the information provided at that time, i.e. Dumbledore is gay, could not have been ascertained solely from the original seven novels), and if readers accept the legitimacy and recognize the authority of extratextual commentary, the *Harry Potter* text can then be said to have entered a state of flux in which presumably stable details may be changed, supplemented or highlighted in new ways at any time. The source of these details, however, according to Rowling, *remains* at all times Rowling herself.

J. K. Rowling and the intentional fallacy

Responding to the claims of Barthes and others concerning the (theoretical) death of the author, Foucault briefly takes up similar questions of authority in his essay, "What Is an Author?" Unlike Barthes, Foucault attempts to extend the argument beyond what an author or a text is *not*, to what it *is* or has become. Of interest to this investigation is Foucault's claim that, "[e]ven when an individual has been accepted as an author, we must still ask whether everything that he wrote, said, or left behind is part of his work."[20] Foucault's problematic assumption is that the author exists only in the past tense—has left, is dead—and that the body of his/her texts and/or extratexts is thus static insofar as it can no longer be expanded upon or added to by the author, whomever or whatever that may be. Rowling, on the other hand, is very *literally* alive, a barely middle-aged woman and a very public one, whose body of work remains exposed to fluctuating media discourse and potential future continuation, as text or otherwise. It does appear, however, that Foucault has not *discounted* extratextual commentary from his consideration of what constitutes a body of work, concluding simply that "[a] theory of the work does not exist."[21] In other words, there is little critical precedence for contending with the extratext, what it means and the degree to which it informs more conventional texts (in the case of Rowling, the *Harry Potter* novels themselves).

M. C. Beardsley and W. K. Wimsatt's "intentional fallacy"—and the discussion and criticism it has engendered—is perhaps a relevant entry point to critically position the potential of an *extra*textuality.[22] Their argument, which they funnel through a discussion of poetry and poetic criticism, is essentially that "the design or intention of the author is neither available nor desirable as a standard for judging the success of a work of literary art"[23]—clarified by George Dickie and W. Kent Wilson to imply the following:

> To commit the intentional fallacy seems to mean something like thinking that an artist's intention is *relevant* to the meaning of the artwork. However, [...] a narrower notion [...] is [...] to think that "the meaning of

the work itself" and "the meaning that the author intended to express in the work" *are identical.*[24]

Dickie and Wilson's distinction between the meaning of the text (which is itself a fairly ambiguous concept) and the apparently irrelevant (and separate) meaning "intended" by the author introduces the question of how meaning is produced by and within texts: whether it is inherent to the text itself as the swish-and-flick product of the author's wand/pen, or is externally created, produced through the reader's *interaction* with the text. Addressing this question, Beardsley and Wimsatt assert that "[t]he poem belongs to the public,"[25] a view since adopted in the privileging of "readerly" or fan involvement, as outlined, perhaps exemplarily, by Henry Jenkins: "fans cease to be simply an audience for popular texts; instead, they become active participants in the construction and circulation of textual meanings."[26] The configuration of the reader/fan within the framework of Rowling's extratextual conversations is an interesting and increasingly tenuous relationship.

The subject of authorial intent and the intentional fallacy is particularly relevant to Rowling's conversational, extratextual outing of the character of Dumbledore. If Rowling "intended" throughout the composition of her novels for Dumbledore to be gay but did not explicitly (and textually) address this intention within the novels, does this make him so? Many fans claim not and those in agreement with Beardsley and Wimsatt would assert that Rowling's comment has no bearing (and should *not* come to bear) on readers' own perceptions of the character's sexuality. Consequently, Beardsley and Wimsatt *do* (if indirectly) address the possibility of an extratext in their original article, if only by *negating* its possibility:

> There is a difference between internal and external evidence for the meaning of a poem [...] [W]hat is [...] external is private or idiosyncratic; not a part of the work as a linguistic fact: it consists of revelations (in journals, for example, or letters or reported conversations) about how or why the poet wrote the poem [...]. But the [...] types of evidence [...] shade into one another so subtly that it is not always easy to draw a line between examples, and hence arises difficulty for criticism.[27]

While "external evidence" could certainly be said to be "idiosyncratic"—the extratext, after all, is in a permanent state of flux, perpetually changing, multiple, and different for all—the absolute refusal of the extratext as "not a part of the work" seems far too definite, especially when reconsidered in the postmodern, plural framework. Conversely, their suggestion that the extratext presents a "difficulty for criticism"—much like the statement cited earlier from Foucault—better characterizes the text-extratext conundrum in its complexity, along with the one concession that "[t]he use of biographical evidence need not involve intentionalism, because while it may be evidence of what the author intended, it may also be evidence of the meaning of his words and the dramatic character of his utterance."[28] It is my contention that the extratext cannot be denounced, at least not entirely. Once made, it cannot be unmade through selective acknowledgment. The question of *how* to acknowledge it, however, is an entirely different matter and one that extends beyond the scope of this investigation.

Having provisionally accepted the extratext as somehow relevant (if nothing more) to the original or initial text, an examination of Gregory Currie's (1991) essay "Interpreting Fictions" offers a rather congruous comparison through which one might consider Rowling's particular extratexts, especially the outing of Dumbledore. His case study not only highlights the potentially absurdist nature of the adoption of the intentional fallacy, but is also particularly applicable to the context of Rowling and *Harry Potter*.

> [I]t is a fallacy to suppose, if anyone does, that something can be true in a fiction just because the author intends it to be [...] Indeed, the author may intend a proposition to be true in a fiction *without* it thereby being true in the fiction. Suppose [Sir Arthur Conan] Doyle had peculiar beliefs about alien beings and their infiltration of our world, and thought of Holmes as a fictional representation of this race of beings [...]. [E]ven if Doyle's private correspondence revealed this intention we should not want to conclude that it was true in the story that Holmes is an alien being. This is just not a reasonable way to read the story that Doyle actually wrote, since Doyle's (hypothetical) intention did not, in this case, find expression in his text.[29]

Currie has a point, though his emphasis on the *written* as designating the "reasonable" limitations of what constitutes a text remains difficult to fully endorse. After all, if a document were to surface containing equally ridiculous information to that cited above, it is rather unlikely that it would be so casually and carelessly overlooked by Holmes scholars. The trials of Conan Doyle and Sherlock Holmes offer a particularly apt comparison to Rowling and the *Potter* texts in terms of their shared mass popularity, serial production, and the predicament of how to maintain authorial control over a popular character post-publication. In fact, prior to the release of *Harry Potter and the Deathly*

Hallows, some critics explicitly compared the two, speculating on whether or not Rowling would *take the plunge*, so to speak, as Doyle did, to ensure that Harry remained within her control:

> Conan Doyle killed Holmes essentially to keep his wildly popular character under control [...]. Rowling evidently has control issues, too [...]. [S]he [...] commented sympathetically on her predecessor's impulse. "I can completely understand the mentality of an author who thinks "Well, I am going to kill them off because that means there can be no non-author written sequels, as they call them, so it will end with me." [Otherwise] after I am dead and gone, they would be able to bring back the character and write a load of ...." That, of course, is exactly what happened to Holmes after Conan Doyle's death [...]. Rowling must know the same will happen to Harry regardless of what she does.[30]

Here, Bethune once again addresses the authorial concern over control and ownership. His mention of the reality of Holmes's post-Doyle-mortem—and the coincident reality Rowling may face (or eventually will not be around to face) in the coming years with Potter—reunites this discussion with the inevitable uncertainty of authorial intention. Intention aside, *in* control or not, Rowling will not always be around to protect, control and police her creation, which is inevitably bound to become less and less *hers*.

J. K. Rowling and the authorial Chamber of Secrets

As I have discussed, since the release of the final *Harry Potter* volume, the content of the *Potter* extratext has expanded considerably. While, as Mark Harris mentions, Rowling's conversations used to consist of "unveiling the *occasional* tantalizing nugget about her decision-making on her website or during an interview or public appearance," Rowling is now, presumably, at liberty to "spill the many-flavored beans herself."[31] The revelation regarding Dumbledore's sexuality was merely one of many during Rowling's post-publication media frenzy, including several additional "nuggets" about other characters and plot points in the narrative past, present, and future. Philip Nel, an associate professor at Kansas State University who has written fairly extensively on the *Harry Potter* texts and phenomenon, in addition to his involvement with *Potter* pedagogically, writes, "All good writers know a lot more about their characters than they tell you...readers are only told what they need to know."[32] However, based on Rowling's unfolding authorial strategies, "needed" information appears to be linked to some sort of slow-release timeframe, becoming progressively relevant as time goes by—or as media attention and product sales wane. Gina Elliott, having attended the Carnegie Hall presentation during which the now infamous Dumbledore remark was first made, states: "Rowling reminded us that there will always be something new to discover about the series. The beauty of the Harry Potter books is that she has it all worked out—she knows everything there is to know about the world she has created, so no question will stump her," claiming, too, that such commentary provided an "entirely different dimension [...] to the series."[33] However, what *is* this dimension and how do critics define and understand it? In addition to the structural and technical problems it provokes, this concept of text in flux—with Author (capital "A") at the helm overseeing the change—also implicates issues regarding who has access to the emergent extratext and who does not. What of those without access to the internet, television or print media (an issue brought to the fore in the case of Pottermore)? If the extratext is to gradually inform the original text in some pivotal way, are these readers missing out? The text via extratext becomes a multitext, with endless possibilities for each individual reader. Granted, the reading experience is always individualized—but should the text be too?

Continuing in the vein of individualization, nowhere is such a concept more apparent than in Rowling's extratextual conversations themselves. It is not only the actual information she reveals each time that is of interest, but also the way in which she rhetorically codifies it as would a protective parent with a child. Rowling's rhetoric betrays a sense of possessiveness, of ownership. In her coverage of Rowling as runner-up for *TIME* magazine's "Person of the Year," Nancy Gibbs comments,

> she will never really be in control of Harry again. She knows he's bigger than she is now and not always in ways she likes [...] you can feel her ambivalence—or even something more fierce and protective—at the prospect of legions of writers who want to take up Harry's story as their own. One declared at last summer's biggest Potterfest that, as Rowling had left the sandbox, it was open for all to play in.[34]

Similarly, in a press conference held days after Carnegie Hall, Rowling responded to the many inquiries regarding her purpose in having outed Dumbledore by saying, "He is my character. He is what he is and I have the right to say what I say about him,"[35] later reiterating this response a few months later on the subject of the character of Harry:

> He's still mine [...]. Many people may feel that they own him. But he's a very real character to me, and no one's thought about him more than I have [...]. No one has mourned more than I have. [The characters

were] inextricably linked with my life for 17 years. No one else has that association with Harry. They may remember where they were when they read it. But to remember where you were when you created it is, I'm afraid to say it, a different experience.[36]

Rowling's assertion here of the legitimacy of authorship and her own authority is fairly self-evident. She has placed herself in a position of privilege over her readers, perceptible, as she claims, in the very "different experience" of writing a text over reading one. Bearing in mind her self-proclaimed close relationship with her texts and characters in addition to her desire to remain in control of extratextual, post-publication details, it is clear that Rowling does not consider herself a casualty of the assault on authorship, but an opponent to its pretence.

Many people have, nevertheless, attempted "to play in Rowling's sandbox," perhaps most notably in online Harry Potter-inspired fan and slash fiction. While Rowling—as Wallace Koehler and Simon Newman explain—generally tolerates fan fiction making use of her *Harry Potter* characters and settings,"[37] a dispute with fan Steven Vander Ark and his publisher, RDR Books, over a formerly forthcoming Harry Potter lexicon to be penned by Vander Ark once again demonstrates Rowling's need to police such activities closely and to maintain her authorial control—as one sees in her claim that *she* was planning to write such a text *herself*. After filing a lawsuit against Vander Ark and RDR (a lawsuit Rowling since won), Rowling reflected on the potential consequences for the Harry Potter fan community with the following statement:

> If RDR's position is accepted, it will undoubtedly have a significant, negative impact on the freedoms enjoyed by genuine fans on the Internet [...]. Authors everywhere will be forced to protect their creations much more rigorously, which could mean denying well-meaning fans permission to pursue legitimate creative activities [...]. I find it devastating to contemplate the possibility of such a severe alteration of author-fan relations.[38]

Notice the rhetorical strategies at work in Rowling's statement: the concern over the "freedoms" of "genuine" or "well-meaning" fans, the need for "permission" and the question over what constitutes a "legitimate" creative activity. These descriptors are vague. How is a well-meaning fan discerned from a fan with malicious intentions? What, according to Rowling, is a legitimate creative activity? How do such activities differ from her own? What type of permission would she expect to bestow? How, exactly, would she go about bestowing it? With the counsel for RDR claiming Vander Ark's project "a very legitimate activity. Like a reference book or guide to literature"[39] and copyright law as it relates to such activities as fan sites and fan fiction remaining somewhat fuzzy, how has Rowling managed to retain such influence? While intellectual property and copyright scholars like Kembrew McLeod[40] and Tim Wu[41] acknowledge the ultimate illegality of much fan production (especially online fan production), they also acknowledge the practice of what Wu refers to—in relation to the Harry Potter fansite *The Leaky Cauldron*, for instance—as the phenomenon of "tolerated use": a practice, as Wu describes it, "that declares many inoffensive activities illegal, with the tacit understanding that the law will usually not be enforced, leaving sanctions hanging overhead like copyright's own Sword of Damocles."[42] Certainly, Rowling has not pursued legal action in response to every fansite and/or fan project that appears and circulates online, thereby, perhaps, implicitly permitting their existence and continuance. That having been said, she is also clearly invested in limiting the terms of this engagement, as evidenced here in her remarks concerning Vander Ark and RDR, and in the design of Pottermore—a topic to be explored more fully later in this chapter.

J. K. Rowling and the negotiation of author/reader interaction

In order to offer some tentative conclusions on the status of contemporary authorship (theory) as it can be read through the case study of Rowling and the *Harry Potter* novels, I would first like to address the role of the reader or "fan" in slightly greater depth, particularly how one might theorize the production of Harry Potter fan and slash fiction in relation to the Rowling-centric extratext(s) discussed thus far. Following the enthusiastic response to her comment about Dumbledore's sexuality that October afternoon at Carnegie Hall, Rowling humorously and suddenly exclaimed, "Oh, my god, the fan fiction!"[43] Her explicit linking of this (and other) extratextual revelation(s) to the Harry Potter fan community is interesting, likely pointed and certainly prescient, especially given the diverse fan responses to the incident that would follow. Broadly speaking, the reactions of Harry Potter fans/readers to Dumbledore's outing can be grouped into four categories: those excited to learn something new about their beloved headmaster, whether specifically because of his queering, or more generally; those offended, disappointed, or even disgusted by the possibility of Dumbledore as a gay man; those who immediately dismissed the suggestion on the grounds that it was not included or suggested in/by the original novels; and perhaps most passionately, those who were not offended by the content of Rowling's comment, but, rather, by what the comment implied, and what the comment prevented: namely the primacy of *Rowling's* interpretation over the infinite, individual interpretations of any and all *Harry Potter* readers, and the implicit denial of alternative interpretations.

In the hours and days that followed Rowling's Carnegie Hall appearance, the blogosphere alighted with fan reactions to Rowling's comment, staking claims to its (il)legitimacy. Romance author Brenda Coulter, for instance, soon posted on her blog, "To insist on ownership (as she has done) and the right to define or re-define those characters as she sees fit after the fact, is to insist on absolute control over the literary experience of her readers she cannot possibly have."[44] Coulter's response is exemplary of this fourth type of fan response, outlined above. Where *Harry Potter* readers such as Coulter formerly counted themselves among Rowling's truest and most supportive fanbase and, before the publication of *Hallows*, were bound to *her* final say, many now became reactive and resistant, denying the very source they had so fully endorsed in months previous.

More pressing than the matter of the limits and limitlessness of the a/Author for many distressed *Harry Potter* fans, however, was and remains the concern that Rowling had not only overstepped her authorial bounds but had, in fact, intruded on the territory *of the fan*: if Rowling believed Vander Ark had transgressed "the role of the reader," so to speak, many fans, especially those fan producers (e.g. writers of fan and/or slash fiction), felt Rowling, by outing Dumbledore in an "official" public announcement, had done the reverse, particularly given what was considered by many to be her casual appropriation of the queer. Harry Potter fan/slash fiction communities are employed by their participants as spaces for subverting and, quite literally in some cases, "coming out of" hegemonic ideas of gender and sexuality via the appropriation of Rowling's characters, settings, and overall Harry Potter universe, often by the adolescents who make up the core of Rowling's fanbase—a potentiality *re*appropriated or taken back by so definitively claiming Dumbledore's sexuality.

Angela Thomas, one of the few critics—along with Jenkins[45]—to explicitly address the production and consumption of adolescent fan fiction, suggests that teenage users are adopting spaces of especially online fan communities as sites of identity exploration: "Cyberspace has been credited with opening up new and liberating spaces [...] to explore aspects of identity [...]. Such uses of cyberspace are also thought to have been a catalyst for challenging the artificial boundaries of the subject as defined by dominant cultures."[46] Fan/slash fiction participants find in these communities the potential for play or performativity of identity, perhaps, as notes Sheenagh Pugh, "because they wanted either 'more of' their source material or 'more from' it."[47] According to Pugh, Harry Potter fan/slash fiction writers either respond to an absence of queer characters or write to extend the queerness they interpret in the texts and would like to perpetuate. Having constructed an entire participatory realm around the queering or "slashing" of Rowling's texts and characters, many found and continue to find Rowling's extratextual note on Dumbledore's sexuality to be running unwanted interference. Of course, not all critics/fans frame the reception and incorporation of Rowling's extratextual comments in terms of what they prevent or deny. Ernest L. Bond and Nancy L. Michelson, for instance, characterize the outing of Dumbledore as "a rather big incentive for new riffs on the Harry Potter storylines," adding, "it is actually indicative of the way popular fictional narratives might be understood in the age of Web 2.0: as ever expanding networks of story."[48] Either way, Rowling's Carnegie Hall comments certainly serve as a useful site for exploring the relationship between the author and his/her reader(s), and the shifting understandings of who "owns" the right (and the means) to production in contemporary culture.

It is useful at this point to turn briefly to Joe Moran's work in *Star Authors: Literary Celebrity in America*,[49] and more specifically his responses to the treatises on authorship by Barthes and Foucault formerly discussed in this chapter. Moran, transitioning the argument from the "academic" realm to the "popular," points out that "while academic criticism has formulated theories about the death, disappearance or absence of the author, this figure still seems to be very much alive in non-academic culture,"[50] quoting Malcolm Bradbury's contention that we now live "in two ages at once: the age of the author typed and promoted, studied and celebrated; the age of the author denied and eliminated, desubjected and airbrushed from writing."[51] Rowling very definitely fits the scenario articulated here by Bradbury/Moran. However, while Moran proposes that "[t]he author becomes gradually less in control not only of her work but also of her image and how it circulates, at the same time as the machinery of celebrity asserts what literary critics call 'the intentional fallacy,' which assumes that she is wholly in control of it,"[52] in terms of Rowling, many would not entirely agree. Or at the very least Rowling would not. For it is not only the machinery of celebrity but Rowling herself perpetuating this control or the *appearance* of it. She has now come to transcend the machine, or, perhaps, make it do her bidding. Her control, too, seems to surpass (to some degree, at least) mere appearance. As seen with the case of Vander Ark, Rowling is not afraid to test her authorial control, even if doing so means taking a fan to court.

Finally, and somewhat unrelatedly, one might also argue that she has benefitted considerably from the sequel format in which the books were composed; as described by Hope Apple and Merle Jacob, sequels are those "books that satisfy both our need to know the outcome and our desire to know more."[53] In fact, it may be the very format of the books which brought these contemporary extratextual conversations into existence. In sum, readers have come to expect that Rowling has secrets to share, and she has perpetuated such expectation post-publication via media incidents such as Dumbledore's outing.

J. K. Rowling and the ongoing *Harry Potter*(more) saga

And then, of course, there's Pottermore: Rowling's latest pseudo-extratextual Harry Potter incarnation, and the presumed equalizing project of author/reader relations. In the aforementioned online video introducing the project, Rowling highlights Pottermore's capacity to allow for a unique reading experience of the *Harry Potter* series in a safe Internet environment. Two things stand out in Rowling's phrasing. First, somewhat paradoxically, the primary adjective she employs to describe an innovative and interactive web experience is "safe"; second, while no doubt self-evident, throughout the short video Rowling once again repetitively insists on the primacy of the original texts: Pottermore is entirely built around and based upon all of the *Harry Potter* books, and therefore all creativity and/or interactivity it begets remain secondary to Rowling's oeuvre (notably available for purchase—and, for many, *re*purchase—in e-formats through the site itself).

Rowling's statements in the Pottermore introductory video have left the author of this chapter somewhat uneasy, and I am not alone in my slight discomfort and disconcertion over Rowling's descriptions of the Pottermore project, the project itself and the *reality* of the space it opens up for reader/fan involvement—or rather, the space it *fails* to open up. It was not particularly surprising to see Henry Jenkins among the first critical respondents to Pottermore. As both a theorist of fan relations and himself a self-professed Harry Potter "fan," the promise of Pottermore certainly suits Jenkins' purview; not to mention, as Jenkins himself points out in the opening lines of his blog response to the project,[54] Pottermore "may be the most highly visible transmedia project to date"—transmedia having been the focus of Jenkins' most recent research (transmedia, convergence culture and, forthcoming in 2012, what Jenkins refers to as "spreadable media," or meme culture). While the Pottermore project certainly seems to hold critical and personal interest for Jenkins, his response to Pottermore's content is less than enthusiastic. He likewise finds concern with the characterization of Pottermore as "safe," referring to the site (based on Rowling's description of it and early glimpses of its content) as a "walled garden": "the term, 'safe,' is a red flag [...;] 'safe' in those terms means censored, regulated, or policed. So, the promise is that 'You,' 'Us,' will help shape the future of the franchise but only in terms specified by Rowling and by the companies involved in overseeing this site."[55] As someone deeply invested in the possibilities of participatory culture and user and community-generated media, Jenkins takes issue with what he considers to be Pottermore's—and, by extension, *Rowling's*—attempt to "capture and commodify participatory culture," or the static establishment of "the terms of our engagement with the storyworld,"[56] instead of those terms being established individually at the level of the user(s)/reader(s).

The tendency identified here by Jenkins in Pottermore, as he goes on to say, is not unique to the Pottermore project; Jenkins, too, finds many instances of control and restrictedness under the guise of freedom and openness elsewhere in Rowling's *Harry Potter* franchise. Drawing from the work of Suzanne Scott and Julie Levine Russo on transmedia and the ways in which some "transmedia practices tend to priviledge [*sic*] some kinds of fans over others,"[57] Jenkins contends:

> Rowling [...] has shown many signs that she wants to continue to shape and control how fans respond to her work well after she finished writing it. We can see this in the epilogue to the last novel, which seems to pointlessly map out futures for all of her characters, including shaping the "ships" (relationships) between them, in what amounts to spraying her territory. Many fans would have preferred a text which was more open ended on that level and allows them more freedom to speculate beyond the ending. She decided to "out" Dumbledore not through the books but via her own discourse around the books. She tried to shut down the Harry Potter Lexicon. So, it is abundantly clear that she likes some of her fans more than others and that any effort to facilitate fan interactions also represents an attempt to bring fandom more under her control.[58]

As I have outlined throughout this paper, Rowling has been and continues to be rigorously concerned with legitimizing her own authority when it comes to all things Harry Potter—a trait no doubt betraying anxieties that such authority is only ever precarious at best. After a lengthy site construction time, and limited Beta release to a select number of fans Pottermore is now available to everyone. Harry Potter fans/readers can only wait to see which creative allowances will be bestowed and which will be denied within the so-called interactive online reading experience. As Jenkins writes, "She's been surprisingly supportive of fan culture in the past, but on a selective basis, which does not give us much guarantee on how this one is going to shape out."[59] Years after the publication of *Potter*'s final volume, it seems, the life-and-death battle of a/Author Rowling and the Harry Potter world rages on—all is not *entirely* well.

Conclusion: J. K. Rowling and the *Harry Potter* past, present, and future

As if aware of Foucault's statement of impending doom—"The work, which once had the duty of providing immortality, now possesses the right to kill, to be its author's murderer"[60]—J. K. Rowling has strategically manipulated her text via her star text and extratextual conversations to avoid, to the best of her abilities, the postmodern sentence of the death of the author and the impossibility of authorship. Rowling returned to the question of the future of Harry Potter (and *Harry Potter*) as recently as October 2010 when, in a special hour-long interview with Oprah Winfrey at the Balmoral Hotel in Scotland,[61] she responded to Winfrey's query about the possibility of subsequent *Potter* volumes by indeterminately stating that she could write more, and she might, but she might not—a comment that once again reaffirms Rowling's right to (the) rei(g)n(s). For the most part, I have merely presented questions relating to the contemporary status of authorship and Rowling's brand of authorship in particular—many remain unanswered, most importantly, the question of whether or not to accept or acknowledge the extratext, and if so, *how* to acknowledge it. Additionally, more questions need to be asked, especially further investigation into fan fiction and fan involvement more generally, as well as the degree to which authorial strategies such as those enacted here by Rowling constrict the ability of a fan/reader to engage with the text. To a certain extent, only time will tell if Rowling outlives her text or if the text outlives Rowling—realistically speaking, the latter scenario is likely to prevail.

Notes

1. B. Bethune, "Will Harry Die?" *Maclean's* (2007): 62–8, at 64.
2. S. Gupta, *Re-Reading Harry Potter* (New York: Palgrave Macmillan, 2003): 34.
3. N. Scamander [J. K. Rowling], *Fantastic Beasts and Where to Find Them* (New York: Arthur A. Levine Books, 2001).
4. K. Whisp [J. K. Rowling], *Quidditch through the Ages* (New York: Arthur A. Levine Books, 2001).
5. J. K. Rowling, *The Tales of Beedle the Bard* (London: Bloomsbury, 2008).
6. R. Barthes, *Image, Music, Text* (Glasgow: Fontana Collins, 1977).
7. M. Foucault, "What Is an Author?" in P. Rabinow (ed.), *The Foucault Reader* (New York: Pantheon Books, 1984): 101–20, at 113.
8. *Ibid.*: 118.
9. Barthes: 142.
10. *Ibid.*: 147.
11. J. Runcie (dir.) *A Year in the Life of J. K. Rowling* (2007) RDF Television.
12. See James Daem's essay titled "'I Knew a Girl Once, whose Hair…': Dumbledore and the Closet", Chapter 12 in this book, for further information on this topic.
13. Quoted in BBC News Online, "JK Rowling Outs Dumbledore as Gay," October 20, 2007, available at: http://www.bbc.co.uk/1/hi/entertainment/7053982.stm (accessed November 10, 2010).
14. Runcie, *op. cit.*, emphases added.
15. Barthes: 147.
16. C. Tosenberger, "'Oh my God, the Fanfiction!' Dumbledore's Outing and the Online Harry Potter Fandom," *Children's Literature Association Quarterly* 33(2) (2008): 200–4, at 201.
17. T. S. Gendler, "Is Dumbledore Gay? Who's to Say?" in G. Bassham (ed.), *The Ultimate Harry Potter and Philosophy: Hogwarts for Muggles* (Hoboken, NJ: John Wiley & Sons, 2010): 143–56, at 152.
18. *Ibid.*
19. *Ibid.*: 144.
20. Foucault: 103.
21. *Ibid.*: 104.
22. M. C. Beardsley and W. K. Wimsatt, "The Intentional Fallacy," *On Literary Intention: Critical Essays Selected and Introduced by David Newton-De Molina* (Edinburgh: Edinburgh University Press, 1976): 1–13.
23. *Ibid.*: 1.
24. G. Dickie and W. K. Wilson, "The Intentional Fallacy: Defending Beardsley," *The Journal of Aesthetics and Art Criticism* 53(3) (1995): 233–50, at 234.
25. Beardsley and Wimsatt: 3.
26. H. Jenkins, *Textual Poachers: Television Fans and Participatory Culture* (New York: Routledge, 1992): 24.

27. Beardsley and Wimsatt: 6–7.
28. Foucault: 7.
29. G. Currie, "Interpreting Fictions," in R. Freadman and L. Reinhardt (eds.), *On Literary Theory and Philosophy* (New York: St. Martin's Press, 1991): 96–112, at 103.
30. Bethune: 63–4.
31. M. Harris, "2007 Entertainer of the Year: J. K. Rowling," *Entertainment Weekly*, November 26, 2007 (emphasis added).
32. Quoted in E. Friedman, "Dumbledore's Gay: Does Anyone Care?" *ABC News*, February 12, 2009.
33. G. Elliott, "Rowling Reveals *Harry Potter* Secrets," *TIME*, October 20, 2007.
34. N. Gibbs, "Person of the Year Runner-Up #3: J. K. Rowling," *TIME* 170(7) (2007): 74.
35. Quoted in M. Roberts, "Dumbledore Brave, Brilliant; Why Not Gay: Rowling," *Reuters*, October 23, 2007, available at: http://www.reuters.com/article/2007/10/23/us-arts-rowling-idUSN2321044620071023 (accessed November 10, 2010).
36. Quoted in Elliott: 76.
37. W. Koehler and S. Newman, "Copyright: Moral Rights, Fair Use, and the Online Environment," *Journal of Information Ethics* 13(2) (2004): 38–57, at 47.
38. Quoted in "Rowling Says Fan-created Potter Book Would Be 'Devastating' to fan Sites," *CBC News*, February 29, 2008.
39. *Ibid.*
40. K. McLeod, *Owning Culture: Authorship, Ownership, and Intellectual Property Law* (New York: Peter Lang, 2001).
41. T. Wu, "Tolerated Use: The Copyright Problem," *Slate*, October 16, 2007, available at: http://www.slate.com/articles/news_and_politics/jurisprudence/features/2007/american_lawbreaking/tolerated_use_the_copyright_problem.html (accessed November 12, 2010).
42. *Ibid.*
43. Quoted in BBC News Online, *op. cit.*
44. Quoted in Gendler: 144.
45. Jenkins (1992), *op. cit.*
46. A. Thomas, "Blurring and Breaking through the Boundaries of Narrative, Literacy, and Identity in Adolescent Fan Fiction," in M. Knobel and C. Lankshear (eds.), *A New Literacies Sampler* (New York: Peter Lang, 2007): 147–75, at 157.
47. S. Pugh, *The Democratic Genre: Fan Fiction in a Literary Context* (Bridgend, UK: Seren, 2005): 19.
48. E. L. Bond and N. L. Michelson, "Writing Harry's World: Children Co-authoring Hogwarts," in E. E. Heilman (ed.), *Critical Perspectives on Harry Potter* (New York: Routledge, 2009): 309–27, at 309.
49. J. Moran, *Star Authors: Literary Celebrity in America* (London: Pluto Press, 2000).

50. *Ibid.*: 58.
51. *Ibid.*: 59.
52. *Ibid.*: 61.
53. H. Apple and M. Jacob, *To Be Continued: An Annotated Guide to Sequels*, 2nd edn (Phoenix, AZ: Oryx Press, 2000): ix.
54. H. Jenkins, "Three Reasons Why Pottermore Matters..." *Confessions of an Aca-Fan*, June 24, 2011, available at: http://www.henryjen kins.org/2011/06/three_reasons_why_pottermore_m.html (accessed December 3, 2011).
55. *Ibid.*
56. *Ibid.*
57. Quoted in Jenkins (2011).
58. *Ibid.*
59. *Ibid.*
60. Foucault: 102.
61. "Oprah and J. K. Rowling in Scotland," *The Oprah Winfrey Show* (2010).

Further Reading

Monographs

M. Anelli, *Harry, A History: The True Story of a Boy Wizard, His Fans, and Life Inside the Harry Potter Phenomenon* (New York: Pocket Books—Division of Simon & Schuster, 2008).

Garnering a foreword by J. K. Rowling, the webmistress of "The Leaky Cauldron" fansite reflects on the *Harry Potter* juggernaut as she experienced the various stages of the project. More of a paean to the project than an addition to *Harry Potter* studies.

G. Beahm, *Muggles and Magic: J. K. Rowling and the* Harry Potter *Phenomenon* (unauthorized) (Charlottesville, VA: Hampton Roads, 2004).

A general, though dated, resource book that provides background information on Rowling and her process, information on the first three films and the first five books, as well as information on *Harry Potter* merchandise and websites. Of some value is "The Final Exam: A Trivia Quiz for Muggles" found therein.

A. Blake, *The Irresistible Rise of Harry Potter* (Brooklyn, NY: Verso Books, 2002).

Locating the *Potter* books in the context of contemporary Britain, this work critiques them as nostalgic, escapist fantasies. Now somewhat outdated with the publication of the last four books in the series.

N. C. Brown, *The Mystery of Harry Potter: A Catholic Family Guide* (Huntington, IN: Our Sunday Visitor Publishing Division, Our Sunday Visitor, Inc., 2007).

Nancy Carpentier Brown addresses issues such as why anyone should read the *Potter* books, whether children could learn spells from the books, whether the stories are compatible with the Catholic faith, the moral and spiritual issues addressed, Harry Potter as a role model, and the differences between the movies and the books. Each chapter offers "Questions to Ponder" that can be adapted for classroom discussions. The book was rushed into publication before *The Deathly Hallows* was published, so some issues raised in the book are left unanswered. Brown incorporates G. K. Chesterton's paradoxes of courage, humility and faith into the explanations, which are further explained in an Appendix interview with Dale Ahlquist, President of the American Chesterton Society.

M. Dickerson and D. O'Hara, *A Handbook on Myth and Fantasy from Homer to Harry Potter* (Grand Rapids, MI: Brazos Press, 2006).

Matthew Dickerson and David O'Hara examine myth and fantasy through the ages, considering the Bible, Homer, Beowulf, Arthur, the Brothers Grimm, and George MacDonald (whose fairy tales influenced J. R. R. Tolkien and C. S. Lewis) to establish a background for exploring some modern works of fantasy. Chapters are devoted to the following authors and works: Ursula Le Guin's *Earthsea* Trilogy, Philip Pullman's *Dark Materials* Trilogy, Walter Wangerin Jr's *The Book of the Dun Cow*, and J. K. Rowling's *Harry Potter* series. The chapter on *Harry Potter* only considers the first five books directly; however, the ideas about the role of myth and fantasy in literature that are generated within the *Handbook* definitely are also applicable to the final two books of the series.

C. Duriez, *Field Guide to Harry Potter* (Downers Grove, IL: IVP Books-InterVarsity Press, 2007).

Colin Duriez reviews Rowling's "Life and Times" before examining "Key Themes" found in the seven books of the series. Separate chapters in Part One cover "Rowling's Spiritual Worldview," "Images of Good and Evil," the series' relationship to "the Great Traditions of Children's Literature," and "The Storyteller's Craft." Part Two provides an alphabetical listing and summary of all the "Beings, Places, Things, and Events" that figure in the series. Also useful are the Appendices that summarize the seven books, provide a timeline of events associated with the storyline, and overview some of the major monographs about the series.

J. Granger, *Harry Potter's Bookshelf: The Great Books Behind the Hogwarts Adventures* (unauthorized) (New York: Berkley Books, 2009).

John Granger analyzes the entire *Harry Potter* series on four levels: surface, moral, allegorical, and mythic, spiritual or anagogical. At each level, he considers similarities between Rowling's work and literary influences on her work—other places to find the techniques and images she embraces being used. On the surface level, Granger examines voice, drive and setting, drawing examples from Charles Dickens, Dorothy Sayers, Jane Austen, and Enid Blyton. The moral level brings in the Brontë sisters; Gothic romances of authors such as Mary Shelley, R. L. Stevenson and Bram Stoker; and works that preach inclusion and tolerance, such as the Arthur Rankin cartoon *Rudolph the Red-Nosed Reindeer*. At the allegorical level, Granger posits connections to Plato's Cave, Gulliver, and Everyman. The final level explores the magic of the circle, alchemy, and the Seeing Eye, using Frances Hodgson Burnett (*The Secret Garden*), E. Nesbit (*The Magic World*, and so on), Shakespeare, Dickens, and Elizabeth Goudge (*The Little White Horse*). Modest use of other *Harry Potter* criticism to support the ideas.

J. Granger, *The Hidden Key to Harry Potter: Understanding the Meaning, Genius, and Popularity of Joanne Rowling's* Harry Potter *Novels* (Haddock, WA: Zossima Press, 2002).

Advertised as "The first book to take J. K. Rowling's *Harry Potter* seriously as literature" (front cover), John Granger provides an excellent resource for the classroom to understand symbols and meaning in the first four books of the series. Also of value is the section that explores "What Will Happen with Harry" (pp. 257–320) to show readers how effective storylines are mapped out with early clues to help readers predict what will happen later.

S. Gupta, *Re-Reading Harry Potter* (Basingstoke: Palgrave Macmillan, 2003).

This substantial, academic monograph on J. K. Rowling covers both the earlier four books and the first two films. It argues for a social and political critique of the series and considers them in terms of aspects of contemporary culture, as well as through close analysis of the individual books. Oddly uneven in certain ways, it does not consider issues of form or of Rowling's relationship to the traditions of fantasy and children's literature. It seems to be of the "books that contain magic must be escapist" school of thought espoused by Todorov, Jackson *et al.*

E. M. Kern, *The Wisdom of Harry Potter: What our Favorite Hero Teaches Us about Moral Choices* (Amherst, NY: Prometheus Books, 2003).

Setting aside religious and social criticism of the series, Edmund M. Kern suggests that "an updated Stoic moral system whose primary virtue is constancy" offers an alternate way of reading the books (pp. 13–14). Expanding on "Harry Potter, Stoic Boy Wonder," his November 16, 2001, essay printed in *The Chronicle of Higher Education*, Kern explores Rowling's use of history in general, and the histories she has created for her characters, to present an updated ethical code that is firmly grounded in an explicit, non-demonic, moral system. Primarily, this book examines the first four books, with an Afterword devoted to a Stoic analysis of *The Order of the Phoenix*, which was released as the book was going to press. While the rest of the book makes positive connections between Stoicism and the story's actions, Kern finds primarily negative examples in *OP*, such as "in failing to exercise self-discipline, Harry places himself and his friends in jeopardy" (p. 234). Kern concludes that *OP* uses negative examples to advance the basic Stoic ethic explained in the rest of the books.

V. G. Lee, *On the Trail of Harry Potter* (Newtown, MA: Pitapat Press, 2011).

Dividing a discussion of the *Harry Potter* series into four sections, the book first explores the trio dynamics of Harry, Ron, and Hermione, along with Dumbledore, then examines aspects of the books' plot as a whole before spending some time with the humor and style of the series. The book ends by considering Harry Potter beyond the series, with the spin-offs and the films before drawing some conclusions about the series as a whole.

B. McCabe, *Harry Potter Page to Screen: The Complete Filmmaking Journey* (New York: Harper Design-Harper Collins, 2011).

This coffee-table sized book is filled with pictures to demonstrate the process artistic teams use to turn an author's words into the magic seen on the silver screen. Each of the characters in the story is covered in some detail as befitting the extent of the character's role. Key set elements are analyzed regarding the choices made as those set pieces were being created, especially as to how they could help convey the essence of the location to enhance the story. A great resource for people undertaking further analysis of the *Potter* movies.

C. Neal, *The Gospel According to Harry Potter: Spirituality in the World's Most Famous Seeker* (unauthorized) (Louisville, KY: Westminster John Knox Press, 2002).

Admittedly using techniques of interpretation to read the *Potter* books selectively, as do those who see the occult influences in the series, Neal explores the many Christian parallels that can be found in the first four books of the series in print when she wrote. Each section opens with a useful look at the major themes found in the book being covered, which can be useful in studying the early books, and presents ideas carried over into the subsequent books.

B. Sibley, *Harry Potter Film Wizardry* (New York: Collins Design-Harper Collins, 2010).

This book explores various aspects of the processes used to create the filmed versions of *Harry Potter*. The production designers' notebooks and producers' diaries are included to provide background to the process used to create the images seen on the silver screen. Each film also merits a character study as well as a location unique to that film. Useful resource for studying the magic of films about magic.

J. Vos MacDonald, *J.K. Rowling: Banned, Challenged, and Censored* (unauthorized) (Berkeley Heights, NJ: Enslow Publishers, Inc., 2008).

The author summarizes each of the seven books, then comments on the values presented in each book. She also covers some of the issues involved in banning books such as the process of getting a book banned and why people want to ban certain books. An appendix offers a timeline of book banning to place the *Harry Potter* series in a historical context that starts with Plato.

P. Nel, *Continuum Contemporaries Series: J. K. Rowling's "Harry Potter" Novels: A Reader's Guide* (unauthorized) (New York: Continuum, 2001).

A short (96 pages) introductory guide for general readers as much as for students, it mainly covers the first three books. Brief, it inevitably does not take into account the more recent criticism.

Essay collections

G. L. Anatol (ed.), *Reading Harry Potter: Critical Essays* (Westport, CT: Greenwood/Praeger, 2003).

The collection of essays locates the books within several strands of criticism: reading *Harry Potter* and child development; literary influences and historical contexts; morality and social values. As a collection, this has several noteworthy pieces that are referenced in this collection of essays.

D. Baggett and S. Klein (eds.), *Harry Potter and Philosophy: If Aristotle Ran Hogwarts* (Chicago: Open Court Press, 2004).

This is an amusing, semi-parodic collection that shows various philosophical approaches to the world of Harry Potter. Essays are split among the four Hogwart's houses, examining aspects most relevant to that particular house: Gryffindor and Character, Hufflepuff and Morality, Slytherin and the Dark Arts/Evil, and Ravenclaw and Metaphysics.

C. W. Hallett (ed.), *Scholarly Studies in Harry Potter: Applying Academic Methods to a Popular Text*, Studies in British Literature Vol. 99 (Lewiston, NY: Edwin Mellon Press, 2005).

This collection divides its discussion into a consideration of "Serious Scholarship and Academic Hocus Pocus" and "Conjuring Harry Potter into the Canon." Essays include explorations of education in Potter's world, the myths and allegories used in the series in addition to several noteworthy pieces that are referenced in this collection of essays.

E. E. Heilman (ed.), *Harry Potter's World: Multidisciplinary Critical Perspectives* (Pedagogy and Popular Culture) (New York: RoutledgeFalmer, 2003).

This collection approaches the material through an emphasis on the critical approaches put into action upon the text: cultural studies perspectives; reader response and interpretive perspectives; literary perspectives: the hero, myth, and genre; critical and sociological perspectives. As a collection, this has several noteworthy pieces that are referenced in this collection of essays.

L. A. Whited (ed.), *The Ivory Tower and Harry Potter: Perspectives on a Literary Phenomenon* (Columbia, MO: University of Missouri Press, 2002).

The first book-length analysis of J. K. Rowling's work from a broad range of perspectives within literature, folklore, psychology, sociology, and popular culture. A significant portion of the book explores the *Harry Potter* series' literary ancestors, especially magic and fantasy works for children and the boarding-school tradition. Other essays explore the religious controversies in the USA. Several of the essays in this volume are reprinted from journals and are referenced in this collection of essays.

G. Wiener and P. J. Parks (eds.), *Readings on J. K. Rowling* (San Diego, CA: Greenhaven Press, 2004).

This collection of essays on *Potter* is more polemical than critically informed, with an emphasis on illustrating debates, though the writers are often not interested in approaching the books as literary texts. For example, Richard

Abanes, "Harry Potter Is Unsuitable for children"; Judy Blume, "Harry Potter Must Not Be Banned"; William Safire, "Harry Potter Is Just for Children"; Alison Lurie, "Harry Potter Upholds the Wonder of Childhood" are perhaps more for readers in secondary school and/or high school markets and the general reader. Nonetheless, the collection has several noteworthy pieces, including the celebrated novelist Alison Lurie's defense of *Harry Potter*, and the fact its editors chose articles in direct contrast to one another is added value.

Teaching Resources

"*Harry Potter and the Chamber of Secrets* by J. K. Rowling." Worksheet published December 25, 2009. *Times Educational Supplement*, TES Editorial, TSL Education London 2008.

The site offers a "comprehensive and thorough resource pack to support teaching of the text" using a "wide range of activities" with a subscription.

"*Harry Potter and the Philosopher's Stone* by J. K. Rowling." Worksheet published December 26, 2009. *Times Educational Supplement*, TES Editorial, TSL Education London 2008.

The site offers a "worksheets including grammar activities, themes, word search, wizard cards, storyboard of events in the novel" with a subscription.

"*Harry Potter and the Goblet of Fire* by J. K. Rowling." Interactive whiteboard published December 27, 2009. *Times Educational Supplement*, TES Editorial, TSL Education London 2008.

"This resource focuses on characterization—Mad Eye Moody. It will encourage children to comment on how writers use tools within their writing. The plans also concentrate on character, setting, structure and mood, through word choice and sentence structure."

"Mad Eye Moody from *Harry Potter and the Goblet of Fire* by J. K. Rowling." Lesson plan published December 25, 2009. *Times Educational Supplement*, TES Editorial, TSL Education London 2008.

"This lesson plan will support children to analyze entry of a main character and comment on how writers use tools within their writing. They will concentrate on character, setting, structure and mood, through word choice and sentence structure. Support notes offer texts and image."

Index

Note: "n" after a page reference refers to a note on that page.